FORMULA ONE 2020

This edition printed in 2020
by Welbeck Non-Fiction Limited
20 Mortimer Street
London W1T 3JW

ISBN 978-1-78739-373-8

Editorial Director: Martin Corteel
Design Manager: Luke Griffin
Designer: James Pople
Picture Research: Paul Langan
Production: Rachel Burgess

Printed in Spain

**Above: The fireworks fly in celebration
as Max Verstappen crosses the line
to win the German GP at Hockenheim
for Red Bull Racing as his 2019
campaign hit a rich seam of form.**

FORMULA ONE 2020

TEAMS | DRIVERS | TRACKS | RECORDS

BRUCE JONES

WELBECK

» CONTENTS

Right: Lewis Hamilton proves that there's no win like a home win at Silverstone.

Wherever Max Verstappen races, the orange army follow, his passionately proud Dutch fans being treated to three wins as Red Bull Racing came on strong on last year's global tour.

ANALYSIS OF THE 2020 SEASON

If the promise of last year's World Championship can be built upon, this year is going to be special. Sure, Lewis Hamilton and Mercedes both claimed their sixth F1 titles, but consider the fact that he was only one of five winning drivers and that teams using engines from three different manufacturers triumphed. The signs are that this season – the last year before major technical changes are introduced – could be a very exciting one indeed.

With 15 wins from last year's 21 grands prix, and continuity of its personnel, Mercedes will start as favourites, but Ferrari's and Red Bull Racing's results in 2019 showed that both raised their game and it's a rare time in F1 when three teams have powerful arguments to fancy their chances.

What marks Mercedes out is not just its technical excellence, but its operational ability too. So complex is the formula for winning a grand prix that there are times when Lewis Hamilton questions the strategy the team has put him on, but then those crunching the numbers on their computers are proved to be right. Team-mate Valtteri Bottas blossomed last year, bolstering Mercedes' attack further.

Ferrari will be expecting to be at the front again in 2020, but the team requires two things above the continued excellence of Charles Leclerc. The first is to eliminate silly mistakes. The second is to get Sebastian Vettel back up to speed again, as he struggled to handle having a faster team-mate and occasionally drove into him.

A year ago, there was concern that Red Bull Racing's challenge spearheaded by Max Verstappen might be hampered by the team using Honda engines, as the Japanese manufacturer had yet to make its engines competitive. As we look ahead to 2020, there is far more reason to be positive about its prospects as not only did Verstappen take three wins but Honda has agreed to stay in F1 until at least the end of 2021, giving the team stability. Don't

forget, that after parting ways with Renault at the end of 2018, and with neither Ferrari nor Mercedes looking to help them out, their choices were limited. Now, Red Bull Racing can afford to smile and will definitely do so if Alex Albon continues to improve through his second F1 campaign.

Not so long ago, two of F1's great teams were in the doldrums. Now it's just one, as McLaren is back on track, but Williams continues to struggle. McLaren's move to rank fourth overall wasn't just down to Renault power, as a lot of credit must go to the steadying hand applied by former Porsche sportscar team principal Andreas Seidel and the technical advances made by tech chief James Key. Like the top teams, it retains its drivers for the season ahead, with Carlos Sainz Jr and Lando Norris quick enough to achieve great things, providing they are given the tools for the job.

Renault had a fitful season in the midfield and will be relying not just on the pace of Daniel Ricciardo but the return of the effervescent Esteban Ocon after a year on the sidelines.

Last year it was Racing Point that appeared to be the latest new team on the block, although it was just a new name for Force India, while Sauber was reinvented as Alfa Romeo Racing. This time around, the new name is that of Scuderia Alpha Tauri, but it's simply Scuderia Toro Rosso with a rebranding. The drivers will remain the same, Pierre Gasly partnering Daniil Kvyat, but neither

expects to be treated to a surprise result like last year.

Racing Point will be looking forward to its second full year under new ownership after having to compete for years under a cloud caused by former owner Vijay Mallya's court cases. In Sergio Perez, it has one of the steadiest drivers around, and he is sure to score whenever the car is good enough, supported by Lance Stroll.

It still seems odd for Alfa Romeo's efforts to be run by what was once Sauber in Switzerland, but expect it to stay true to its longstanding habit of starting the season strongly, then tailing off as a lack of development budget prevents them from keeping up. Yet, with Kimi Raikkonen again leading its attack, points will come, while Antonio Giovinazzi began to show progress at the end of last year, so expect more from him.

Haas F1 needs to bounce back after falling from fifth in 2018 to ninth last year, and has retained Kevin Magnussen and Romain Grosjean to help it.

On last year's woeful form, it's hard to see Williams getting off the back row. George Russell deserves a better car, while rookie Nicholas Latifi can only learn as he goes.

In 12 months' time, all teams will be hoping that they have got it right as they face up to one of the most comprehensive technical rule changes for decades. This time around, it's more about improving on what they have already.

MERCEDES-AMG PETRONAS

It seemed that Ferrari was going to mount a challenge in 2019, but Mercedes did enough to hold them off for its sixth constructors' title in a row. With the same line-up, it's set to be another golden year for the silver arrows.

If Lewis Hamilton can add this year's F1 drivers' title to his tally, he will equal the record set by Michael Schumacher between 1994 and 2005.

Anyone who watched Mercedes-Benz arrive with a huge splash when it entered the World Championship midway through 1954 and then dominated that season and the next wouldn't be surprised to find Mercedes at the front in 2020. Yet, there is no association between these two periods, except for the cars carrying the same name and racing in a silver livery, as there was a 54-year hiatus.

Mercedes' first period was all about raising the bar. Its W196 was a technical tour de force that Juan Manuel Fangio and Stirling Moss used to the best possible effect, winning nine of the 12 grands prix they contested. However, even before Fangio landed the 1955 crown it was known that Mercedes was pulling out at the end of the season in response to one of its cars flying into the crowd at the Le Mans 24 Hours and killing more than 80 spectators.

The decades passed before Mercedes returned to F1 in 1994, albeit only as an engine supplier. Starting with Sauber in the Swiss team's second season, Mercedes motors found their way to McLaren for 1995 and had their first win in the opening race of 1997 – David Coulthard in Melbourne – and their first title by 1998 thanks to Mika Hakkinen. The partnership continued to blossom

KEY PEOPLE & 2019 ROUND-UP

TOTO WOLFF
Racing is in Toto's blood, as he competed in Formula Ford before heading off to forge a career in the world of business. Later, having made a small fortune, he returned to race in GTs and try rallying too. Business was still king, though, and Toto raised enough money to become an investor in Williams in 2009 and, showing his ambition, was soon the man in charge for Frank Williams. Not one to stand still, Toto then took a 30 percent stake in the Mercedes team and in 2013 took it over from Norbert Haug.

CONTINUING TO LEAD FROM THE FRONT
It seemed, before the season, that Ferrari might have found the pace to challenge Mercedes but, as soon as the racing started, Mercedes did what it does best: win races. There were times when Ferrari had a faster car, but too often the Italian team made a mess of things. By the time Ferrari started winning in the second half of the campaign, Lewis Hamilton and Mercedes had headed over the horizon and it duly collected its sixth pair of championship titles.

2019 DRIVERS & RESULTS

Driver	Nationality	Races	Wins	Pts	Pos
Valtteri Bottas	Finnish	21	4	326	2nd
Lewis Hamilton	British	21	11	413	1st

but, inevitably, Mercedes wanted to take all the credit for any success so elected to run a team under its own name.

To start a team from scratch means spending several years sorting out a host of technical and operational problems, so Mercedes' top brass decided to take over an established team. The one chosen was based close to Silverstone, at Brackley, and had started life in 1999 as BAR (British American Racing) then had three years competing under the Honda Racing name before its one, title-winning season as Brawn GP in 2009. The new Mercedes came into being in 2010, with Nico Rosberg and a driver brought back from retirement, one they had fielded in sports-prototypes as a junior star 20 years earlier, and with seven F1 titles to his name: Michael Schumacher.

Brawn GP's glory came because it cleverly exploited a technical loophole that wasn't likely to be repeated and Jenson Button and Rubens Barrichello put away the wins before the rival teams could respond to Brawn GP's aerodynamic advantage of double-decked diffusers. However, even with Ross Brawn at the helm, it took longer than planned before Mercedes AMG Petronas hit winning form, with Rosberg triumphing in the 2012 Chinese GP. At the end of that year, Schumacher retired again, disappointed not to have added at least one more win to the incredible tally he racked up with Benetton and especially Ferrari. In his place, Lewis Hamilton was brought in from McLaren with the aim of giving the team a change of momentum.

This change certainly worked and in 2014 Mercedes exploded into action, mastering the new hybrid engine rules to such an extent that it took until the 11th round before another team, Red Bull Racing, got to record a win as Hamilton landed his second F1 title and the team its first. Key to this success was clear management from Toto Wolff, harnessing the decades of experience of three-time world champion Niki Lauda, along with technical leadership from Paddy Lowe and Geoff Willis plus great engines built in Northamptonshire.

With five more drivers' titles – four for Hamilton and the 2016 crown for Rosberg – the team continues to set the standard,

with Hamilton still its lead driver, supported ably since 2017 by Valtteri Bottas.

Ferrari looks best placed to attempt to tip Mercedes from the top of the table, but considerable investment and strong technical leadership from James Allison ought to keep Mercedes as the team to beat for some time to come.

"Last year was the team's biggest year of growth and I hope that this will put us in a good position for 2020. I've had some great races with Valtteri, Max and Charles and anticipate that it will be even tougher in 2020."

Lewis Hamilton

James Allison has been in F1 since 1991 and his expertise has yielded three titles in a row.

LEWIS HAMILTON

Lewis has a target to aim for this year, to claim his seventh F1 title and so equal Michael Schumacher's record tally. If Mercedes can supply him with machinery as competitive as the past six years, he will start as favourite to achieve it.

Lewis drew considerable pride from his sixth title, as he really had to work for it.

Lewis was that rare thing when he reached single-seaters: a kart driver already known within car racing circles. This was because he'd been taken under the wing of McLaren boss Ron Dennis and so had a profile.

Reaching Formula Renault for the 2001 winter series, it took Lewis until 2003 to win the British title, doing so in dominant form with 10 wins for Manor Motorsport. Staying with Manor, he ranked fifth in the European F3 series, finishing a single point behind his old karting team-mate Nico Rosberg. In 2005, after swapping to race for ASM, he took control, winning 15 races as he swept to the title.

GP2 was next, and Lewis edged out Nelson Piquet Jr for the crown, by which time he knew that he was in the running for promotion to F1 in 2007, with McLaren. It was rare for a rookie to join a top team, but Lewis made the most of it and could have won the title, but was edged out by Ferrari's Kimi Raikkonen at the final round in Brazil, ending up on the same score as team-mate, Fernando Alonso. F1 insiders were very impressed.

In 2008, Lewis almost came second again, but gained a place on the last corner of the final lap in the season-ending Brazilian GP to edge out Felipe Massa and become World Champion. At this point, to suggest that a second F1 title wouldn't follow for another six years would have seemed crazy, but Red Bull began to dominate and it took a move to Mercedes in 2013 for his fortunes to change, with titles being earned in 2014, 2015, 2017, 2018 and now 2019.

TRACK NOTES

Nationality:	**BRITISH**
Born:	**7 JANUARY 1985,**
	STEVENAGE, ENGLAND
Website:	**www.lewishamilton.com**
Teams:	**McLAREN 2007-12,**
	MERCEDES 2013-20

CAREER RECORD

First Grand Prix: **2007 AUSTRALIAN GP**
Grand Prix starts: **250**
Grand Prix wins: **84**
2007 Canadian GP, United States GP, Hungarian GP, Japanese GP, 2008 Australian GP, Monaco GP, British GP, German GP, Chinese GP, 2009 Hungarian GP, Singapore GP, 2010 Turkish GP, Canadian GP, Belgian GP, 2011 Chinese GP, German GP, Abu Dhabi GP, 2012 Canadian GP, Hungarian GP, Italian GP, United States GP, 2013 Hungarian GP, 2014 Malaysian GP, Bahrain GP, Chinese GP, Spanish GP, British GP, Italian GP, Singapore GP, Japanese GP, Russian GP, United States GP, Abu Dhabi GP, 2015 Australian GP, Chinese GP, Bahrain GP, Canadian GP, British GP, Belgian GP, Italian GP, Japanese GP, Russian GP, United States GP, 2016 Monaco GP, Canadian GP, Austrian GP, British GP, Hungarian GP, German GP, United States GP, Mexican GP, Brazilian GP, Abu Dhabi GP, 2017 Chinese GP, Spanish GP, Canadian GP, British GP, Belgian GP, Italian GP, Singapore GP, Japanese GP, US GP, 2018 Azerbaijan GP, Spanish GP, French GP, German GP, Hungarian GP, Italian GP, Singapore GP, Russian GP, Japanese GP, Brazilian GP, Abu Dhabi GP, 2019 Bahrain GP, Chinese GP, Spanish GP, Monaco GP, Canadian GP, French GP, British GP, Hungarian GP, Russian GP, Mexican GP, Abu Dhabi GP

Poles: **88**
Fastest laps: **47**
Points: **3431**
Honours:
2008, 2014, 2015, 2017, 2018 & 2019 F1 WORLD CHAMPION, 2007 & 2016 F1 RUNNER-UP, 2006 GP2 CHAMPION, 2005 EUROPEAN F3 CHAMPION, 2003 BRITISH FORMULA RENAULT CHAMPION, 2000 WORLD KART CUP & EUROPEAN FORMULA A KART CHAMPION, 1999 ITALIAN INTERCON A CHAMPION, 1995 BRITISH CADET KART CHAMPION

LEWIS'S 2019 HAD SIX APPEAL

Another year, another title could be Lewis's F1 mantra, such has been his record since joining Mercedes. Last year was no different to every season since the engine rules changed for 2014 and Mercedes moved past Red Bull Racing to the head of the pack. There was a stern challenge from Ferrari as the 2019 season wore on, and then a late charge from Red Bull Racing too, but Lewis already had too many points to have to worry too much as he notched up 11 wins to cruise to the 2019 world crown. What was impressive was the way that he watched the challenge gather pace, metaphorically rolled up his sleeves and competed at an even higher level to see it off. Despite his unbelievable tally of wins and titles, Lewis continues to learn, especially the way that he has to work with his race engineer and strategy crew to go for wins with strategies that don't immediately seem obvious.

VALTTERI BOTTAS

Last year started with a win for Valtteri, ahead of Lewis Hamilton, and a general upturn in form, but then everything fell back to usual form. The talented Finn had to play the back-up role at Mercedes, just as it will be for him in 2020.

Valtteri proved last year that he can not only push Lewis on occasions, but beat him too.

Valtteri was an ace kart-racer and was more than ready to step up to single-seater racing when he was 17. That was in 2007 and he displayed good pace in Formula Renault. Back for a second crack in 2008, he landed not only the minor championship for northern European countries, but the main European title too, his five wins just enough to edge out Daniel Ricciardo.

In time-honoured fashion, F3 followed, and he showed well in a year dominated by Jules Bianchi. Back for more in 2010, he ranked third again, winning the one-off F3 Masters for a second year in a row.

Valtteri didn't have the backing to graduate to GP2, something not unusual for Finns. Instead, he raced in less powerful GP3 and duly won that, coming on strong in the second half of the year. His prize for this was to have an F1 test with Williams. This is normally for show, but Valtteri's approach really impressed them, so he was signed as a test driver for 2012 and gained useful experience as he was usually sent out for the first practice session on the Friday morning of a grand prix meeting.

For 2013, with Williams' management delighted by his unflashy approach to all he did and the way that he operated as a team player rather than a prima donna, Valtteri was rewarded with a race seat and did what he could as the team struggled with Renault engines. Mercedes power for 2014 was a huge improvement and Valtteri ranked fourth overall, standing on the podium six times. In 2015, he was fifth.

Valtteri got a dream ticket, a ride with Mercedes, for 2017. By year's end, he had three wins to his name – in the Russian, Austrian and Abu Dhabi GPs – and finished third in the World Championship. However, he has always been seen as support to Lewis Hamilton, even on the days when he has outpaced him.

TRACK NOTES

Nationality:	**FINNISH**
Born:	**28 AUGUST 1989,**
	NASTOLA, FINLAND
Website:	**www.valtteribottas.com**
Teams:	**WILLIAMS 2013-16,**
	MERCEDES 2017-20

CAREER RECORD

First Grand Prix:	**2013 AUSTRALIAN GP**
Grand Prix starts:	**139**
Grand Prix wins:	**7**
	2017 Russian GP, Austrian GP,
	Abu Dhabi GP, 2019 Australian GP,
	Azerbaijan GP, Japanese GP, US GP
Poles:	**11**
Fastest laps:	**13**
Points:	**1289**
Honours:	**2019 F1 RUNNER-UP,**
	2011 GP3 CHAMPION, 2009 & 2010
	FORMULA 3 MASTERS WINNER, 2008
	EUROPEAN & NORTHERN EUROPEAN
	FORMULA RENAULT CHAMPION

BETTER SPEED, BUT STILL SECOND

Two wins, in Melbourne and Baku, and two seconds in the first four rounds of the 2019 season, along with a pair of poles, suggested that Valtteri would have a far better season than ever before. However, this run was as good as it got, and he rarely finished ahead of Lewis Hamilton thereafter as his team-mate upped the pace. There was a degree of frustration later in the season when team tactics didn't favour the Finn and he was reduced to being the support player again as Hamilton went after his sixth F1 title. Pleasingly, he had a second spell in the limelight in the closing stages of the season, winning the Japanese GP and the United States GP as well. This impressive flourish was sufficient in the face of improved form from both Ferrari and Red Bull Racing for Valtteri to end the campaign with his best ever ranking: second overall. Yet, he still knows that he's good enough only to be second at Mercedes.

» FERRARI

After an up and down season in which its decisions seemed less than the best, Charles Leclerc gave Ferrari the long-craved home win at Monza, and it's time for the sport's most famous team to step up in 2020 and deliver on a consistent basis.

Sebastian Vettel led Charles Leclerc in last year's Canadian GP, but the team will have to be wary of further internecine battling in 2020.

Anyone who thinks that Ferrari's seven decades in F1 have been one long run at the very top of the sport needs to think again, as its ride has been cyclical. Highs have included Alberto Ascari's romp in the early 1950s, Niki Lauda's pomp in the mid-1970s and then Michael Schumacher's dominance from 2000 to 2004. Yet there have also been lows, which is natural in a sport in which the technical rules change, but less forgivable as Ferrari has seldom been anything other than extremely well-funded.

Last year, Ferrari seemed all set for its best season since Schumacher's days, having set the pace in testing. Then the racing started and Mercedes' continued excellence put the team back in its place. In terms of speed of car, there was little in it, but factors went against them, such as Charles Leclerc being thwarted by mechanical failure when set to win the second round in Bahrain, but also by less than sparkling strategic calls, and this highlighted a perennial problem: management.

Back in the early years of the World Championship, Ferrari arrived with a reputation and soon started proving why, taking over after Alfa Romeo quit at the close of 1951. Much of its strength came from Enzo Ferrari's predominance and single-mindedness. However, by the 1970s, with parent company Fiat

KEY PEOPLE & 2019 ROUND-UP

MATTIA BINOTTO

Mattia took a couple of degrees in motor vehicle engineering and joined Ferrari's F1 engine department in 1995, at the age of 25. He was there through Michael Schumacher's period of domination at the start of the 21st century and assumed control of the engine department in 2013. A loftier post awaited, though, as James Allison's departure midway through 2016 enabled Mattia to be appointed as the team's chief technical officer. Then, when Maurizio Arrivabene left the team ahead of the 2019 season, Mattia became team principal.

FAST ENOUGH, BUT POOR MANAGEMENT

Had Charles Leclerc not been hit by an engine malfunction when heading for victory in Bahrain on his second Ferrari outing, the season might have been different, but it was a year of squandering their pace. Ferrari's decision that Binotto could add the role of team principal to his one of technical director overloaded his plate, especially when Sebastian Vettel began to be unco-operative when the incoming Leclerc outpaced him.

2019 DRIVERS & RESULTS

Driver	Nationality	Races	Wins	Pts	Pos
Charles Leclerc	Monegasque	21	2	264	4th
Sebastian Vettel	German	21	1	240	5th

FOR THE RECORD

Country of origin:	**Italy**
Team base:	**Maranello, Italy**
Telephone:	**(39) 536 949111**
Website:	**www.ferrari.com**
Active in Formula One:	**From 1950**
Grands Prix contested:	**991**
Wins:	**237**
Pole positions:	**228**
Fastest laps:	**253**

THE TEAM

President:	**Louis Camilleri**
Team principal & technical director:	
	Mattia Binotto
Chief designer, chassis:	**Simone Resta**
Chief designer, power unit:	
	Lorenzo Sassi
Head of aerodynamics:	**Loic Bigois**
Director of aero development:	
	Enrico Cardile
Sporting director:	**Claudio Albertini**
Head of race activities:	**Jock Clear**
Operations director:	**Gino Rosato**
Chief race engineer:	**Matteo Togninalli**
Test driver:	**tba**
Chassis:	**Ferrari SF91**
Engine:	**Ferrari V6**
Tyres:	**Pirelli**

attempting to call the shots, and political appointments being made, team management was a trickier matter. Luca di Montezemolo, allied with Lauda, made winning a habit in the mid-1970s and Jean Todt and Ross Brawn worked wonders alongside Schumacher three decades later. Since then, though, the management has been less than special.

Yet, the Ferrari name still carries more glamour and weight than any other on the F1 grid. It's the go-to team, its red racers the most photographed.

Ascari became Ferrari's first world champion in 1952, when F1 ran to F2 regulations and Ferrari had just the car and engine for the job. Indeed, Ascari set off on a nine-race winning streak that landed him two titles in a row, his Ferrari 500 the class of the field. Juan Manuel Fangio became champion when Ferrari ran Lancia chassis in 1956, then Mike Hawthorn became the first British World Champion when pipping Vanwall's Stirling Moss to the 1958 crown,

Ferrari was slow to adapt to British teams – like Cooper and Lotus which mounted the engine behind the driver rather than in front – but it claimed the 1961 title when Phil Hill landed the title ahead of team-mate Wolfgang von Trips. The rules, however, again had been changed to suit

them, with the engine size being slashed to 1500cc. Three years later, John Surtees became Ferrari's next champion, almost despite the management, as he stuck to his guns and benefitted from the fragility of Jim Clark's Lotus.

However, it then took until Lauda joined the team in 1974 for the team to start acting like one that was serious about winning. Two titles in three years was Ferrari's reward.

Ground-effects transformed F1 in the late 1970s and Ferrari came out on top in 1979, with Jody Scheckter edging out team-mate Gilles Villeneuve. But this championship wasn't built on and it took another 21 years before Ferrari ended a period of dominance by British teams McLaren, Williams and Benetton.

It was hoped that Sebastian Vettel might be Ferrari's next champion after he joined in 2015, but he hasn't been able to get the better of Mercedes' Lewis Hamilton on a consistent enough basis. Ferrari's decision to take a driver with minimal F1 experience when it signed

Leclerc for 2019 was a rare one for this most conservative of teams, but the *tifosi* was able to show its approval when he won last year's Italian GP for their first home win since Fernando Alonso answered their Monza prayers in 2010.

> **"When we started last season, we had a rookie and an experienced driver, but if you look at the later races of 2019, our drivers were free to race and this is where we will start from for 2020."**

Mattia Binotto

Ferrari finished first and second in 1979, with Jody Scheckter outscoring Gilles Villeneuve.

15

SEBASTIAN VETTEL

Last year was one in which the four-time World Champion's abilities came into question as he was increasingly overshadowed by Ferrari team-mate Charles Leclerc and made a series of errors. Nobody can tell what this year will bring.

Sebastian scoffed at talk of him quitting F1 last year, but he must raise his game.

Some drivers have to fight for every corner as they work their way towards the top of the sport. Others appear simply to glide through the challenges, and Sebastian was definitely one of the latter.

He started winning in his first year in the ADAC Formula BMW series, then blitzed the field at the second time of asking in 2004 by winning 18 of the 20 races. Sebastian was top rookie on the European F3 series in 2005, then was beaten to the title by Paul di Resta in 2006. However, he had had a winning outing in the more powerful World Series by Renault and advanced to that formula in 2007. He didn't have a full year, because Robert Kubica was injured in the Canadian GP and Sebastian was promoted from Sauber's test team, making him an F1 driver just before his 20th birthday. He then landed a ride with Scuderia Toro Rosso later in the year.

Staying on with Red Bull's junior team, Sebastian shocked everyone by qualifying on pole then winning the 2008 Italian GP in the wet. As a result, Red Bull Racing had his name straight onto a contract for 2009. Having been runner-up to Brawn GP's Jenson Button in 2009, Sebastian came through at the final round to win the 2010 title and become the youngest world champion, at 23. He followed that with titles in each of the next three seasons.

With Mercedes moving to the front of the pack, Sebastian elected to join Ferrari for 2015, succeeding Fernando Alonso. Despite wins aplenty to move to third all-time in F1 wins, there have been no more titles as Lewis Hamilton has ruled the roost.

BEING SHOWN UP BY A JUNIOR

In any sport, after time, there will be a changing of the guard, when the greats become somewhat less so, when perhaps the desire to chase every opportunity begins to ebb away. Many felt that 2019 was when this happened for Sebastian, as he was overshadowed by his team-mate Charles Leclerc. Sebastian's pace was still acceptable, but it was the second year F1 racer who was taking the poles and then the wins. There were mistakes in the races too, most notably when crashing out of the lead at Hockenheim, and also at Monza. Perhaps stung by the criticism that he had fallen below his best, Sebastian then won in Singapore, but the impression remained that he had slipped below his best. Then came the Russian GP, and Sebastian's decision to go against a pre-race agreement had echoes of Senna and Prost in their days together at McLaren in 1989. The team management wasn't impressed.

TRACK NOTES

Nationality:	**GERMAN**
Born:	**3 JULY 1987,**
	HEPPENHEIM, GERMANY
Website:	**www.sebastianvettel.de**
Teams:	**BMW SAUBER 2007,**
	TORO ROSSO 2007-08, RED BULL
	RACING 2009-14, FERRARI 2015-20

CAREER RECORD

First Grand Prix:	**2007 UNITED**
	STATES GP
Grand Prix starts:	**241**
Grand Prix wins:	**53**

2008 Italian GP, 2009 Chinese GP, British GP, Japanese GP, Abu Dhabi GP, 2010 Malaysian GP, European GP, Japanese GP, Brazilian GP, Abu Dhabi GP, 2011 Australian GP, Malaysian GP, Turkish GP, Spanish GP, Monaco GP, European GP, Belgian GP, Italian GP, Singapore GP, Korean GP, Indian GP, 2012 Bahrain GP, Singapore GP, Japanese GP, Korean GP, Indian GP, 2013 Malaysian GP, Bahrain GP, Canadian GP, German GP, Belgian GP, Italian GP, Singapore GP, Korean GP, Japanese GP, Indian GP, Abu Dhabi GP, United States GP, Brazilian GP, 2015 Malaysian GP, Hungarian GP, Singapore GP, 2017 Australian GP, Bahrain GP, Monaco GP, Hungarian GP, Brazilian GP, 2018 Australian GP, Bahrain GP, Canadian GP, British GP, Belgian GP, 2019 Singapore GP

Poles:	**57**
Fastest laps:	**38**
Points:	**2985**
Honours:	**2010, 2011, 2012 & 2013**

F1 WORLD CHAMPION, 2009, 2017 & 2018 FORMULA ONE RUNNER-UP, 2006 EUROPEAN FORMULA THREE RUNNER-UP, 2004 GERMAN FORMULA BMW ADAC CHAMPION, 2003 GERMAN FORMULA BMW ADAC RUNNER-UP, 2001 EUROPEAN & GERMAN JUNIOR KART CHAMPION

CHARLES LECLERC

Last year was a remarkable one for Charles as he settled in at Ferrari without a backward glance and belied the fact that this was only his second year of F1. He led on his second outing and left Sebastian Vettel in his wake.

Last year's fabulous form earned Charles a five-year Ferrari contract.

Born in Monaco to a racing-mad father, it was all but inevitable that Charles would race. What is never inevitable, however, is that a second-generation racer will be any good. Father Herve, who competed in Monaco's grand prix-supporting F3 race each year from 1986 to 1990 – coming eighth in 1988 – backed him as far as he could and Charles's results in karting showed huge promise.

Charles was French cadet kart champion aged 11 in 2009, won the Monaco Kart Cup the next year and, as a 13-year-old, won the 2011 FIA Academy Trophy title. Second place in the 2012 world KF series, behind Max Verstappen, showed that he was ready for car racing.

Starting with second place in a regional Formula Renault series, Charles then advanced to F3 in 2015 and ended the year fourth in the European championship, also placing second in the famous Macau F3 GP.

For 2016, without a budget to step up to GP2, Charles turned to GP3 and did what he had to do to keep his career momentum going: he won the title ahead of Alex Albon thanks to three wins. Being managed by Jean Todt's son Nicolas helped further as Ferrari put him on its academy books and the team gave him his first F1 test.

For 2017, he moved up to F1's new feeder formula, F2, and duly won that for Prema Racing, his seven wins leaving him way out front. Sadly, his father Herve never saw him clinch the title, as he died, aged 54, midway through the year.

After an impressive test for Sauber, Charles joined the Ferrari-powered team for 2018 and produced one of the most impressive F1 rookie seasons for years, placing his car much further up the grid than was expected, even finishing in sixth place at the Azerbaijan GP. He followed this with four seventh-place finishes in the final six rounds to demonstrate he was blessed not just with speed but also with the ability to deliver in all conditions and this was seen by people the length of the pitlane as remarkable.

TRACK NOTES

Nationality:	MONEGASQUE
Born:	16 OCTOBER 1997,
	MONTE CARLO, MONACO
Website:	www.charles-leclerc.com
Teams:	SAUBER 2018,
	FERRARI 2019-20

CAREER RECORD

First Grand Prix:	2018 AUSTRALIAN GP
Grand Prix starts:	42
Grand Prix wins:	2
	2019 Belgian GP, Italian GP
Poles:	7
Fastest laps:	4
Points:	303
Honours:	2017 FIA F2 CHAMPION, 2016 GP3 CHAMPION, 2015 MACAU F3 RUNNER-UP, 2014 FORMULA RENAULT ALPS RUNNER-UP, 2013 WORLD KZ KART RUNNER-UP, 2012 UNDER 18 WORLD KART CHAMPIONSHIP RUNNER-UP & EURO KF KART RUNNER-UP, 2011 ACADEMY TROPHY KART CHAMPION, 2010 JUNIOR MONACO KART CUP CHAMPION, 2009 FRENCH CADET KART CHAMPION

17

SHOWING HE IS THE MAN FOR NOW

Charles was tipped to make an impression with Ferrari after his outstanding maiden F1 season with Sauber. Indeed, he could have won his second race for Ferrari, in Bahrain, but a mechanical glitch hampered his charge. He bounced back from this and fought to lead the chase to the dominant Mercedes and, despite some poor tatctical decisions from Ferrari, found himself ever more of a threat and was unlucky to lose out in a bruising battle for honour with Max Verstappen in Austria. Finally, that breakthrough first win came at Spa-Francorchamps and he immediately backed this up with a second in, of all places, Italy. The *tifosi* went wild and hailed Charles as Ferrari's new leader. With Sebastian Vettel not entirely on song as his team-mate, it seemed that he had already assumed that mantle, with his form in qualifying being particularly noteworthy, as shown by a run of five pole positions in six rounds.

There can be no mistaking which team is the focus of the fans at Monza, with the *tifosi* going wild with delight when Charles Leclerc won for Ferrari in 2019.

RED BULL RACING

Not able to take the battle to Mercedes and Ferrari on a regular basis through 2019, Red Bull Racing will be looking for a bit more power from its Honda engines this year so that Max Verstappen can go for gold.

Max Verstappen took the first of his three 2019 victories in Austria and the team knows it only needs small gains to secure more.

With its strong branding of a dark blue car tipped with a yellow nose and topped with a huge red bull, this team's cars appear to have changed little over the years. Of course, the shape of nose, wings, sidepods and engine covers have been altered according to changes in regulations. However, whether in that first year as Red Bull Racing in 2005 or in its most recent campaign, there is an unusual homogeneity.

This hasn't meant that the results have always stayed the same, as the team struggled at first, dominated from 2010 to 2013, when Sebastian Vettel guided it to four titles, and since then has had to act as the lead chaser of Ferrari and pace-setters Mercedes.

The team started back in 1997 when three-time World Champion Jackie Stewart and son Paul decided to take their team up the final step from F3000 to F1. It upgraded its facilities at Milton Keynes and signed Rubens Barrichello and Jan Magnussen for its inaugural season. Thanks to Jackie's

influence, Ford supplied the engines and rewards came when Barrichello finished a surprise second in Monaco. Two years later, in a wet/dry race at the Nurburgring,

he was third, but was eclipsed on the day by team-mate Johnny Herbert, who gave the team its breakthrough win that helped it rank fourth overall in the Constructors' Cup.

KEY PEOPLE & 2019 ROUND-UP

PIERRE WACHE
While Adrian Newey is assumed to be the man calling the technical shots at Red Bull Racing, it is more normally Pierre who does so. He broke the family trend of studying medicine by becoming an engineer instead and joined Michelin. When Michelin stopped supplying F1 tyres, he joined BMW Sauber, then, in 2013, moved to Red Bull Racing, becoming performance director the following year. Then, in 2018, when Newey focused more on the Aston Martin Valkyrie and later the Veloce Extreme E team, Pierre became technical director.

STILL TRYING TO GET BACK INTO THE TOP
With Ferrari raising its game last year and Mercedes continuing to set the standard in F1, it was always going to be hard for Honda-powered Red Bull Racing to keep up, yet alone step up. Max Verstappen got stuck in, but Pierre Gasly never seemed to find his feet and was dropped after the Hungarian GP to be replaced by the more impressive Alex Albon. Fittingly, Verstappen was able to win at Austria's Red Bull Ring and at Hockenheim, before adding the best of them, a controlled victory in the Brazilian GP.

2019 DRIVERS & RESULTS

Driver	Nationality	Races	Wins	Pts	Pos
Alex Albon	British	9	0	92	8th
Pierre Gasly	French	12	0	95	7th
Max Verstappen	Dutch	21	3	278	3rd

Ford then took over the team for 2000, keeping the majority of personnel, and branding it as Jaguar Racing to push its premium brand. The cars were invariably quick, especially in the hands of Eddie Irvine and Mark Webber, but the management had become hampered by interference from the manufacturer, something that never works in the fast-on-its-feet world of F1.

Then, refreshed again, the team became Red Bull Racing in 2005, with the experienced David Coulthard leading its attack. Beefing up the technical side, too, Coulthard attracted Adrian Newey to follow him from McLaren and the team form was expected to change in Red Bull's favour sooner rather than later.

Webber returned and started to record some decent results, but was frustrated when, at the 2008 Italian GP, sponsor Red Bull's junior team – Scuderia Toro Rosso – beat it to become the first team in the energy drink company's colours to enjoy a grand prix victory, Sebastian Vettel at the wheel. The German was promoted to Red Bull Racing for 2009, but they were beaten by the technical wizadry of Brawn GP. Newey got it right with his 2010 chassis as Vettel overhauled both Webber and Ferrari's Fernando Alonso in the final round at Yas Marina to take the crown, with the team taking constructors' honours to double its delight.

This was the start of a purple patch, with Vettel landing the next three drivers' titles, each time with Red Bull Racing as the champion team too. It always feels that a team this dominant will continue winning forever, but a change of regulations – enforcing the use of smaller capacity turbocharged engines in 2014 – swung the pendulum Mercedes' way. Red Bull's engine supplier Renault was unable to respond.

A further shock for Vettel came with the arrival of Daniel Ricciardo, stepping up from Toro Rosso, as the Australian surprised everyone by outscoring him. Vettel joined Ferrari in 2015, leaving Ricciardo to be partnered by Daniil Kvyat. However, the Russian was dropped after the fourth race of 2016, and was replaced by Max Verstappen who rocked everyone

FOR THE RECORD

Country of origin:	**England**
Team base:	**Milton Keynes, England**
Telephone:	**(44) 01908 279700**
Website:	**www.redbullracing.com**
Active in Formula One:	**As Stewart GP 1997-99, Jaguar Racing 2000-04, Red Bull Racing 2005 on**
Grands Prix contested:	**402**
Wins:	**62**
Pole positions:	**62**
Fastest laps:	**65**

THE TEAM

Chairman:	**Dietrich Mateschitz**
Team principal:	**Christian Horner**
Chief technical officer:	**Adrian Newey**
Technical director:	**Pierre Wache**
Chief engineering officer:	**Rob Marshall**
Chief engineer, aerodynamics:	**Dan Fallows**
Chief engineer, car engineering:	**Paul Monaghan**
Team manager:	**Jonathan Wheatley**
Chief engineer:	**Guillaume Roquelin**
Test driver:	**tba**
Chassis:	**Red Bull RB16**
Engine:	**Honda V6**
Tyres:	**Pirelli**

by winning on his first outing, in Spain.

Since then, it has been the young Dutchman's team, with Red Bull Racing's driver scout Helmut Marko chopping and changing his second driver on a fairly regular basis. It seems fairly harsh, with some given little time to settle. Yet, the pace displayed last year when he dropped Pierre Gasly for Alex Albon showed that he can get it right.

"For us, it was very much a transitionary year with Honda, but we can be proud of our achievements and Alex learnt so much in the nine races he did with us last year that I'm sure we will see a great deal from him in 2020."

Christian Horner

Team chief Christian Horner celebrates with Sebastian Vettel in 2010 when Red Bull went top.

MAX VERSTAPPEN

Red Bull Racing fell away from the pace last year as its Honda engines couldn't match the best from Ferrari and Mercedes. Max, however, pressed as hard as he could and will demand that the team helps him to close the gap in 2020.

Max continued to enhance his reputation last year and more wins will surely follow.

Mexican star Ricardo Rodriguez was the original teenage hotshot in F1 in the early 1960s but, for decades, few drivers reached motor racing's top category until they had many more years on the clock. Max's father Jos was considered a young one when he burst from F3 to F1 in 1994 at the age of 22, bypassing the final feeder formula, F3000. Impressively, he hadn't moved too high too soon after an apprenticeship that included being

Benelux Formula Opel champion then winning the German F3 title.

Wind the clock forward to 2015, and Max proved that because most up-and-coming stars have years of kart racing behind them, a car racing apprenticeship doesn't have to be so long. Indeed, he was only 17 when he made his F1 debut with Scuderia Toro Rosso in 2015, after just one season of car racing. That had been in the European F3 Championship and he won 10 of the races to rank third as Esteban Ocon took the title.

There was plenty of advice coming from the family, but it wasn't just from Jos, because Max's mother Sophie (Kumpen) had been a handy kart racer too. That maiden F1 season showed enormous promise, with Max not in awe of anyone and he laid down a marker by taking a pair of fourth-place finishes.

His second campaign with Toro Rosso didn't last long as, after just four rounds, he swapped rides with Daniil Kvyat and was promoted to Red Bull Racing. Everyone was keen to see how he would fare, but no one would have predicted what happened at the Spanish GP, as he took victory first time out.

With Mercedes dominant and Ferrari fast but inconsistent, any win is hard earned, but Max has managed multiple each year since, notably a double in Mexico, with the form that suggests that if he was in a Mercedes or Ferrari he'd be notching up a whole lot more.

TRACK NOTES

Nationality:	**DUTCH**
Born:	**30 SEPTEMBER 1997, HASSELT, BELGIUM**
Website:	**www.verstappen.nl**
Teams:	**TORO ROSSO 2015-16, RED BULL RACING 2016-20**

CAREER RECORD

First Grand Prix: **2015 AUSTRALIAN GP**
Grand Prix starts: **102**
Grand Prix wins: **8**
2016 Spanish GP, 2017 Malaysian GP, Mexican GP, 2018 Austrian GP, Mexican GP, 2019 Austrian GP, German GP, Brazilian GP
Poles: **2**
Fastest laps: **7**
Points: **948**
Honours: **2013 WORLD & EUROPEAN KZ KART CHAMPION, 2012 WSK MASTER SERIES KF2 CHAMPION, 2011 WSK EURO SERIES CHAMPION, 2009 BELGIAN KF5 CHAMPION, 2008 DUTCH CADET KART CHAMPION, 2007 & 2008 DUTCH MINIMAX CHAMPION, 2006 BELGIAN ROTAX MINIMAX CHAMPION**

PRESSING ON, FALLING SHORT

Winning "only" three grands prix last year will have been a disappointment to Max, as it was only one win more than he managed to claim in each of the preceeding two seasons. However, although he might have hoped for more, there was no escaping from the fact that the Honda-powered Red Bull RB15 was a few horsepower short of its leading rivals and so just couldn't match the best across the full season. Red Bull Racing duly dropped away from the ultimate pace set by the quartet of cars entered by Mercedes and Ferrari until the team came on strong through the season's closing rounds, peaking with an impressive win in from pole position in Brazil. Even including the win at Interlagos, the highlight for F1 fans was his cracking scrap with Charles Leclerc at the Red Bull Ring, when they fought all the way to the flag.

22

ALEX ALBON

Impressive in his maiden season of F1 with Scuderia Toro Rosso, Alex was then promoted midway through the year to Red Bull Racing and shone even more brightly, earning the right to keep the seat for a full season in 2020.

Alex has the pace, now knows the circuits and is set for his best year.

Alex's father Nigel contested the British Touring Car Championship in 1994 and then became a Ferrari 355 Challenge champion in the Asian-Pacific series in 1998 and 1999. This set the ball rolling, as his passion was passed on to his son, Alex, who started racing karts as soon as permitted, at eight, and was soon making rapid strides through the divisions. That was in 2005 and he advanced up the levels, taking the British Super 1 Honda title in 2009. Two years later, aged 15, he was runner-up in the World KF1 series. This was enough to prove that he was more than ready to move up to car racing.

Alex's first year out of karts was in Formula Renault, and he had already made a good connection, having been signed to be part of the Red Bull Junior Team programme. Unfortunately, his second year in Formula Renault didn't yield the progress expected and he was dropped by Red Bull. Alex wanted to prove Red Bull wrong and shone in 2014 by ranking third behind his karting nemesis Nyck de Vries.

Formula 3 followed, but ending 2015 only seventh in the European series suggested that perhaps Red Bull had been right. However, a second place overall finish, behind Charles Leclerc, in GP3 in 2016 was a step forward.

F2, the last stop before F1, was next. Two podium visits were promising, but ending yup 10th overall was less than he'd hoped for. Back for a second year in F2 in 2018, Alex came on strong and beat de Vries but, despite recording four wins, he ended the year third in the standings, behind fellow British drivers George Russell and Lando Norris.

With no doors opening in F1, it looked as if Alex would head to Formula E, but his half Thai heritage eased open the door at Scuderia Toro Rosso, and he became only the second driver to represent Thailand at the sport's top level, following on six decades after Prince Birabongse Bhanudej Bhanubandh, better known as "B Bira".

TRACK NOTES

Nationality:	**BRITISH/THAI**
Born:	**23 MARCH 1996, LONDON, ENGLAND**
Website:	**www.alexalbon.com**
Teams:	**TORO ROSSO 2019, RED BULL 2019-2020**

CAREER RECORD

First Grand Prix:	**2019 AUSTRALIAN GP**
Grand Prix starts:	**21**
Grand Prix wins:	**0 (best result: 4th 2019 Japanese GP)**
Poles:	**0**
Fastest laps:	**0**
Points:	**92**
Honours:	**2016 GP3 RUNNER-UP, 2011 WORLD KF1 KART RUNNER-UP, 2010 EUROPEAN KF3 KART CHAMPION, 2009 SUPER 1 HONDA KART CHAMPION**

MEETING ALL THE CHALLENGES

Alex showed impressive speed but suffered from appalling luck in the first half of the season. Points were scored, peaking with sixth at Hockenheim. However, Pierre Gasly did not achieve the results Red Bull Racing expected of him and Helmut Marko demoted him to Scuderia Toro Rosso, with Alex going the other way. Fifth place first time out at the Belgian GP was no fluke, as Alex then repeated the result three races later, in Sochi, despite starting from the tail of field. The minimum that should be achieved by a driver for the third most competitive team ought to be sixth, and he hit this target in his first seven races in a row (and the run only ended when, lying second in Brazil, Lewis Hamilton collided with him), peaking with fourth in Japan, where he exactly matched Verstappen in qualifying. What made this all the more impressive was that Alex showed remarkable accuracy in working his way up through the field. His technical feedback is reportedly excellent. Natural out of the car, Alex proved a welcome addition to the paddock and now gives Thai fans a driver to cheer for.

McLAREN

All fans ought to have been delighted last year as McLaren's slump was reversed. By its loftiest standards, no wins and only one podium were disappointing, but team principal Andreas Seidl's arrival from Porsche steadied the ship and its drivers performed well.

Life was very much on an upswing for McLaren last year and Carlos Sainz Jr will aim for even greater results as the team continues its fightback.

Seldom has a team been so rooted in one man as McLaren was in its founder Bruce McLaren. Taking the lead from his late 1950s Cooper team-mate Jack Brabham, the New Zealander used all his engineering ingenuity to build sports racers that people wanted to drive in the early 1960s and this, in turn, allowed him to start building single-seaters and, in time, enter a team in the World Championship.

That was in 1966 and considerable earnings from winning the Can Am sportscar series in the USA and Canada filled the McLaren purse not only with substantial amounts of prize money but also with lucrative orders of cars for customers, with McLarens making up most of the field by 1970. Sadly, Bruce was killed when testing his latest Can Am car at Goodwood that year, and it took great fortitude for his lieutenants to carry on.

Success in F1 was harder to come by, but was achieved by Bruce at Spa-Francorchamps in 1968. Matra, Lotus, Tyrrell and Ferrari set the pace into the 1970s, but the wins became more frequent and Emerson Fittipaldi became McLaren's first champion driver in 1974. Two years later, James Hunt became its second, pipping Ferrari's Niki Lauda.

McLaren lost ground as others harnessed ground effect technology in the late 1970s and it took the arrival of

KEY PEOPLE & 2019 ROUND-UP

ANDREAS SEIDL

After graduating in mechanical engineering from the Technical University of Munich, Andreas moved into motor racing with BMW Motorsport in 2000. After six years there, he gained a first taste of F1 as head of track operations for BMW Sauber until 2009. After joining Porsche and, as head of its LMP1 programme, Andreas oversaw its mastering of hybrid technology and dash to victory at the 2015 Le Mans 24 Hours. With Porsche closing its World Endurance Championship project, Andreas joined McLaren as team principal last May.

FLASHES OF SPEED SUGGEST BETTER THINGS

There were times last year when McLaren looked sure to pick up the sort of point hauls of which they could only have dreamt in 2017, such as at the Belgian GP when Lando Norris looked set for its third fifth-place finish in a row, only to have an engine problem with a lap to go. Carlos Sainz Jr lost strong results too, but came on strongly as the season came to its end, peaking with third place in the Brazilian GP, but it was clear that the trend was upwards as McLaren advanced from sixth in 2018 to fourth.

2019 DRIVERS & RESULTS

Driver	Nationality	Races	Wins	Pts	Pos
Lando Norris	British	21	0	49	11th
Carlos Sainz Jr	Spanish	21	0	96	6th

FOR THE RECORD

Country of origin:	**England**
Team base:	**Woking England**
Telephone:	**(44) 01483 261900**
Website:	**www.mclaren.com**
Active in Formula One:	**From 1966**
Grands Prix contested:	**864**
Wins:	**181**
Pole positions:	**154**
Fastest laps:	**154**

THE TEAM

Executive director:	**Zak Brown**
Team principal:	**Andreas Seidl**
Technical director:	**James Key**
Racing director:	**Andrea Stella**
Sporting director:	**Gil de Ferran**
Production director:	**Piers Thynne**
Chief engineering officer:	**Matt Morris**
Chief engineer, aerodynamics:	
	Peter Prodromou
Director of design & development:	
	Neil Oatley
Head of design:	**Mark Inham**
Team manager:	**Paul James**
Test driver:	**Sergio Sette Camara**
Chassis:	**McLaren MCL35**
Engine:	**Renault V6**
Tyres:	**Pirelli**

Ron Dennis as team principal to propel it forward again, with the breakthrough being provided by designer John Barnard pioneering carbonfibre monocoque technology.

By 1984, with Niki Lauda leading the way, the titles started flowing again, with rising star Alain Prost matching that in 1985 and 1986. Changing from TAG engines to Honda units for 1988 was a springboard for even greater things as these were combined with the lowline MP4/4 chassis with which Prost and new signing Ayrton Senna won all but one of the 16 rounds. Their rivalry became ever more intense through 1989 when Prost came out ahead, and it was perhaps best that they were separated when Prost moved to Ferrari for 1990 and Senna won that title and the next.

It seemed that nothing would stop McLaren, but designer Adrian Newey took Williams to new heights in 1992. After McLaren lost its Honda engine deal, it took until 1998 for the team, now with Newey-designed chassis, to reassert itself, and Mika Hakkinen bagged the first of two consecutive titles with Mercedes power.

From 2000 it was Ferrari's turn, but Kimi Raikkonen ended the 2003 and 2005 campaigns as runner-up. In 2007, a McLaren driver should have been champion, but Fernando Alonso and rookie Lewis Hamilton fought too much and Raikkonen, now with Ferrari, pipped them to the crown. Happily, with Hamilton as team leader in 2008, McLaren hit the top again, but it didn't last as Red Bull Racing took over, succeeded by Mercedes with its own team. Mercedes poached Hamilton after 2013 to lead its attack and, a year later, McLaren lost its Mercedes engine deal. From 2015, life became much tougher for McLaren, with the team struggling with returning Honda before changing to Renault power in 2018.

Dennis masterminded the opening of an extraordinary technical centre outside Woking in 2003 and this was from where it started making its stunning supercar, the F1, creating a new element of McLaren, a road-car building wing. This gargantuan project appeared to take Dennis's eye off the F1 division, and he was removed from the helm in 2016.

The change of tack, with Zak Brown heading the team and Eric Boullier running it for Alonso, was disappointing. Much of the blame was laid at Honda's door, but it took a while for things to improve when it took on Renault engines, suggesting that other changes needed to be made. These were done last year, with Boullier standing down and Andreas Seidl being brought in.

> **"Finishing last year in fourth place overall in the constructors' World Championship, with sixth and 11th places for Carlos and Lando respectively, is a great achievement."**
>
> Andreas Seidl

Ayrton Senna and Alain Prost formed a pacy but combustible pairing for McLaren in 1988.

CARLOS SAINZ JR

Carlos drove very well last year and must be hoping that McLaren continues its return to form in the season ahead as it aims to tackle the top three teams and so give him a chance to pitch for the podium results he now craves.

Carlos Jr displays great maturity and adds welcome experience to his pace.

It might have been expected that Carlos Jr would follow his multiple world title-winning father of the same name into rallying, but his desire was always more likely to be circuit racing as he ripped up the kart racing ladder.

His highlight was winning the Monaco Kart Cup in 2009 and then, aged 15, it was time to advance to car racing in 2010. Carlos Jr's first year was spent in Formula BMW and he impressed by taking a win en route to fourth place overall.

Carlos Jr went better still in his second year of car racing, finishing as runner-up in European Formula Renault and claiming the northern European series title. Formula 3 was the obvious next step and he was helped towards this by being part of Red Bull's driver talent programme. Sixth in the British series and ninth in Europe was acceptable, but a move to GP3 for 2013 yielded only 10th place in that series as fellow Red Bull scholar Daniil Kvyat dominated. It suggested that his days in the Red Bull programme might be limited.

However, Carlos Jr opted for more power for 2014 and stepped up to Formula Renault 3.5. The move worked as he easily bagged the title, ahead of Pierre Gasly. This set him up for promotion to F1 with Scuderia Toro Rosso and the Red Bull programme's decision to stick with him proved to be right.

All Toro Rosso drivers hope they will be promoted to Red Bull Racing and an opening came in 2016 when Kvyat wasn't recording the results expected of him. However, it was a bitter blow for Carlos Jr when rookie team-mate Max Verstappen was given the drive instead of him.

A move to the Renault team part way through 2017 gave Carlos Jr a change of scene, but the team wasn't going through a good period and, pragmatically, he chose to move to McLaren – a team below its best – for 2019 in the hope of a better long-term future.

TRACK NOTES

Nationality:	**SPANISH**
Born:	**1 SEPTEMBER 1994, MADRID, SPAIN**
Website:	**www.carlossainzjr.com**
Teams:	**TORO ROSSO 2015-17, RENAULT 2017-18, McLAREN 2019-20**

CAREER RECORD

First Grand Prix:	**2015 AUSTRALIAN GP**
Grand Prix starts:	**102**
Grand Prix wins:	**0 (best result: 3rd, 2019 Brazilian GP)**
Poles:	**0**
Fastest laps:	**0**
Points:	**267**
Honours:	**2014 FORMULA RENAULT 3.5 CHAMPION, 2011 EUROPEAN FORMULA RENAULT RUNNER-UP & NORTHERN EUROPEAN FORMULA RENAULT CHAMPION, 2009 MONACO KART CUP WINNER & EUROPEAN KF3 RUNNER-UP, 2008 ASIA/PACIFIC JUNIOR KART CHAMPION, 2006 MADRID CADET KART CHAMPION**

MATURE DRIVING GATHERS POINTS

A pair of consecutive fifth-place finishes in the German and Hungarian GPs showed how strong Carlos's form was in mid-season and his run to sixth place in the Russian GP was further proof of this. Yet, as the McLaren team increasingly got its act together, so too did Carlos Jr. The points kept on flowing in and the cruellest moment of the season was when he finished fourth in Brazil. Although happy enough with that, he didn't get to celebrate what became his first top-three finish, as the podium ceremony was over before Lewis Hamilton - second on the track - was hit with a 5s penalty for tipping Alex Albon into a spin. Still, the Spanish driver can be proud of this like no season before it as he fought right to the last corner of the last lap of the year in Abu Dhabi, with his move to pass both Renault drivers giving him 10th place, enough to ensure that he ended the year ranked a career-best sixth.

LANDO NORRIS

The results didn't always go his way last year, with mechanical failures costing Lando some of his best drives, but he was extremely impressive in his maiden year and is sure to deliver even more in his second F1 campaign in 2020.

Lando brought pace, poise and humour to his impressive rookie season.

The word "champion" comes up a lot when you skim through Lando's curriculum vitae. That is a good thing, as a racing driver's very purpose is to beat all those around them. This is precisely what little Lando did in karting, landing numerous championship titles, including the world title in 2014, to prove that he was ready for the jump up to car racing.

He started in the Ginetta Junior series in 2014, when he was 14, finishing third in that. In 2015, Lando advanced to single-seaters, running in the MSA Formula, and winning the title, but also racing in F4 and winning races in the British and German series.

With a good degree of backing from his father's financial services business, Lando was able to spread his wings further in 2016, starting off in New Zealand, in the northern hemisphere winter, when he landed the Toyota Racing Series title. He then kept that momentum going through his main campaign in Formula Renault, winning both the European and the lesser northern Europe titles. He even found time to emphasize his flexibility by winning four races in British F3. All of this, plus strong form in the end-of-year McLaren *Autosport* BRDC award test days, landed him that prestigious title and the associated F1 test run with McLaren.

For 2017, Lando wanted the European F3 crown, and this he duly claimed thanks to winning nine races for Carlin. He just missed out on winning the F3 street race in Macau and then rounded out his year by contesting the final F2 round.

A full year in F2 with Carlin followed in 2018. Lando won the opening race, at Sakhir, and must have thought that the year would be his, but George Russell won seven races for the ART Grand Prix team to dominate a three-way battle between the best of the Brits, with Lando pipping Alex Albon to second in the rankings.

Lando has brought much needed humour to the F1 paddock, often being moved to tears of laughter if near Daniel Ricciardo in a press conference.

TRACK NOTES

Nationality:	**BRITISH**
Born:	**13 NOVEMBER 1999, GLASTONBURY, ENGLAND**
Website:	**www.landonorris.com**
Teams:	**McLAREN 2019-20**

CAREER RECORD

First Grand Prix:	**2019 Australian GP**
Grand Prix starts:	**21**
Grand Prix wins:	**0 (best result: 6th, 2019 Bahrian GP & Austrian GP)**
Poles:	**0**
Fastest laps:	**0**
Points:	**49**
Honours:	**2018 F2 RUNNER-UP, 2017 EUROPEAN F3 CHAMPION, 2016 EUROPEAN FORMULA RENAULT CHAMPION & FORMULA RENAULT NEC CHAMPION & TOYOTA RACING SERIES CHAMPION, 2015 MSA FORMULA CHAMPION, 2014 WORLD KF KART CHAMPION, 2013 WORLD KF JUNIOR KART CHAMPION & EUROPEAN KF KART CHAMPION & KF JUNIOR SUPER CUP WINNER**

LANDING ON HIS FEET IN F1

McLaren did a far better job in 2019 than it had in the previous few seasons before Lando joined the team. So, instead of racing around at the back of the field, he really landed on his feet as he and Carlos Sainz Jr started to get the MCL34 really motoring up the order, up into the points again. Lando's sixth place on his second outing, in the Bahrain GP at Sakhir, was exceptional, and a similar result in Austria was proof of his continued improvement. Both might have been eclipsed by a fifth place finish in the Belgian GP, but a power unit failure on the last lap cruelly scuppered that. However, it's always important to end a season strongly and Lando certainly did that, by finishing seventh then twice eighth in the final three rounds in the United States of America, Brazil and Abu Dhabi. He ranked 11th overall and, with a little more luck, would deservingly have ended his rookie F1 campaign in the top 10.

RENAULT

Renault is still finding its feet as it tries to make an impact as a team again after many years in F1 as an engine supplier. Daniel Ricciardo has established himself as team leader but he will have a challenge from the returning Esteban Ocon.

Daniel Ricciardo gave his all for Renault last year and won't be satisfied if all he can do is shoot for the minor points positions again in 2020.

Glance through the history books of the World Championship, and you might surmise that there have been three Renault teams in F1. There was a Renault team 1977–85, another 2002–11 and a third since 2016. It would be more accurate, however, to say that there have been just two. The first team, 1977–85, was run from Viry-Chatillon in France and it has a place in F1 history for introducing turbocharged engines. The second, is the team that runs as Renault today and, despite increasing input from the French manufacturer, is still simply a British team that has had many names.

This team, as Toleman, reached F1 in 1981, four years after the first Renault debuted. Toleman was formed by car transport magnate Ted Toleman, having shone in F2. Yet, this pedigree wasn't enough to help it make a splash. In fact, the cars seldom qualified.

By 1984, Toleman was making moves, thanks to chassis design by Rory Byrne and the pace of F1 rookie Ayrton Senna

who, if the Monaco GP had run for one more lap before being stopped early due to rain, might have given the team its first win. Senna then moved to Lotus

and, by 1986, the team had its first new name, being rebadged as Benetton, with cars continuing to be based in Witney. Powered by flame-spitting turbocharged

KEY PEOPLE & 2019 ROUND-UP

CYRIL ABITEBOUL

Cyril seems like a Renault "lifer", having joined in 2001. After working for the manufacturer in France and then the Renault F1 team in Enstone, he rose to executive director of the F1 outfit and then returned to Viry as Renault moved its focus to engine supply. In 2012, Cyril became team principal of the Caterham F1 Team, but Renault drew him back in late 2014 to be managing director of its F1 programme in preparation of it rebranding the team from Enstone with its own name for 2016.

TOO LITTLE TOO LATE TO CHALLENGE

When Renault's Daniel Ricciardo and Nico Hulkenberg raced to fourth and fifth places in the Italian GP, it showed what might have been, but it was a day in which two of the drivers for the three top teams stumbled, so that showed more accurately what the Renault drivers could hope for as they strove simply to be best of the rest, the leaders of the midfield. The RS19 was sleek and worked best on low downforce circuits, but it was never going to be a winning car, whatever Ricciardo and Hulkenberg did.

2019 DRIVERS & RESULTS

Driver	Nationality	Races	Wins	Pts	Pos
Nico Hulkenberg	German	21	0	37	14th
Daniel Ricciardo	Australian	21	0	54	9th

FOR THE RECORD

Country of origin:	**England**
Team base:	**Enstone, England**
Telephone:	**(44) 01608 678000**
Website:	**www.renaultsport.com**
Active in Formula One:	**Toleman**
	1981-85, Benetton 1986-2000, Renault
	2002-11 & 2016 on, Lotus 2012-15
Grands Prix contested:	**655**
Wins:	**48**
Pole positions:	**34**
Fastest laps:	**54**

THE TEAM

Managing director:	**Cyril Abiteboul**
President:	**Jerome Stoll**
Executive director:	**Marcin Budkowski**
Engineering director:	**Pat Fry**
Team chassis technical director:	
	Nick Chester
Team engine technical director:	
	Remi Taffin
Chief aerodynamicist:	**Dirk de Beer**
Sporting director:	**Alan Permane**
Operations director:	**Rob White**
Chief engineer:	**Ciaron Pilbeam**
Team manager:	**Paul Seaby**
Test drivers:	**Jack Aitken &**
	Guanyu Zhou
Chassis:	**Renault RS20**
Engine:	**Renault V6**
Tyres:	**Pirelli**

BMW engines, the multi-coloured cars were spectacular in qualifying for Teo Fabi and Gerhard Berger, with Berger going on to win the Mexican GP. Williams was the team to beat and the loss of BMW engines to them hit Benetton hard. Then after McLaren had taken over at the top of F1 in 1988, Benetton, led by Thierry Boutsen advanced to third overall.

Nelson Piquet won the final two races of 1990 as a career swansong, but it was the arrival of Michael Schumacher, late in 1991, that gave the team its golden ticket. Now operating out of a new base at Enstone, the team came on strong as Schumacher won the Belgian GP and did well enough to help Benetton match its best ranking of third overall.

Byrne was still in charge of design and worked wonders with Ross Brawn to produce a front-running car. The 1994 season came down to a clash, literally, with Damon Hill at Adelaide, and Schumacher took the title. Joining Williams in being powered by Renault engines kept Benetton in the hunt in 1995 and Schumacher won a second title and the team's first, but then he, Byrne and Brawn moved to Ferrari.

Berger and Jean Alesi kept Benetton near the front in 1996, but its ranking dwindled over the following years and led to Renault's decision to add finance for 2002 and change it to race simply as Renault.

Fernando Alonso stepped up to be the team's "second Schumacher", claiming the 2005 and 2006 crowns as Ferrari's dominance was brought to an end. His decision to then join McLaren cost Renault momentum and it spent the rest of the decade in the midfield. A third change of name for 2012 saw the team race as Lotus although, as is F1's way, it had nothing to do with the team that had shaped F1 in the 1960s and 1970s. Kimi Raikkonen won in Abu Dhabi to finish third in the drivers' championship, but this was to be as good as it got. The team ranked fourth in both 2012 and 2013 but, by 2014, was on the slide. It fell to eighth out of 11 in the Constructors' Cup as Mercedes took F1 to new levels of excellence and Renault's engines simply couldn't keep up. Budgets were also tight and this meant a lack of development

that hit it hard for a couple of years.

Thus Renault decided to take it over again in 2016 and Nico Hulkenberg led its return to respectability.

> **"Esteban has shown his ability to score points, has great professionalism on and off the track, plus his recent experience as reserve driver to the current world champions will be a valuable asset to the development of our team."**
>
> *Cyril Abiteboul*

Michael Schumacher really put the team on the map when it raced as Benetton in 1994.

DANIEL RICCIARDO

The Australian racer was still smiling through 2019, but life with Renault team was very different to his previous life at Red Bull Racing and Daniel had to adjust for tilting at podium finishes rather than possible grand prix wins.

Daniel faced new challenges in 2019 and now has Esteban Ocon to keep in place.

Western Australia is a great place to grow up, with a wonderful climate and huge swathes of space in which to go out and play. The trouble is, it's an awfully long way away from everywhere, even from the rest of Australia.

So, when Daniel's father guided him from karting into car racing, long-distance travel was always going to be an essential part of the package. Indeed, instead of contesting an Australian single-seater championship, Daniel entered the 2006 Asian Formula BMW series. Third place in that was a precursor to finishing fifth in the end-of-year world Formula BMW finals.

For 2007, distances grew greater as 17-year-old Daniel, headed to Europe to compete in Formula Renault. Snapped up as a future talent by the Red Bull driver search programme, he finished second behind Valtteri Bottas in the European championship in 2008. Next came Formula Three and he won the British title with the Carlin team.

Formula Renault 3.5 was next up and Daniel ended 2010 as runner-up in that, just two points short of the title. Back for more in 2011, he suddenly found himself as an F1 driver when Narain Karthikeyan was dropped by the tail-end HRT team.

This promotion came courtesy of backer Red Bull, which then gave him a full-time ride with Scuderia Toro Rosso in 2012 and he did well enough to move up to a ride with Red Bull Racing in 2014 after compatriot Mark Webber retired. A real clue to Daniel's potential was shown when he outscored his team-mate, the then reigning world champion Sebastian Vettel, through the course of the season thanks to landing his breakthrough F1 win in the Canadian GP and then backing that up with two more to finish third in the drivers' table behind Mercedes' Lewis Hamilton and Nico Rosberg.

Mercedes dominated the next few years, too, making wins hard to come by. By the end of 2018, feeling that he was now seen as number two to Max Verstappen at Red Bull Racing, Daniel played contractual hardball before opting to move to Renault for 2019.

TRACK NOTES

Nationality:	**AUSTRALIAN**
Born:	**1 JULY 1989, PERTH, AUSTRALIA**
Website:	**www.danielricciardo.com**
Teams:	**HRT 2011, TORO ROSSO 2012-13, RED BULL RACING 2014-18, RENAULT 2019-20**

CAREER RECORD

First Grand Prix:	**2011 BRITISH GP**
Grand Prix starts:	**171**
Grand Prix wins:	**7**
	2014 Canadian GP, Hungarian GP, Belgian GP, 2016 Malaysian GP, 2017 Azerbaijan GP, 2018 Chinese GP, Monaco GP
Poles:	**3**
Fastest laps:	**13**
Points:	**1040**
Honours:	**2010 FORMULA RENULT 3.5 RUNNER-UP, 2009 BRITISH FORMULA THREE CHAMPION, 2008 EUROPEAN FORMULA RENAULT RUNNER-UP & WESTERN EUROPEAN FORMULA RENAULT CHAMPION**

LIFE AFTER RED BULL RACING

Everyone saw Daniel's move from Red Bull Racing to Renault as a risk, as the team from Enstone had finished 2018 with just 122 points compared to Red Bull's 419. However, these things can happen when contract negotiations don't go as planned. Typically, Daniel still appeared to go about his racing with a smile on his face, just from rather further back down the grid. There were a host of retirements that left further him down the points table than he should have been, followed by a series of first-lap incidents towards the end of the season. This left him simply trying to win the battle to score more points than team-mate Nico Hulkenberg. Usually a few tenths of a second faster in qualifying, Daniel finished in the points less often, but peaked with fourth place in the Italian GP, and this kept him ahead in the final reckoning.

ESTEBAN OCON

This talented French racer was pretty hungry before, but a year spent on the sidelines will have strengthened his appetite and it will be intriguing to see whether he can take the battle to Daniel Ricciardo within the Renault camp.

A year on the sidelines will have made Esteban extra hungry for the year ahead.

Back in the 1980s, the F1 grid was packed with French racing drivers, with Alain Prost, Patrick Tambay, Didier Pirioni and Rene Arnoux – all grand prix winners – leading the way, and all were helped up the racing ladder by a cluster of French sponsors seeking to promote rising French talent. Then a drought started, triggered by the banning of tobacco advertising on television. A very

rare bright moment was Olivier Panis's victory for Ligier in the 1996 Monaco GP.

Almost two decades later, France had a rising wave of talent coming out of kart racing. Among them were Esteban Ocon, Pierre Gasly, Charles Leclerc and Anthoine Hubert. Suddenly, the cupboard was full again.

Esteban's first year out of karting, in 2012, was spent racing in Formula Renault. He learnt well enough to rank third in the European series the following year when Gasly took the spoils. This was good enough for Esteban to advance to Formula 3 in 2014 and he shone for the Prema Powerteam, landing nine wins as he swept to the European championship title, with Max Verstappen ranking third. As a member of the Lotus F1 Junior Team, Esteban had his first F1 test and went well.

However, no F1 drive beckoned for 2015, so Esteban went into GP3 instead, and he made it two titles in two years by landing the crown, this time for ART Grand Prix. This ought to have been enough for Esteban to move up to at least GP2, but his family didn't have

enough money and so he opted to be paid instead by becoming a touring car racer for Mercedes in the DTM.

This move paid dividends in an unexpected way too. Rio Haryanto was dropped by the Manor F1 team and, as Mercedes supplied the team's engines, the German manufacturer placed Esteban there for the final nine grands prix of the 2016 season.

Two years with Force India followed in 2017 and 2018, when he was up against Sergio Perez, often quite literally and often leading to collisions as they scuffled in an attempt to get the upper hand.

TRACK NOTES

Nationality:	FRENCH
Born:	17 SEPTEMBER 1996, EVREUX, FRANCE
Website:	www.esteban-ocon.com
Teams:	MANOR 2016, FORCE INDIA 2017-18, RENAULT 2020

CAREER RECORD

First Grand Prix:	2016 BELGIAN GP
Grand Prix starts:	50
Grand Prix wins:	0 (best result: 5th, 2017 Spanish GP, Mexican GP)
Poles:	0
Fastest laps:	0
Points:	136
Honours:	2015 GP3 CHAMPION, 2014 FIA EUROPEAN FORMULA THREE CHAMPION

FORCED TO WAIT AND OBSERVE

A racing driver is most agitated when forced to have no role in racing and watch their rivals out on the track doing what they want to do. In fact, doing what they need to do themselves, just to feel as though they exist. Being a racing driver defines them and no amount of simulator work can replace this. Even the most confident drivers know there might be a new rising star who will usurp them. So, it was with agitation that Esteban spent 2019 trackside, having lost his F1 ride as the Force India team morphed into Racing Point, and he had to make way for team owner Lawrence Stroll's son Lance. Testing for Mercedes was not fully satisfying, so it was with relief that Esteban was named as this year's Renault number two driver in place of Nico Hulkenberg, even if there was a time when he thought that Mercedes made take a punt on him and promote him to its race team in place of Valtteri Bottas.

Daniel Ricciardo heads out of the Renault garage to attempt to improve his lap time in 2019 when the team from Enstone lived its life in F1's midfield pack.

SCUDERIA ALPHA TAURI

Red Bull's second team continues to be used as a training ground and feeder for Red Bull Racing, and it produced a shock when Daniil Kvyat came third in Germany, but expect it to be back closer to the tail of the field, even with it new name.

Daniil Kvyat came away with the team's best result of 2019, third in the German GP, but it will take more than a new name to reproduce that.

Competing alongside Red Bull Racing with cars that look only a little different, as both teams sport dark blue cars topped with a large bull, can make this Italian team seem merely as a support act. In many ways it is precisely that, a training ground financed by the Red Bull energy drink company that serves only to bring on talented young drivers and prepare the best of them to step up to Red Bull Racing when a vacancy arises.

This all seems a very far cry from the way it went for its first 21 years in F1 when it ran as Minardi, a team loved for its plucky approach to being perennial tailenders. The Minardi story goes back to the early 1970s when it stepped up to F2 and had the honour of running Ferrari engines. Unfortunately, these weren't competitive and it was only when the team from Faenza built its own chassis and ran them with BMW power that they began to feature, with Michele Alboreto scoring a breakthough win at Misano in 1981.

Sticking with its lead F2 driver, Alessandro Nannini, Minardi elected to step up to F1 in 1985, just as F2 was superceded by F3000 as F1's feeder category. Held back by running Motori Moderni engines, it took Italy's second team until 1988 to score a point, although it was harder then as they were awarded only down to sixth place.

KEY PEOPLE & 2019 ROUND-UP

FRANZ TOST

This 64-year-old Austrian is old school in that he was a racer first – in F3 – before hanging up his helmet to turn to team management. Running the Walter Lechner Racing School was his first step on this course, followed by joining Willi Weber's driver management company to help look after the Schumacher brothers. He followed Ralf Schumacher to Williams in 2000 as he oversaw its new supply of BMW engines. In 2006, Franz became team principal of new Scuderia Toro Rosso as it was transformed from Minardi.

THIRD WAS A SURPRISE NOT REPEATED

Daniil Kvyat must have expected that the best his third spell at Toro Rosso might deliver would be a sixth place or so on a day of attrition for the top three teams. So, with a best result of seventh place at Monaco to his name, the Russian will have been shocked and delighted to smile down from the podium after finishing in third place in the German GP at Hockenheim. However, this was a flash in the pan and it was team-mate Alex Albon who got the call mid-season to step up to Red Bull Racing.

2019 DRIVERS & RESULTS

Driver	Nationality	Races	Wins	Pts	Pos
Alex Albon	British	12	0	92	8th
Pierre Gasly	French	9	0	95	7th
Daniil Kvyat	Russian	21	0	37	13th

FOR THE RECORD

Country of origin:	**Italy**
Team base:	**Faenza, Italy**
Telephone:	**(39) 546 696111**
Website:	**www.alphatauri.com**
Active in Formula One:	**As Minardi 1985-2005, Toro Rosso 2006-19, Alpha Tauri 2020 onwards**
Grands Prix contested:	**609**
Wins:	**1**
Pole positions:	**1**
Fastest laps:	**1**

THE TEAM

Team owner:	**Dietrich Mateschitz**
Team principal:	**Franz Tost**
Technical director:	**Jody Egginton**
Chief designers:	**Paolo Marabini & Mark Tatham**
Head of aerodynamics:	**Brendan Gilhome**
Head of vehicle performance:	**Guillaume Dezoteux**
Team manager:	**Graham Watson**
Team co-ordinator:	**Michele Andreazza**
Chief engineer:	**Marco Matassa**
Chief race engineer:	**Jonathan Eddols**
Test driver:	**tba**
Chassis:	**Toro Rosso STR15**
Engine:	**Honda V6**
Tyres:	**Pirelli**

The driver on that day, Pierluigi Martini, was later able to shock the establishment when the 1990 season-opening United States GP was held on a street circuit in Phoenix. The team's Pirelli tyres were very much the ones to have in qualifying and Martini qualified second behind McLaren's Gerhard Berger, but could finish only seventh in the race.

Giancarlo Minardi was patriotic and his intention was always to bring on young Italian talent, giving an F1 break to future grand prix winners Giancarlo Fisichella and Jarno Trulli, as well as Spanish great Fernando Alonso and Australia's Mark Webber. However, as finding money was always crucial to this underfinanced team, with the cost of F1 continuing to rocket, Minardi continued to be even slightly competitive by also fielding cars for drivers with markedly lesser talent.

Once F1 became beyond its budget, Minardi sold out to Dietrich Mateschitz, co-founder of the Red Bull energy drink. As a result, from the start of the 2006 season, the team was rebranded as Red Bull Racing's "mini me" sidekick and would race as Scuderia Toro Rosso, ditching its longstanding black, yellow and white livery for something more corporate. F1's perennial but popular underdog had a new coat.

This was when the team's form gained a new trajectory, as it also benefitted from advice from Red Bull Racing's technical division. That said, no one expected Toro Rosso to beat its senior partner to a first F1 win, but this is what happened when Sebastian Vettel dominated a wet/dry Italian GP from pole position in 2008.

Toro Rosso hasn't won since, settling back into its role of bringing on the best of Red Bull's many scholarship drivers if they have shone in the junior categories. By dint of numbers, most are discarded, found not up to the exacting standards required by Mateschitz's talent scout, former F1 racer Helmut Marko.

The pick of the drivers coming through after Vettel have been Daniel Ricciardo and Max Verstappen, both of whom started winning on being promoted to Red Bull Racing, with Verstappen stunning onlookers by claiming victory first time out when he stepped up a few races in to the 2016 campaign.

Just as others have stepped up so some, such as Daniil Kvyat in 2016 and Pierre Gasly in 2019, been made to step down to Toro Rosso again, something from which few careers recover.

"I must thank the team, both in Faenza and Bicester, as the upgrades from the aero department we got through 2019 worked very well. Honda's developments were impressive too to enable us to be competitive."

Franz Tost

This was the result that no-one predicted, the team's one and only win, at Monza in 2008.

DANIIL KVYAT

Scuderia Toro Rosso went better last year as engine supplier Honda made strides, but this Russian driver must be feeling that if he doesn't advance in 2020 with Scuderia Alpha Tauri that his time in Formula One must be coming to an end.

Daniil was frustrated last year but is unlikely to take another podium in 2020.

Daniil's racing career has been stop-start, which is odd as he was adjudged good enough to be promoted to race in Formula One before his 20th birthday. Yet, six years on, it has been an interrupted career dotted with a few amazing results but peppered with disappointments.

It started with so much promise as he was notably quick in karts and took to single-seaters with aplomb when he started in Formula BMW having turned 16 in 2010. Backing from Red Bull, which was keen to bring on a Russian driver for the obvious commercial reasons, gave him wings and these took him out to New Zealand to get his 2011 campaign on the road in the Toyota Racing Series.

His main campaign in 2011 was in European Formula Renault and Daniil ranked third, then second the following year, when he and Stoffel Vandoorne scored double the tally of the next best driver. Daniil mastered more powerful machinery to win the 2013 GP3 title, then ended his year with an F1 test for Scuderia Toro Rosso.

For most drivers, a year in F3 then a year or two in GP2 would have been the expected route, but Daniil was promoted straight to an F1 ride for 2014, the year of the first Russian GP. In the points in the first two races, he was clearly not overawed and Red Bull promoted him to Red Bull Racing for 2015 as Sebastian Vettel had gone to Ferrari. This wasn't a like-for-like replacement, but Daniil impressed as he scored enough to outrank team-mate Daniel Ricciardo, with a surprise second place in Hungary boosting his tally.

The following season wasn't so kind and, after just four races, Daniil was dropped to Toro Rosso, with Max Verstappen going the other way, even though he had finished third in China. The rest of the year was less kind.

Daniil didn't get to complete the 2017 season with Toro Rosso, as he was dropped to make space for Pierre Gasly and then spent 2018 on the sidelines.

TRACK NOTES

Nationality:	**RUSSIAN**
Born:	**26 APRIL 1994, UFA, RUSSIA**
Website:	**www.daniilkvyat.com**
Teams:	**TORO ROSSO 2014 & 2016-17 & 2019, RED BULL RACING 2015-16, ALPHA TAURI 2020**

CAREER RECORD

First Grand Prix:	**2014 AUSTRALIAN GP**
Grand Prix starts:	**95**
Grand Prix wins:	**0 (best result: 2nd, 2015 Hungarian GP)**
Poles:	**0**
Fastest laps:	**0**
Points:	**170**
Honours:	**2013 GP3 CHAMPION, 2012 FORMULA RENAULT RUNNER-UP & ALPS CHAMPION, 2011 FORMULA RENAULT NORTHERN EUROPE RUNNER-UP, 2009 WSK KART RUNNER-UP**

THIRD IN GERMANY WAS A SHOCK

Racing for Scuderia Toro Rosso tends to mean that any points scored will have been hard-earned as the team is not often among the top five teams. So, if it finds a better than usual vein of form, as it did early last season, these opportunities must be grabbed. So, with Honda offering more punch than before, Daniil will have been pleased that he bounced back from a year away from racing by scoring in four of the first seven races. What wasn't so impressive was that his rookie team-mate Alex Albon was hard on his heels, often in races that included setbacks. So, when the extraordinary German GP resulted in a career-best second place, up from 14th on the grid as his rivals spun, the Russian must have felt he was in for possible promotion to a second stint at Red Bull Racing. Yet, to his disappointment, not only did he not get the team's second seat for 2020, but Albon already had been promoted to it.

PIERRE GASLY

Any step backwards in Formula One is hard to recover from, yet a poor first half of the year with Red Bull Racing was redeemed when Pierre Gasly was demoted to Scuderia Toro Rosso and bounced back by finishing second in Brazil.

Pierre is undoubtedly quick and needs this year to rebuild his reputation.

Study the history of the international kart racing and there are more names that don't make it in car racing than do. Pierre is one that did.

He was on the pace in his first year in cars, in French F4, but took two seasons to hit the top in the European Formula Renault Championship, his three wins helping him land the 2013 title.

In 2014, thanks to backing from Red Bull, Pierre advanced to the much more powerful Formula Renault 3.5 cars. It was a larger jump than most would have taken, but he did very well and, although he failed to win a race, was still able to be ranked second behind the more experienced Carlos Sainz Jr. The following season, spent in GP2, was less exceptional. It produced four podium visits, but Pierre could rank only eighth as Stoffel Vandoorne dominated.

Then came the season in which Pierre stood out: 2016. Staying on in GP2, he knew that he had to win the title and duly did with Prema Racing, his four wins enough to help him to pip Antonio Giovinazzi.

Red Bull liked him a lot, but had no opening for him either with Red Bull Racing or Scuderia Toro Rosso for 2017, so he was placed in Japan's Super Formula and his reputation soared as he won races at Motegi and Autopolis. Then, with the title in his grasp, he faced a conundrum: he had been given his F1 debut by Toro Rosso in the Malaysian GP in place of Daniil Kvyat and did well

enough to be asked back. This meant that he wouldn't be able to go for the Super Formula title. Toro Rosso let him return to Japan, but the final round was rained off and he ended the season half a point down on Hiroaki Ishiura.

However, it was clear that F1 was his future and so he was kept on for 2018 by Toro Rosso and stunned with fourth place in Bahrain, a drive that earned him a Red Bull ride for 2019 as Daniel Ricciardo moved to Renault.

TRACK NOTES

Nationality:	**FRENCH**
Born:	**7 FEBRUARY 1996, ROUEN, FRANCE**
Website:	**www.pierregasly.com**
Teams:	**TORO ROSSO 2017-18 & 2019, RED BULL RACING 2019, ALPHA TAURI 2020**

CAREER RECORD

First Grand Prix:	**2017 MALAYSIAN GP**
Grand Prix starts:	**47**
Grand Prix wins:	**0**
(best result: 2nd, 2019 Brazilian GP)	
Poles:	**0**
Fastest laps:	**2**
Points:	**124**
Honours:	**2017 JAPANESE SUPER FORMULA RUNNER-UP, 2016 GP2 CHAMPION, 2014 FORMULA RENAULT 3.5 RUNNER-UP, 2013 EUROPEAN FORMULA RENAULT CHAMPION, 2010 EUROPEAN KF3 KART RUNNER-UP**

FAILING TO MATCH VERSTAPPEN

Last year was when Pierre should have taken his natural course towards becoming a regular podium visitor, yet it didn't shape out that way, as this driver who had always impressed through the single-seater categories came up short. Certainly, his yardstick was not one that many could match in that it was Max Verstappen, the driver around whom Red Bull Racing has revolved. However, 2019 just didn't gel for him and he was nowhere near as effective at taking the battle to Mercedes and Ferrari as Max. Indeed, Pierre had only fourth place at the British GP to smile about by mid-season. Two races later, he was dropped back to Scuderia Toro Rosso, unseated by F1 rookie Alex Albon. How humiliating must that have felt? Then, defying logic, Pierre restored his reputation with one sweep by finishing second at Interlagos. His lofty finishing position was due in part to the Ferraris colliding and Lewis Hamilton knocking Albon out of second, but also to Pierre's refusal to let his head drop and keep pressing to improve.

RACING POINT

After a less than spectacular first season under its latest name, Racing Point has opted to keep its line-up of Sergio Perez and Lance Stroll to see if this continuity can help it score points on a more consistent basis in 2020.

Lance Stroll finished up just off the podium in last year's German GP and will be hoping to impress his team-financing father further in 2020.

Most team bosses and owners running teams in the stepping-stone single-seater formulae used to dream that, one day, they might be able to take their team up to F1. The stratospheric budgets of F1 over the past 20 years has increasingly required all but a few of these dreams to be put on hold. Back at the early 1990s, though, it was still possible, just...

One person who long had ambitions to make the jump was former racer Eddie Jordan, and he gave his project the green light to go F1 in 1991, moving up from the front ranks of F3000, in which the Jordan team had propelled Jean Alesi to the 1989 title. Operating from a team base just across the road from Silverstone's front gates, his team was a revelation, ranking fifth at its first attempt and shaking the established order.

Trouble was, this form was hard to maintain, and landing an engine deal was one of the few ways to keep the budget in check, but Jordan learnt a vital lesson in 1992 when its Yamaha motors left it

languishing at the back of the pack. It took until 1994 for Jordan to rediscover its 1991 form, this time with Hart engines and promising drivers Rubens Barrichello

and Eddie Irvine helping the team to rank fifth. When Barrichello and Irvine finished second and third in the 1995 Canadian GP, it hinted that a win may not be far away, but

KEY PEOPLE & 2019 ROUND-UP

ANDREW GREEN

This is a man who knows the team inside out, as he joined it when it stepped up to F1 as Jordan in 1991. First a designer, he then got hands-on experience as a race engineer before moving to Tyrrell in 1998. Andrew stayed on as the team morphed into BAR, before being signed by Red Bull Racing in 2005. He later had a spell at Virgin Racing before returning home to the team in its Force India days as technical director.

GOING BACKWARDS TO ADVANCE

Seventh in last year's constructors' standings, like in 2018, suggests that it was status quo for Racing Point in F1's midfield, but this ignores the fact it had lost 59 points in 2018 – for changing its name from Force India – points that would have put it fifth. There were regressive steps last year, but moments of promise too, such as a pair of sixth place finishes for Sergio Perez and an out-of-the-blue fourth for Lance Stroll in the crazy wet German GP. Perez ended the season really strongly, scoring points in each of the final six rounds, suggesting that better things might lie ahead.

2019 DRIVERS & RESULTS

Driver	Nationality	Races	Wins	Pts	Pos
Sergio Perez	Mexican	21	0	52	10th
Lance Stroll	Canadian	21	0	21	15th

it didn't prove to be the case. Nonetheless, sixth, fifth and fifth in the Constructors' Cup 1995–97 showed it remained in the mix.

Jordan's breakthrough win came after a change from Peugeot to Mugen engines in 1998 and, not only did Damon Hill triumph in the wet/dry Belgian GP, but it was also a team one-two, with Ralf Schumacher instructed not to try to overtake, lest they clash. That helped them to beat Benetton to fourth in the constructors' points table.

Better still was to follow in 1999, when Jordan clocked up wins in the French and Italian GPs, both through Heinz-Harald Frentzen, and ended the year behind only Ferrari and McLaren. However, these two teams then accelerated off into the distance over the next few seasons, leaving Jordan with just its win in the 2003 Brazilian GP to cheer it and Eddie Jordan realised that the budget required to keep up was beyond him.

The team was sold to become Midland in 2005, then sold again to become Spyker in 2007. Spyker lasted just a year before a third sale saw the team renamed Force India as Indian drinks industry tycoon Vijay Mallya took over. For a while, things looked good, with its deal in 2009 to run with Mercedes engines a clever one. Giancarlo Fisichella then came close to giving the team its second Belgian GP victory when he finished second at Spa-Francorchamps.

What followed was a number of years in which the team took the battle to the grandee teams that had all the money, running lean and hungry, picking up their scraps, with Paul di Resta and Sergio Perez leading the way. Sadly, Mallya became more focused on fighting court cases against him and the long-serving staff never knew whether the team would survive, yet they pressed on and

ranked fourth overall in 2016. Force India continued to punch above its weight in 2018, despite Perez and Esteban Ocon appearing to be at war with each other as they fought to establish supremacy within the team. Their clashes squandered more than a few points.

Mallya's reign concluded towards the end of the 2018 season when, after agreeing to pay off the team's creditors, Lawrence Stroll took control.

Since then, Stroll and his investors have stabilized the team and ought to reap greater rewards in 2020.

FOR THE RECORD

Country of origin:	**England**
Team base:	**Silverstone, England**
Telephone:	**(44) 01327 850800**
Website:	**www.racingpointf1.com**
Active in Formula One:	**As Jordan 1991-2004, Midland 2005-06, Spyker 2007, Force India 2008-18, Racing Point 2019 on**
Grands Prix contested:	**518**
Wins:	**4**
Pole positions:	**3**
Fastest laps:	**7**

THE TEAM

Team principal:	**Otmar Szafnauer**
Technical director:	**Andrew Green**
Sporting director:	**Andy Stevenson**
Production director:	**Bob Halliwell**
Chief designers:	**Akio Haga & Ian Hall**
Aerodynamics director:	**Simon Phillips**
Chief engineer:	**Tom McCullough**
Operations manager:	**Mark Gray**
Test driver:	**tba**
Chassis:	**Racing Point RP20**
Engine:	**Mercedes V6**
Tyres:	**Pirelli**

"I am happy to re-sign as I see that this team has big potential. I really believe in the plans that we have for the coming years although last year, as expected, was a bit of a transition."

Sergio Perez

Sergio Perez competed for the team when it raced as Force India. This is Baku in 2018.

SERGIO PEREZ

Sergio backed up another consistent season by putting his name on a contract that will keep him racing for Racing Point for the next three seasons, emphasizing the extremely high esteem in which he is held for delivering all a car can achieve.

Sergio knows how competitive it can be in the midfield, but expects points every time.

Drivers looking to advance their careers have it relatively easy if they live in Europe, as there are leading championships close at hand, whether in their home country or the one next door. For the likes of Sergio, who grew up in Mexico, a little more travel is required and a lot more sacrifice.

He headed north to the USA when only 14 in 2004 to get his break in single-seaters, competing in the Barber Dodge series. Anxious to move further up the racing ladder, he went way further in 2005, to Europe. This was to race in Formula BMW, and he spent two years in the German series, growing up both in and out of the cockpit.

In 2007, Sergio moved to Britain and raced in Formula 3, with his first season landing him the lesser National class title and then showing good progress to rank fourth in 2008 by taking four wins as Jaime Alguersuari landed the title.

GP2 came next and Sergio really seemed to take well to the extra power, winning two races in the early-season 2009 Asian GP2 championship. He went on to claim a couple of podium finishes in the main GP2 series as future F1 team-mate Nico Hulkenberg dominated. At his second attempt, in 2010, Sergio raced to five wins, but ended the year runner-up behind Pastor Maldonado.

However, he was ready for promotion to F1 and a couple of tests with Sauber landed him a ride with the Swiss team for 2011. He boosted his chances by bringing a budget from Mexican sponsors as the country began to consider mounting a return to the World Championship calendar.

Sergio's light has never shone more brightly than in his second season when he harried Fernando Alonso's Ferrari for victory in Malaysia. A further second place later in the year at Monza cemented his reputation. Yet, after a year at McLaren in 2013 and then the next six years with Force India, now Racing Point, he has never placed as well. Through this time, notably for his ability to conserve tyres, Sergio's reputation has remained strong.

TRACK NOTES

Nationality:	**MEXICAN**
Born:	**26 JANUARY 1990, GUADALAJARA, MEXICO**
Website:	**www.sergioperezf1.com**
Teams:	**SAUBER 2011-12, McLAREN 2013, FORCE INDIA 2014-18, RACING POINT 2019-20**

CAREER RECORD

First Grand Prix:	**2011 BAHRAIN GP**
Grand Prix starts:	**176**
Grand Prix wins:	**0 (best result: 2nd, 2012 Malaysian GP, Italian GP)**
Poles:	**0**
Fastest laps:	**4**
Points:	**581**
Honours:	**2010 GP2 RUNNER-UP, 2007 BRITISH FORMULA THREE NATIONAL CLASS CHAMPION**

LEADING THE TEAM FORWARDS

Sergio's sixth year with the team from Silverstone – his first with it competing under the Racing Point name – was a strong one as he yet again outperformed a team-mate, on this occasion the far less experienced Lance Stroll. As with all drivers beyond the three top teams, though, collecting championship points consistently was an achievement and this consistent Mexican racer peaked with a pair of sixth-place finishes in the Azerbaijan and Belgian GPs when he proved himself to be the best of the rest. His seventh-place finish in the Italian and Russian GPs were the fruits of another couple of strong runs and he then rounded out the year with another seventh place in the championship finale at Yas Marina as he ended the year in a stream of points and earned the ranking of 10th overall, which wasn't bad for a driver racing for a team good enough only to be classified seventh out of the World Championship's 10 teams.

LANCE STROLL

Competing alongside the rapid and experienced Sergio Perez was always going to be difficult as Lance moved to join the Racing Point team for 2019, but he was the one who produced the best finish with a surprise fourth place at Hockenheim.

Lance is ambitious for greater things from his fourth year of F1.

With a billionaire father who loves racing, it wasn't a major job for Lance to convince him that he'd like to go karting. Using some of the considerable wealth he'd built up in the fashion industry, Lawrence Stroll set the wheels in motion and Lance did the rest.

He kicked off his car-racing career at the age of 15 in Ferrari's Florida-based Winter Series. He then headed from his home in Canada to contest the Italian F4 Championship and ended the year as champion, by which time he had joined the Ferrari Driver Academy. Lance kept up that momentum at the start of 2015 by heading south in the northern hemisphere winter to contest the New Zealand-based Toyota Racing Series and won that title as well.

So, people now realized that Lance was quick as well as unusually wealthy. Not chosing to hang around, he moved up to Formula 3 in 2015, coming on strong to win the final round of the European series and rank fifth overall. Unfortunately, he also gained a reputation for having accidents, knowing that he could always afford to keep racing.

In 2016, Lance tried something different by turning to sportscars to contest the Daytona 24 Hours. He returned to Europe to build on the F3 experience he had gained with the Prema Powerteam, staying on with the crack Italian team and winning the title by a considerable margin, taking 14 wins from 30 races.

Attracted both by his natural speed and his father's wealth and possible involvement with their team, Williams gave him a test run and Lance performed well.

In 2017, he stepped directly from F3 to F1, lining up alongside Felipe Massa for Williams. Impressively, Lance overcame early-season retirements to be in the right place at the right time to take third place in the Azerbaijan GP. A second season with Williams buoyed him, but the team was losing ground and Lance moved to what had been Force India for 2019 as his father led a consortium to buy it out and rename it Racing Point.

TRACK NOTES

Nationality:	CANADIAN
Born:	29 OCTOBER 1998, MONTREAL, CANADA
Website:	www.lancestroll.com
Teams:	WILLIAMS 2017-18, RACING POINT 2019-20

CAREER RECORD

First Grand Prix:	2017 AUSTRALIAN GP
Grand Prix starts:	62
Grand Prix wins:	0 (best result: 3rd, 2017 Azerbaijan GP)
Poles:	0
Fastest laps:	0
Points:	67
Honours:	2016 FIA EUROPEAN FORMULA THREE CHAMPION, 2015 TOYOTA RACING SERIES CHAMPION, 2014 ITALIAN FORMULA FOUR CHAMPION

FOURTH PLACE WAS NOT TYPICAL

Fourth at the topsy-turvy German GP was a wonderful boost for this young Canadian and the team in its first year since changing its name from Force India to Racing Point. However, it was certainly not representative of the regular run of results that the drivers could hope for with the RP19. Indeed, getting into the points at all was something of a bonus for either of the drivers, as the team was effectively only the seventh most competitive of the 10 teams, meaning that if no cars retired, then 13th and 14th were the best finishes that he and Sergio Perez could expect. All too often, Lance ended up finishing just out of the points, despite having given his all, frequently tussling with the drivers from closest rival Scuderia Toro Rosso. With the exception of that freak result at Hockenheim, Lance's other points came from a quartet of ninth-place finishes, in Australia, Azerbaijan, Canada and Japan.

ALFA ROMEO

This Swiss-based team had an up and down first season racing under the Alfa Romeo name, making it similar to recent years when it was entered as Sauber. Kimi Raikkonen remains the team's key component, delivering excellent performances as a matter of course.

Kimi Raikkonen started 2019 with a run of point-scoring drives, but Alfa Romeo must improve to ensure he can score at the end of the season too.

After a year in Alfa Romeo's white and red branding, the big question is whether fans think of the team from Hinwil as Alfa Romeo or Sauber. After all, most fans considered the team to still be Sauber in the five years from 2006 to 2010 when it was BMW Sauber. Although the cars raced in BMW's corporate white and blue colours, it always felt like a team run by an individual – Peter Sauber – rather than by a corporation.

Peter Sauber started his competition career in a VW Beetle, taking part in hill-climbs because his native Switzerland didn't permit any circuit racing following the dreadful death toll when Pierre Levegh's Mercedes flew into the crowds during the 1955 Le Mans 24 Hours. To move to circuit racing, Peter had to go abroad. His chosen arena was sportscars and, to keep costs down, he began building his own cars. Rivals looked on and some formed a queue to buy his machinery, which is why he quit competing and turned this into a business.

By the mid-1980s, his entries into the World Sports-Prototype Championship were boosted by covert funding from Mercedes-Benz, with Henri Pescarolo and Mike Thackwell taking a breakthrough win in a Mercedes-powered Sauber C8 at the Nurburgring 1000Kms in 1986. By 1988, Sauber's team was a works outfit and this

KEY PEOPLE & 2019 ROUND-UP

ERIC GANDELIN
An engineering graduate, Eric is one of Alfa Romeo Racing's long-stay employees, as this year will be his 19th with the Swiss team. His first experience in F1 came with Prost Grand Prix, joining as a composite design engineer in 1999. After three years with the French team, Eric moved to Switzerland and joined Sauber to perform a similar role. By the start of 2008, he was promoted to be head of concept design. After five years of that, Eric became the team's chief designer midway through 2013.

WORKS NAME BRINGS NO PROGRESS
The final season racing as Sauber ended with a ranking of eighth overall. The first racing as Alfa Romeo last year brought precisely the same result. One could quibble and say that some progress had made in celebration of the team's marketing tie-up with the Italian manufacturer that of course dominated F1 when the World Championship kicked off in 1950, as its final tally was 57 points to 2018's 48, but that would be an exaggeration. Kimi Raikkonen scored when possible, with a surprise fourth in Brazil.

2019 DRIVERS & RESULTS

Driver	Nationality	Races	Wins	Pts	Pos
Antonio Giovinazzi	Italian	21	0	14	17th
Kimi Raikkonen	Finnish	21	0	43	12th

blossomed as his cars won four of the 11 rounds. In 1989, Team Sauber Mercedes won the title and Jean-Louis Schlesser took the drivers' title ahead of team-mates Mauro Baldi and Jochen Mass, with the outfit coming top again in 1990.

Sauber wanted the next step to be F1 and Mercedes helped to fund a factory at Hinwil in north-eastern Switzerland, but then Mercedes changed its mind about direct involvement. However, Sauber pressed on and entered F1 in 1993. Its first F1 car, the Sauber C12, was designed by Leo Ress and proved to be effective, with JJ Lehto guiding it to fifth on its debut. However, that was as good as it got. Hoping for better things in 1994, when its Ilmor-built V10 engines were rebadged with Mercedes' name, Sauber was disappointed that it didn't move up the championship table. That was nothing, however, compared to Mercedes' decision to take its engines to McLaren instead for 1995, marking one of many twists and turns of fortune across the decades for Sauber's team.

Sauber then settled into life in the midfield, usually finishing seventh overall as it pressed on with Ford engines. A change to Ferrari customer engines in 1997 was observed with interest, but even the likes of Jean Alesi and Johnny

Herbert couldn't move the team up the order as the 1990s drew to a close. One reason, many thought, was that the team's base was nowhere near any other part of the motor racing world, and design and engineering experts didn't want to uproot their families from England or Italy to go there.

The 2001 season marked a new high, with Nick Heidfeld and rookie Kimi Raikkonen propelling Sauber to fourth overall. It took the arrival of BMW money in 2006 to give Sauber its next shove and it finished second in the constructors' championship in 2007. Then in 2008, Sauber had its day of days in the Canadian GP, when Robert Kubica claimed its only win.

Since then, Sauber's cars have always run with Ferrari power, but they have never been at the cutting edge as these are always one specification behind the works engines and the team's meagre budget has held it back. In 2016, when in a financial peril, the team was bought out by Swiss investment company Longbow Finance and Peter

> **"The midfield was the most competitive it has ever been, but we fought bravely last year and we can learn from last season to come back even stronger this year."**
>
> Frederic Vasseur

FOR THE RECORD

Country of origin:	Switzerland
Team base:	Hinwil, Switzerland
Telephone:	(41) 44 937 9000
Website:	www.sauber-group.com
Active in Formula One:	From 1993
	(as BMW Sauber 2006-2010)
Grands Prix contested:	485
Wins:	1
Pole positions:	1
Fastest laps:	5

THE TEAM

Chairman:	Pascal Picci
Team principal:	Frederic Vasseur
Technical director:	Jan Monchaux
Chief designer:	Eric Gandelin
Head of aerodynamics:	Nicolas Hennel de Beaupreau
Head of engineering:	Giampaolo Dall'ara
Head of track engineering:	Xevi Pujolar
Head of aerodynamic development:	Mariano Alperin-Bruvera
Head of aerodynamic research:	Seamus Mullarkey
Head of vehicle performance:	Elliot Dason-Barber
Team manager:	Beat Zehnder
Reserve driver:	Robert Kubica
Chassis:	Alfa Romeo C39
Engine:	Ferrari V6
Tyres:	Pirelli

43

Sauber stood down to let Frederic Vasseur become team principal, with rookie Charles Leclerc taking it to loftier finishes in 2018.

Sauber started 1993 in style, with JJ Lehto scoring points at Kyalami on the team's F1 debut.

KIMI RAIKKONEN

Although he has turned 40, don't expect Kimi to deliver anything less than his all for Alfa Romeo in the second year of his two-year deal, as he will continue to score points whenever the car is good enough to let him do so.

All Kimi asks for is a competitive car and he will, with no fuss, do the rest.

Kimi vaulted from karts to F1 after a ludicrously short car-racing apprenticeship of just 23 races. Some rookie racers get through that many outings in their first year of cars. Yet, no one who watched Kimi's first year in F1 has ever said that he wasn't ready for the challenge. Indeed, he finished sixth on his debut in Melbourne.

Picked out of karting to try Formula Renault at the end of 1999, Kimi raced four times and followed up with a full season in which he won the 2000 British Formula Renault title.

It was expected that F3 would follow, but Dave Robertson, who was managing him, suggested to Sauber that they might like to give him a run in its F1 car. It seemed premature, but he took to it like a natural and was the shock signing for the 2001 season.

Few had even heard of Kimi, but they were certainly aware of him after that debut run to sixth in Australia. McLaren signed him for 2002 and he rewarded them by ranking sixth as Michael Schumacher dominated for Ferrari. In 2003, the difference between them was just two points as Kimi scored his first win, in Malaysia. Second overall again in 2005, this time with seven wins – he lost out to Renault's Fernando Alonso – Kimi then joined Ferrari in 2007 and promptly came through in the last round to beat the McLaren duo of Lewis Hamilton and Fernando Alonso to the title.

The PR demands of F1 life had never appealed so, ever the individual, Kimi preferred to quit and compete in rallying instead in 2010 and 2011. Tempted back to F1 by Lotus in 2012, Kimi won again at Abu Dhabi and ranked third in the Championship. By 2014, he was back at Ferrari. However, although regularly in the points, Sebastian Vettel usually outpaced him and he won only once, in the 2018 United States Grand Prix, ending a record-setting winless streak of 113 races. Kimi moved on to Alfa Romeo last year.

FORGING ON AS TEAM LEADER

Points-scoring drives in the first four of last year's 21 grands prix proved to be something of a false illusion, as the team that had previously raced as Sauber before being renamed as Alfa Romeo seldom had that sort of pace again, except for a three-race run at the French, Austrian and British GPs. Kimi continued to do what he has done throughout his career: he raced to the best points haul available, without fuss. As the year wore on, the Alfa Romeo C38 became less and less competitive, but the sign of his continued excellence was provided by Kimi outscoring team-mate Antonio Giovinazzi by 43 points to the Italian's 14, with both boosted by an unexpected run to fourth and fifth places respectively in the penultimate race of the year, at Interlagos. For now, this keeps Kimi interested, but one never can tell when he might opt again for a different life in rallying or other forms of motorsport, just for the craic.

TRACK NOTES

Nationality:	**FINNISH**
Born:	**17 OCTOBER 1979, ESPOO, FINLAND**
Website:	**www.kimiraikkonen.com**
Teams:	**SAUBER 2001, McLAREN 2002-06, FERRARI 2007-09, LOTUS 2012-13, FERRARI 2014-18, ALFA ROMEO 2019-20**

CAREER RECORD

First Grand Prix: **2001 AUSTRALIAN GP**

Grand Prix starts:	**315**
Grand Prix wins:	**21**

2003 Malaysian GP, 2004 Belgian GP, 2005 Spanish GP, Monaco GP, Canadian GP, Hungarian GP, Turkish GP, Belgian GP, Japanese GP, 2007 Australian GP, French GP, British GP, Belgian GP, Chinese GP, Brazilian GP, 2008 Malaysian GP, Spanish GP, 2009 Belgian GP, 2012 Abu Dhabi GP, 2013 Australian GP, 2018 United States GP

Poles:	**18**
Fastest laps:	**46**
Points:	**1859**
Honours:	**2007 FORMULA ONE WORLD CHAMPION, 2003 & 2005 FORMULA ONE RUNNER-UP, 2000 BRITISH FORMULA RENAULT CHAMPION, 1999 BRITISH FORMULA RENAULT WINTER SERIES CHAMPION, 1998 EUROPEAN SUPER A KART RUNNER-UP, FINNISH & NORDIC KART CHAMPION**

ANTONIO GIOVINAZZI

Alfa Romeo's challenge gradually faded through the course of last season, but Antonio's first full year of F1 was clearly one of improvement and longtime backer Ferrari saw enough to convince them to urge Alfa Romeo to keep him for 2020.

Antonio will have learnt a lot from Raikkonen in 2019 and needs to put that into practice.

Antonio laid down his marker in kart racing at World and European levels and immediately landed a single-seater title in his first year of car racing in 2012. This wasn't in a conventional Italian or European series but in Formula Pilota China instead. In 2013, though, Antonio returned to Europe and finished second in the British Formula 3 Championship.

A full campaign in the European series followed in 2014 and Antonio impressed by winning a couple of races in the year Esteban Ocon won the title.

For 2015, Antonio trebled his wins total, but had to make do with being runner-up to Felix Rosenqvist. His team-mate Sean Gelael then enticed him to share a sportscar programme through the close season, finishing third in the Asian Le Mans Series. However, it was back to single-seaters for 2016 as he advanced to GP2 with the crack Prema Racing team. This was his strongest season to date, with five wins to his name, as Pierre Gasly only pipped him to the title at the final round. This form attracted Ferrari's attention, and it added Antonio to its squad of drivers. Antonio's love of sportscar racing was boosted by a pair of outings in the World Endurance Championship and a singleton run in the European Le Mans Series.

His new life began in 2017 when there was no race programme, but his tie-up with Ferrari meant that he was appointed as Sauber's F1 reserve driver. Expecting to perform testing duties on the team's simulator, attend grands prix to support the team and observe the off-track duties of the two race drivers, Antonio was given a shock debut in the opening race of the season when Pascal Wehrlein failed to recover from a back injury. He got to contest the second round, too.

The 2018 season was spent as Sauber's reserve driver, but a welcome distraction came when he went racing, making his debut in the Le Mans 24 Hours, sharing a GTE Pro class Ferrari 488 with "Pipo" Derani and Toni Vilander.

TRACK NOTES

Nationality: **ITALIAN**
Born: **14 DECEMBER 1993, MARTINA FRANCA, ITALY**
Website: www.antoniogiovinazzi.com
Teams: **SAUBER 2017, ALFA ROMEO 2019-2020**

CAREER RECORD

First Grand Prix: **2017 AUSTRALIAN GP**
Grand Prix starts: **23**
Grand Prix wins: **0**
(best result: 9th, 2019 Italian GP)
Poles: **0**
Fastest laps: **0**
Points: **14**
Honours: **2016 GP2 RUNNER-UP, 2015 FORMULA 3 MASTERS WINNER & EUROPEAN FORMULA 3 RUNNER-UP, 2013 BRITISH FORMULA 3 RUNNER-UP, 2012 FORMULA PILOTA CHINA CHAMPION, 2010 & 2011 WSK MASTERS SERIES KF2 KART CHAMPION**

SLOW AT FIRST BUT GAINING PACE

Having spent 2018 largely on the sidelines as Sauber's test driver, Antonio was raring to go when the 2019 World Championship swung into action in Australia. Racing for the team that used to be Sauber, he knew that his best chance of points was going to come in the early races, as the team always struggles for development as the season progresses and so loses ground to its rivals. Team-mate Kimi Raikkonen showed that points were possible, scoring in each of the first four rounds, but the Italian peaked with an 11th place in Bahrain. While no one expected him to match the Finn, there was concern that he wasn't closer in pace, but a mid-season step up in his performance encouraged the team. Antonio's first points came for 10th in Austria, he then lost eighth place in Germany for the use of driver aids at the start, with a 30s penalty demoting him to 13th, and later finished ninth at Monza. This was enough for the team to retain his services for a second season.

Looking down on the grid for the Australian GP in the final few moments before the team personnel are signalled to leave the starting grid in the final countdown to the grand prix.

HAAS F1

Four years have passed since this American team was created to contest the World Championship and its initial impact has not been maintained, despite its connection with Ferrari, with occasional early-season speed early being lost due to a lack of consistency.

Kevin Magnussen and team-mate Romain Grosjean clashed occasionally, but this was the least of the team's problems as it struggled for pace.

Formula One and the United States of America are like extraordinarily long-term suitors who fail ever to truly commit. For the first decade of the drivers' World Championship, the USA's involvement was the annual Indianapolis 500 being counted as a round. The trouble was, there was no crossover, so it was largely irrelevant. Then, in 1959, the first United States GP was held at Sebring in Florida and the USA had a proper F1 race. While the grand prix then moved around the country before settling at Watkins Glen in upper New York State and American drivers like Dan Gurney, Phil Hill, Richie Ginther and Mario Andretti enjoyed success, there were no long lasting American teams.

Gurney put that right with his All American Racers team that fielded and won with its Eagles in the mid-1960s. Parnelli and Penske teams then came and went, so American fans have rarely had a team of their own to cheer on. It's long been a frustration on both sides of the Atlantic. Then, with F1 becoming

more global in the 21st century, a team called US F1 tried to land a place when there was an invitation for new teams to enter. Sadly, the team was stillborn and it took until 2016 for there to be another bid from the USA. This was Haas F1, the team formed by industrial magnate Gene Haas. His prior involvement in the sport

KEY PEOPLE & 2019 ROUND-UP

GENE HAAS

This dynamic American industrialist's career began when he opened a machine shop in 1978 and its gargantuan growth from then to now has led to an expansion of his workforce from two to 1,500 and a billion-dollar turnover. From setting up a NASCAR team in 2002, it took an allegiance with champion driver Tony Stewart to move it to the top, with its first title landed in 2011. Repeating this in F1 went from a business study in 2014 to scoring sixth place on its debut in Australia in 2016.

TAKING A SERIES OF BACKWARD STEPS

Haas's first race in 2016 yielded a sixth place, and so too did its first in 2019, also in Melbourne, but the team's initial form did as it has done before and dropped away. This left the team towards the back of the midfield rather than towards the front, with the team' drivers struggling as its VF-19 proved fast over a single lap, but less so over a longer stint. Apart from that sixth place finish, Haas's drivers gathered six more top 10 finishes, but coming 14th and 15th in the final round told the story.

2019 DRIVERS & RESULTS

Driver	Nationality	Races	Wins	Pts	Pos
Romain Grosjean	French	21	0	8	18th
Kevin Magnussen	Danish	21	0	20	16th

FOR THE RECORD

Country of origin:	USA
Team bases:	Kannapolis, USA, & Banbury, England
Telephone:	(001) 704 652 4227
Website:	www.haasf1team.com
Active in Formula One:	From 2016
Grands Prix contested:	83
Wins:	0
Pole positions:	0
Fastest laps:	2

THE TEAM

Team owner:	Gene Haas
Team principal:	Gunther Steiner
Chief operating officer:	Joe Custer
Technical director:	Rob Taylor
Vice-president of technology:	Matt Borland
Team manager:	Dave O'Neill
Chief aerodynamicist:	Ben Agathangelou
Group leader aerodynaicist:	Christian Cattaneo
Head of logistics:	Peter Crolla
Chief engineer:	Ayao Komatsu
Test driver:	tba
Chassis:	Haas VF-20
Engine:	Honda V6
Tyres:	Pirelli

went from sponsoring a team in NASCAR to going into partnership with former NASCAR champion Tony Stewart before the wins started to flow.

Inspired by the publicity following the team's successes which helped to promote his machine tool company, Haas considered having a crack at F1. He studied the form and opted to have a base in North Carolina, alongside Stewart-Haas Racing, but to have another base in Europe when it was where the races were held during the middle part of the season. He signed former Jaguar technical chief Gunther Steiner to orchestrate the endeavour.

Landing a good engine deal is a real key to success and Haas went for Ferrari power. To augment this, he even bought a chassis designed by Dallara, to help make the learning curve less steep. It clearly worked well, as Romain Grosjean raced to sixth place first time out, then fifth at the second time of asking. Life has never been so sweet again.

The arrival of Kevin Magnussen for 2017 in place of Esteban Gutierrez meant that Haas had two hard chargers.

One of the hardest things to achieve when starting a team is to forge an identity for it. If a manufacturer enters the fray, the team will adopt some of its corporate image. If a junior team steps up to the top step of the racing ladder, it will arrive with at least some history to build on. Haas F1 had none of these and it certainly doesn't use any of the Stewart-Haas NASCAR team image. In fact, it doesn't even really push the American angle, which perhaps it might if it had an American driver. Instead, it has become identifiable largely because a TV documentary realised that it had a surprise star in gruff-mannered team principal Steiner, his no nonsense and outbursts after his drivers have clashed yet again becoming cult viewing.

With Grosjean and Magnussen seemingly drawn magnetically to each other, whether starting near the front of the grid or from near the back, he had plenty of material to work with through the 2019 season.

There was also a minor soap opera as the team's Rich Energy sponsorship fluctuated as to whether or not it was happening. So, Haas F1 stayed in the news when its result deserved little more than occasional praise.

"Romain and Kevin's understanding of how we work as a team, and our knowledge of what they can deliver behind the wheel, gives us a valued continuity and a strong foundation to keep building our team around."

Gunther Steiner

Gunther Steiner has often had to broker peace between his drivers in recent years.

49

KEVIN MAGNUSSEN

Back for a fourth year with Haas F1, Kevin is largely considered to be the team leader, but being mired in the midfield comes with frustrations as trouble is often close at hand – sometimes supplied by a team-mate. As a result of this, points are hard to come by.

Kevin has a nose for points and will be hoping they're more available in 2020.

Kevin's father Jan was once seen as the shining light who would become a star of F1. Although he made his debut with McLaren in 1995, after racing to 14 wins in the British series and going on to drive for Stewart Grand Prix, his light turned out not to be as bright as expected and by 1999 he had moved on to race sportscars in the United States with great success.

Kevin was six when Jan left F1 and he did a little karting before starting car racing in 2008, winning the Danish Formula Ford title at his first attempt. Having also gained experience of cars with wins in the ADAC Formula Masters series, Kevin finished second in the northern European Formula Renault series in 2009.

Formula 3 came next in 2010, and Kevin opened eyes by winning at his first meeting before ending the year ranked third in the German series. With Carlin showing interest, Kevin entered the British F3 series in 2011 and scored seven wins as he finished the year as runner-up to Felipe Nasr. Carlin kept him on to race in the more powerful Formula Renault 3.5 in 2012 and he came good to land the title at his second attempt in 2013, his five wins leaving him 60 points clear of Stoffel Vandoorne.

Having had a number of successful days of F1 testing, Kevin was given a race seat with McLaren for 2014 and made people sit up when he finished second at his first race, in Australia. This, sadly, remains his best result to date. He was demoted to the test team for 2015 when Fernando Alonso arrived, but bounced back to drive for Renault in 2016.

Renault wasn't at the top of its game though, and Kevin was happy to sign a multi-year deal with Haas F1, starting in 2017. He has gone well whenever the car is competitive and remains one of F1's toughest competitors, which is probably why he and team-mate Romain Grosjean have had more than a few clashes.

The 2018 season remains Kevin's best to date, as he ranked 11th overall.

TRACK NOTES

Nationality:	**DANISH**
Born:	**5 OCTOBER 1992,**
	ROSKILDE, DENMARK
Website:	www.kevinmagnussen.com
Teams:	**McLAREN 2014,**
	RENAULT 2016, HAAS F1 2017-20

CAREER RECORD

First Grand Prix:	**2014 AUSTRALIAN GP**
Grand Prix starts:	**103**
Grand Prix wins:	**0**
(best result: 2nd, 2014 Australian GP)	
Poles:	**0**
Fastest laps:	**2**
Points:	**157**
Honours:	**2013 FORMULA RENAULT 3.5**

CHAMPION, 2011 BRITISH F3 RUNNER-UP, 2009 FORMULA RENAULT NORTHERN EUROPE RUNNER-UP, 2008 DANISH FORMULA FORD CHAMPION

STILL BATTLING AGAINST ROMAIN

Sixth place at the opening round in Australia was as good as it got for Kevin last year, as Haas struggled to keep up with the standard rate of in-season development achieved by rival teams. The Haas VF-19 could be quick on occasion, but it proved to be far from consistent and never competitive through a race distance, with obvious limiting effect. As in 2018, if not more so, there were also clashes with his team-mate Romain Grosjean. It would certainly have made for some "colourful" debriefs with team principal Gunther Steiner, but it did little to boost morale. Eventually, after collecting three more top 10 finishes, Kevin was able to rank 16th out of the world championship's 20 drivers at year's end, which wasn't much of a reward for a season in which he was clearly giving it all in attack. Kevin will have spent much of the year urging the team to build a more competitive car for the season ahead.

ROMAIN GROSJEAN

Although he has raced for Haas F1 since its first year, Romain was nearly replaced for 2020 as the team tired of his too-frequent clashes with team-mate Kevin Magnussen before opting for continuity. He remains fast but flawed.

Romain was outperformed last year and knows that he will have to raise his game.

The signs in Romain's early racing career were that he was a driver destined for the top, someone capable of rising to the increasing challenge as he ascended racing's ladder to the top. Yet, his is a story of how you have to land on your two feet when you make it to F1, preferably with at least a halfway-competitive team, as you seldom get another chance if you fail to impress.

Romain's first season out of karting, 2003, resulted in a dominant title success, as he won all 10 rounds of the Swiss Formula Renault 1.6 series. Full-blooded two-litre Formula Renault followed, with a race win in the French series in 2004 then the title, after taking 10 wins for SG Formula, in 2005.

Formula 3 turned into another two-year project, with 13th place in the European championship in 2006 followed by the title in 2007 for the ASM Formule team.

Stepping up to GP2 in 2008, Romain entered the Asian series at the start of the year and won that, before ranking fourth in the Europe-based main series with a couple of wins. Back for more in 2009, he bagged a couple of early-season wins but was diverted into F1 in the second half of the year after Renault dropped Nelson Piquet Jr for his role in crashing to fix the outcome of the 2008 Singapore GP. This was great, except his seven outings didn't yield a point and he was dropped.

No other F1 team signed him, so Romain spent the next two years in Auto GP then GP2 again, where he did all he could and won both titles. In 2012, his old team Renault, now racing as Lotus, brought him back to F1 and three podium finishes were enough to rank eighth overall. In 2013, he rose to seventh.

Then, when Haas F1 joined the series, he moved to the new American outfit and gave the team points on its first two outings. Unfortunately, Romain has yet to end a year in the top 10 of the World Championship since this move.

TRACK NOTES

Nationality:	**FRENCH**
Born:	**17 APRIL 1986,**
	GENEVA, SWITZERLAND
Website:	**www.romaingrosjean.com**
Teams:	**RENAULT 2009,**
	LOTUS 2012-15, HAAS F1 2016-20

CAREER RECORD

First Grand Prix:	**2009 EUROPEAN GP**
Grand Prix starts:	**166**
Grand Prix wins:	**0 (best result: 2nd,**
	2012 Canadian GP, 2013 United States GP)
Poles:	**0**
Fastest laps:	**1**
Points:	**389**
Honours:	**2012 RACE OF CHAMPIONS CHAMPION, 2011 GP2 CHAMPION, 2010 AUTO GP CHAMPION, 2008 & 2011 GP2 ASIA CHAMPION, 2007 FORMULA THREE EUROSERIES CHAMPION, 2005 FRENCH FORMULA RENAULT CHAMPION, 2003 SWISS FORMULA RENAULT 1600 CHAMPION**

DOING JUST ENOUGH TO STAY ON

There were too many retirements for a large gathering of points in 2019. Yet, a season containing a seventh-place finish for a driver in a team ranked ninth out of the 10 teams in terms of its level of competitiveness is commendable. There could have been more points for Romain through the World Championship's 21 grands prix too, had he and team-mate Kevin Magnussen not continued to clatter into each other infuriatingly in races in which they had been in a position for a stronger result than usual. This showed just how much pressure they were under to deliver in a season in which their team simply couldn't do so itself. Both drivers are aware that introducing an American driver might produce the publicity for the team that their drives cannot until they are equipped with a competitive car. So, it's small wonder that they scrapped for every inch of space, even if that meant running into each other.

Oil tankers are hard to turn when heading in the wrong direction. The same can be said of F1 teams, as poor finishes result in reduced prize money, thus diminished funds for development. Williams really needs to find its feet in 2020 after two years of coming last.

George Russell will lead the Williams attack again and ought to have learnt a lot in his rookie year but knows that he deserves a better car.

When a team is in its pomp, it's hard to imagine it doing anything other than continuing to win races and titles. Yet, Williams' golden periods in the mid-1980s and early 1990s now seem a very long time ago. Even scoring a point for 10th place seems beyond its reach, showing just how far this team has fallen.

Frank Williams realised in the 1960s that he wasn't quite there as an F3 racer, but he soon found that he was pretty handy at running cars for others. At the end of the decade he swapped from the former role to the latter. Two second-place finishes for his charge Piers Courage in 1969 were proof of that, but a desire to become a works team led to a deal with sportscar manufacturer de Tomaso for 1970. Sadly, disaster struck as Courage crashed and was killed in the Dutch GP.

This brought the house of cards down on Williams and his team and it took the thick skin and resilience for which he is renowned to keep plugging on through

the 1970s, invariably trying to do the job on what was at best a meagre budget. Yet, doggedly, Williams kept going,

spurred on by highlights like Jacques Laffite's drive to second place in the 1975 German GP. In 1976, Williams went

KEY PEOPLE & 2019 ROUND-UP

CLAIRE WILLIAMS
Williams' deputy team principal sees more of her father now than she did as a child when he was away at the races. She was coaxed from working at Silverstone to join the team in 2002 as communication officer, before being put in charge of investor relations then later all commercial aspects of the team. Claire stepped up to her current role in 2013, taking on the day-to-day running of the team and the responsibilities of also trying to steer the team back towards more competitive days.

WILLIAMS BRINGS UP THE REAR AGAIN
It wasn't for want of trying, but there was little that Williams could do about last year's FW41's lack of speed. Technical director Paddy Lowe was fired even before the opening race of the season and the disarray in the ranks was clear for all to see. That Robert Kubica was able to score a point at Hockenheim was down to the fact that the German GP turned into a lottery. On all other outings, bringing up the rear was all that he and rookie George Russell could reasonably expect.

2019 DRIVERS & RESULTS

Driver	Nationality	Races	Wins	Pts	Pos
Robert Kubica	Polish	21	0	1	19th
George Russell	British	21	0	0	20th

FOR THE RECORD

Country of origin:	**England**
Team base:	**Grove, England**
Telephone:	**(44) 01235 777700**
Website:	**www.williamsf1.com**
Active in Formula One:	**From 1972**
Grands Prix contested:	**783**
Wins:	**114**
Pole positions:	**128**
Fastest laps:	**133**

THE TEAM

Team principal:	**Sir Frank Williams**
Co-founder:	**Patrick Head**
Deputy team principal:	**Claire Williams**
Chief executive officer:	**Mike O'Driscoll**
Chief technical officer:	**tba**
Head of performance engineering:	**tba**
Chief engineer:	**Doug McKiernan**
Head of aerodynamics:	**Dave Wheater**
Senior race engineer:	**Dave Robson**
Team manager:	**David Redding**
Development driver:	**Dan Ticktum**
Chassis:	**Williams FW43**
Engine:	**Mercedes V6**
Tyres:	**Pirelli**

into partnership with Canadian oil tycoon Walter Wolf to rebrand his cars. This wasn't a partnership made in heaven, though, and Williams fell out with the autocratic Wolf.

The next step was to run a March for Patrick Neve in 1977. Although this left the team in F1's midfield, Williams was boosted that season when designer Patrick Head came on board. By the following season, Williams Grand Prix Engineering had the first car of its own design, and what a first Williams that was, with Alan Jones peaking with second place in the US GP.

Better was to follow in 1979. Head had looked at the pioneering Lotus 78 and observed how it utilised ground effect to boost its road-holding and then produced the FW07 that came on stream partway through 1979. Clay Regazzoni gave the team its breakthrough win, then Alan Jones added four more victories in the final six races. Starting 1980 as the favourite felt novel and Jones didn't disappoint, landing the team its first drivers' and constructors' titles.

Carlos Reutemann stumbled in the 1981 finale but, 12 months, later Keke Rosberg became Williams' second world champion, and there would have been

a third, Nigel Mansell in 1986, but for a last round tyre blow-out in Australia. The following year, Nelson Piquet hit gold for the team.

The loss of Honda engines to rival McLaren reduced Williams' hopes of further glory, but the key to its return to the top was landing Renault's V10 engine. This, combined with the remarkable FW14B chassis, a car that took driver aids to a new level, gave Mansell a cruise to the 1992 crown, in which he won the first five rounds and later added four more.

Williams and Head could be ruthless, though. Knowing that Alain Prost was looking to return after a year's sabbatical, it dropped Mansell and welcomed the French world champion to its ranks. He duly landed the 1993 crown. Then Damon Hill was knocked off in the 1994 finale by Michael Schumacher, but made amends to lift the drivers' title in 1996, only to be dropped like Mansell before him, leaving team-mate Jacques Villeneuve to be crowned in 1997.

Since then, life has been title-free, despite wins from Juan Pablo Montoya and Ralf Schumacher then, out of the blue, from Pastor Maldonado in 2012. Worse than that, for the ever-competitive team founders, it has been ever harder to land a top engine and without that, the top results required to keep the essential investment flowing.

> **"George has served his first season in F1 in difficult circumstances, however his talent, drive and enthusiasm are obvious and it is clear he has everything he needs to be an exceptional F1 driver."**
>
> Dave Robson

Nigel Mansell was in almost total command when Williams dominated the 1992 season.

GEORGE RUSSELL

With Williams the least competitive of F1's 10 teams again last year, it was difficult to assess George's form, but his pedigree is of the highest order and you can be sure that he will maximise all that the car can offer in 2020.

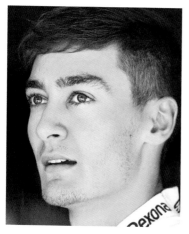

George now knows the tracks. All he wants is a car with which to shine.

With a glut of talented British and French drivers dominating the European kart racing scene as George worked his way up towards car racing, he showed his talent by landing the 2012 European KF3 title at the age of 14.

As soon as he was old enough to move up to single-seaters, he did. This was in 2014 and George grabbed five wins as he won the British F4 title, also gaining useful experience in Formula Renault.

At this point, he looked good. In 2015, however, George looked even better than that as he skipped the next level and advanced to Formula 3, impressively finishing sixth in the European series and second in the F3 Masters race. He then ranked third in 2016 as Lance Stroll dominated the European series.

Then came two outstanding seasons, starting with a title-winning campaign in GP3 in 2017 for ART Grand Prix. All four of his wins came in the first race of the two-race format. These are the more prestigious ones to win, as the top eight finishers in the first race start the other one in flipped order, i.e. the first-race winner starts eighth on the grid and vice versa. The year also included his first taste of F1, and this came with Mercedes and would have a bearing on his racing future.

In 2018, George not only advanced to F2, staying on with ART Grand Prix, but also racked up a stunning tally of seven wins – at Baku, Barcelona, Paul Ricard, the Red Bull Ring, Monza, Sochi and Yas Marina – in F1's immediate feeder formula. It helped him to score enough points to become champion, well clear of Lando Norris and Alex Albon as British drivers filled the top three positions.

Further F1 testing with Force India and Williams, as well as Mercedes, impressed the teams, and George was thought too good to ignore. He was duly signed by Williams for 2019 – placed by Mercedes – to develop his talent with a view towards possibly landing a ride with Mercedes in the years ahead.

TRACK NOTES

Nationality:	**BRITISH**
Born:	**15 FEBRUARY 1998,**
	KING'S LYNN, ENGLAND
Website:	**www.georgerussellracing.com**
Teams:	**WILLIAMS 2019-20**

CAREER RECORD

First Grand Prix:	**2019 AUSTRALIAN GP**
Grand Prix starts:	**21**
Grand Prix wins:	**0 (best result: 11th**
	2019 German GP)
Poles:	**0**
Fastest laps:	**0**
Points:	**0**
Honours:	

2018 FORMULA 2 CHAMPION, 2017 GP3 CHAMPION, 2015 F3 MASTERS RUNNER-UP, 2014 BRITISH F4 CHAMPION & McLAREN AUTOSPORT YOUNG DRIVER AWARD, 2012 EUROPEAN KF3 KART CHAMPION

RACING FOR RESPECT, NOT FOR POINTS

When a driver has achieved a childhood dream to reach F1, that dream will surely include celebrating on the podium and looking down at the team and fans. For George, that wasn't an option in 2019, and his best result during his rookie F1 season was 11th in the German GP. In mitigation, the reason it wasn't any higher is because it was realistically as high as he could expect to place for Williams, a team that was clearly the least competitive of the 10 contesting the World Championship, almost invariably by a large margin the slowest. What George did do was outpace his team-mate, the once great but now injury-hampered Robert Kubica. He also learnt the inner workings of the Williams team and tried all those F1 circuits not visited by F2, so he has knowledge that one feels sure will be used by a more competitive team in the seasons ahead. He's too good for it not to be.

NICHOLAS LATIFI

Having gained experience as Williams' reserve driver, this Canadian racer has stepped up to a race seat for 2020, helped in no small part by his father's considerable financial clout. It's up to him to prove that he's worth his ride.

Nicholas spent last year watching the Williams team. This year, he's racing for it.

Nicholas is unusual among current racers in that he didn't spend his childhood racing karts. In fact, he didn't try one until he was 13, but although he loved it he couldn't wait to graduate to car racing. Fortunately, money has never been an issue, as his father Michael has a considerable fortune to spend, having made it in the food industry and recently bought a 10 percent share in the McLaren Group.

Aged 16, Nicholas contested the Italian F3 Championship, one level above the point at which most people start their car career. He did well to become a winner before the year was out. This encouraged him to try the European series in 2013 and he struggled at this higher level, ranking only 15th. Staying on for a second year was a wise choice, but he was able to advance only to 10th as Esteban Ocon cleaned up. He ended his F3 career on an upswing, finishing fifth in the Macau F3 GP.

With the money to shoot for loftier targets, Nicholas rounded out his 2014 season by competing in the final three Formula Renault 3.5 rounds, claiming a second place at Jerez, and then contesting the final GP2 round.

Opting for Formula Renault 3.5 again in 2015, Nicholas ranked only 11th in a season peppered with retirements. He also competed in GP2 in the second half of the year, but never finished higher than 15th. Unusually, Nicholas also raced in the British Porsche Carrera Cup series.

Many a driver would feel thwarted, but Nicholas did something wise and joined the DAMS team for a first full crack at GP2. Second place in the opening race suggested a turnaround, but it was to remain his best result and he ranked 16th at the season's end.

Back for more in 2017, when GP2 was rebranded as F2, Nicholas took his first win, at Silverstone, and ended fifth overall as Charles Leclerc was crowned champion.

So, a third campaign at this level followed in 2018, again with DAMS, but the hoped for title bid came to naught. Despite winning at Spa-Francorchamps, team-mate Alex Albon overshadowed him and Nicholas ended the year ninth overall.

TRACK NOTES

Nationality:	**CANADIAN**
Born:	**29 JUNE 1995,**
	TORONTO, CANADA
Website:	**www.nicholaslatifi.com**
Team:	**WILLIAMS 2020**

CAREER RECORD

First Grand Prix:	**2020 Australian GP**
Grand Prix starts:	**0**
Grand Prix wins:	**0**
Poles:	**0**
Fastest laps:	**0**
Points:	**0**
Honours:	**2019 F2 RUNNER-UP**

PREPARATION FOR F1 IN 2020

Nicholas already had his foot in the door with Williams last year, as reserve driver. This meant that not only did he get to observe the inner workings of the team but he had the invaluable benefit of doing six practice sessions. This wasn't his first taste of F1, though, as he had a single test for Renault in 2017 and then three runs with Force India in 2018. Yet, Nicholas's main aim was to land the F2 title, something that was vital for his credibility, as it was his fourth year in F1's immediate feeder category. The season could hardly have started better as he won the opening race at Sakhir, then added two more wins from the next two starts. At this point, he led the championship, but then Nyck de Vries got up to speed and it wasn't until August that Nicholas won again, at the Hungaroring. Across the year, de Vries was just that little bit more consistent and so he took the title, while Nicholas was left to rue failing to score at Monaco and again at Monza.

PITSTOP TALKING POINTS:
THE RETURN OF THE DUTCH GP

The Dutch have always loved racing, but Max Verstappen's surge into F1 has swelled their ranks hugely, with the rise of the "orange army" key to Zandvoort being brought back into the F1 fold. It has been chopped since it last held the Dutch GP but will still make a charismatic venue.

In many ways, Zandvoort was one of the first modern circuits, as it was shaped into the crook of the North Sea sand dunes. This was no circuit laid out around an old airfield, like Silverstone, but a track crafted by John Hugenholtz to offer the drivers a flowing course in and out of the dunes. It was an instant hit when it opened in 1948, and attracted a pair of non-championship grands prix in 1950 and 1951, before joining the World Championship in 1952.

With access made easy by a direct rail link to Amsterdam, the crowds were huge. This was despite there being no Dutch drivers of note. Indeed, the home fans would have to wait decades to have one of their own performing as an F1 frontrunner.

What made Zandvoort so popular were the viewing opportunities, especially at Tarzan, the double-right at the end of the ultra-long main straight. Not only did the lofty dunes offer fabulous viewing points, but also they kept the worst of the winds coming off the sea away from the track. Blowing sand was a problem, however, changing the amount of grip that a driver might face from lap to lap, and keeping them guessing.

The first World Championship Dutch Grand Prix was a Ferrari benefit, Alberto Ascari leading a Ferrari 1-2-3, with the best of the rest – Mike Hawthorn's Cooper – two laps behind. Since then, though, Zandvoort is best remembered for some really close races. One that stands out was in 1975, when James

Hunt hit the front at one-fifth distance on a drying track and stayed there despite relentless pressure from Niki Lauda's Ferrari to give the frivolous Hesketh team its one and only win. He would win there again, as a McLaren driver, the following year, chased to the finish by Ferrari's Clay Regazzoni, and this went a long way to cutting into Lauda's points lead while the Austrian was away recovering from his dreadful burns suffered at the Nurburgring.

Eight years before Hunt's first win, Zandvoort gained a place in F1 history when Lotus turned up with Ford's new Cosworth DFV engine. Despite teething problems, Graham Hill put his car on pole and then team-mate Jim Clark waltzed off to victory. It began a new chapter in the sport as the DFV would open the way for privateer teams to enter F1 and challenge the established order.

Sadly, the 1985 Dutch GP, in which Lauda pipped McLaren team-mate Alain Prost, proved to be the end of the circuit's run, with its confines no longer considered safe enough for ever faster F1 cars due to a lack of run-off. Also, Zandvoort's paddock was considered too small for F1 purposes as team transporters and support vehicles required ever more space. Then, in the years that followed, without the Dutch GP to boost its coffers, the circuit struggled financially and was taken over by the town council. Although Zandvoort continued to host racing, pressure from local parties over noise

pollution led to its lap being chopped from 2.642 miles to 1.569 and its eastern edge was moved further away from a holiday camp. Fortunately, some of the lost circuit, including the marvellous, dipping Scheivlak, were reinserted as the lap grew again in 1999 to 2.672 miles through the addition of a twisting return leg.

Despite the Netherlands' love of motor racing, and the best attempts of Jan Lammers, the fans didn't have a potential home-grown grand prix winner until Jos Verstappen came along. This was in the mid-1990s, but alas there was no way then that the circuit was going to get its grand prix back. It took the passage of much time and the injection of considerable money for safety improvements to get the circuit back up to scratch. This was happening while Jos's son, Max, started performing wonders after hitting F1 at just 17 and it corresponded with a new Dutch love affair with F1.

With a grand prix deal in the bag, further modifications had to be made The banking of the final corner is a notable new feature and the orange army of Max fans are sure to fill the dunes.

Opposite top: Alberto Ascari leads away at the start of the 1952 Dutch GP.

Opposite centre left: James Hunt kept his Hesketh ahead of Niki Lauda in 1975.

Opposite centre right: Lauda holds off McLaren team-mate Alain Prost in 1985.

Opposite below: The sweep of the final corner onto the main straight to Tarzan.

TALKING POINT: **MAKING FORMULA ONE CHEAPER AND CLOSER**

Keeping costs in check is always a concern in Formula One, so there will be a budget cap from 2021 to ensure that the less successful teams don't get priced out of becoming competitive. Better still, technical changes should make the racing more exciting.

The top teams never like it when the owners of Formula One try to stop them from winning everything. Ever ambitious, they have a history of trying to preserve their advantage by voting down any change that will threaten their position. They know that as long as they are winning they will attract more money than their rivals and this can help preserve their predominance by enabling them to spend more on vital research and development. However, after two years of consultation, F1's owners decided to do something about it by imposing an annual budget cap of $175m as one of a raft of changes for 2021.

In addition to the budget cap, another proposed way of limiting costs put forward by F1 Chairman & CEO Chase Carey is compressing the grand prix schedule from four days to three, moving the scrutineering process to the Friday morning, with the first practice session shifted to the afternoon, thus cutting costs. Better still for the less successful teams, there is going to be a new system of profit-sharing.

Explaining the rationale, Carey said: "The goal has always been to improve the competition and action on the track and, at the same time, make the sport a healthier and more attractive business for us all."

Ross Brawn, Managing Director of F1 Motorsports concurred: "F1 is almost a victim of its own success in that the rewards of that success are so valuable that the justification keeps coming."

More importantly for F1 fans who want the racing to be as close as possible and not have the less well-funded teams dropping to the tail of the field or even out of existence, F1 has pushed for new technical regulations for 2021. These were masterminded by Brawn and former Ferrari design chief Nikolas Tombazis, and their aim is to make the cars easier to drive in close proximity. Current F1 cars create a lot of turbulence, making it hard for a chasing car to follow closely enough to be in a position to attempt a passing move. Tombazis highlighted how limiting that can be: "A 2019-spec F1 car would lose roughly half of its downforce when running a car-length behind a rival's car. With the changes that the World Motor Sport Council has approved, that figure ought to increase to keeping 86 percent of the downforce of the car in front."

To reduce turbulent wake, the new-look cars will be much simpler in appearance, with fewer aero parts, most notably not being allowed bargeboards, making them look not dissimilar to F1 cars from the mid-1980s. As a result, they will have less downforce, with a greater proportion of what is available being generated under the car as ground-effects return. Better still, the reduction of aerodynamic parts ought to reduce the scope for the best-funded teams to find an aerodynamic advantage and thus reduce the performance gap between the pace of the best cars and the worst. It will also reduce the damage suffered by modern cars from minor contact, keeping

more of the drivers in the running.

Fans shouldn't worry about limiting the number of elements, forcing all cars to appear the same, as Tombazis pointed out: "We expect there to be numerous areas where cars will look different to each other, including the nose, front wing, sidepod and inlet, engine intake and rear wing."

In the name of simplification, there will also be a freeze on transmission development, banning hydraulic suspension and simplifying inboard suspension.

The 2021 cars will have a greater minimum weight, up 25kg to 768kg, largely due to a rise in the weight of the power unit, which was specified to help manufacturers to reduce the cost of the components used.

These new technical regulations will slow the cars by as much as 3.5s per lap. This seems a lot, but the eye can seldom detect that difference and all it's doing is reverting them to the pace they had before 2017.

Going with the zeitgeist, F1 is under increasing pressure to offer environmental sustainability and the new rules specify doubling the renewable content of the fuel to 20 percent. More changes will surely follow as F1 aims at a carbon neutral future by 2030.

Opposite top: Computer renditions give the 2021 car clean, mean lines.

Opposite centre: Last year's F1 drivers examine a model of a 2021 F1 car.

Opposite bottom: A computer rendition of how the 2021 McLaren might look.

TALKING POINT: DOES HOSTING A GRAND PRIX CREATE DRIVING TALENT?

Over the past quarter of a century, the Formula One World Championship has spread its wings by inviting nations beyond its European centre-ground to host grands prix, yet just one of the countries admitted to the circus has produced a driver of its own since gaining a race.

As recently as the late 1990s, the World Championship's 16 grands prix comprised 11 races in Europe with five "flyaways": in Australia, Brazil and Argentina at the start of the campaign, one in Canada in the middle and the final round held in Japan. Although Europe was very much the home of F1, it was decided that to boost the sport's following, more races were needed further afield. Since then, the World Championship has introduced 10 new grands prix, with Vietnam extending that number this year, and dropped some long-standing European rounds to make space for them.

Things began to change in 1999 with the introduction of a grand prix at a new facility in Malaysia. Sepang was built from scratch near Kuala Lumpur's airport and set new standards thanks to government investment, something that most of the organizers of races in Europe had been seeking for decades. This was great as it gave F1 a foothold in burgeoning South-East Asia.

All that was needed to boost this new race's appeal was for Malaysians to have a driver of their own and, within three years, they got one, with Alex Yoong stepping up after building on the experience gained in the nascent Asian racing scene with spells in Europe then Japan. Yoong's season with Minardi didn't produce any fireworks, but it was hoped that this pattern would be repeated at other new venues as they came on stream.

Bahrain and China both joined the show in 2004 and China was seen as

the more likely to produce a driver, as the country was rapidly building circuits and a racing scene of its own, whereas Bahrain had no circuits at all before building Sakhir. Surprisingly, China has not yet managed to get a driver of its own to compete in a grand prix. Ma Qing Hua had runs in a few Friday practice sessions, but never landed a race seat. There are other Chinese nationals making progress, led by F2 racer Guanyu Zhou, but it can be a slow process.

Bahrain has the oil wealth to finance the development of one its own but, 16 years later, there's no star in the pipeline. In fact, most of its hopefuls race in the Middle Eastern Porsche Cup.

Turkey opened its brilliant Istanbul Park circuit in 2005, but it was confined to F1 history after 2011 and no frontline Turkish driver has emerged since. This failure suggested a pattern was forming: countries lacking motorsport history or national racing scene couldn't produce top-level drivers either.

Singapore was next to join, in 2008, and its street race has become one of the key events of the year, as it's a great spectacle. Yet, there's not a local driver who has come to the fore in the intervening dozen years.

Bahrain's lack of success in producing a driver of its own has been repeated by Abu Dhabi since 2009. Some countries spend years courting F1 and get nowhere, while South Korea suddenly found itself at the front of the queue in 2010. Sadly, the Korea International Circuit lost its

race after 2013 and no Korean has since climbed the single-seater ladder.

What followed when India and then Russia joined the F1 show was different, as both had drivers who had reached F1 before they got their race – Narain Karthikeyan and Karun Chandhok plus Vitaly Petrov, respectively. India's grand prix lasted only three years, 2011–13, but no Indian has followed Karthikeyan and Chandhok. Russia, an F1 host since 2014, at least has Daniil Kvyat, who debuted that same year, and a few more talents lining up to have a shot at F1.

Azerbaijan, in F1 since 2017, is perhaps the least likely to achieve this goal, as its street venue is temporary, leaving its wannabe racers with nowhere to compete unless they head abroad, making this considerably more expensive and thus limiting the likelihood of finding one.

So, the host of this year's new grand prix in Hanoi will be aware of the challenge ahead, not just to run a grand prix but to develop a driver of their own. It won't be something that happens overnight, especially as the Hanoi circuit is Vietnam's first, so there are no home-grown drivers waiting in the wings.

Opposite top left: Daniil Kvyat got into F1 in time for Russia's home race.

Opposite top right: India had tow drivers before it hosted F1, but none since.

Opposite centre right: Alex Yoong made it to F1 after Malaysia entered F1.

Opposite below: Turkey had a fabulous circuit but no racing history.

» KNOW THE TRACKS 2020

The teams are going to have to fit in more races than ever before as F1 owners Liberty Media expand the World Championship to 22 grands prix in 2020, with a new event in Vietnam and a return to the Netherlands. To achieve this without burn-out among team personnel, clever grouping of races through the season was required to ensure that there were enough gaps for recovery.

For decades, there were few changes to the World Championship. The teams and fans knew what to expect as the 16-race programme worked its way around Europe with a few flyaways at either end of the season. Now, the World Championship is not only truly global but is ever expanding, with this year's programme the largest yet.

F1's sporting regulations state that it requires the agreement of all the teams if the agreed number of grands prix, 21, is to be exceeded. Liberty Media pushed to go to 22. The extra starting money was attractive, but teams are all aware of how

disruptive being on the road for an extra week can be for the family life of their employees. Some teams talked of agreeing to an extra grand prix provided that they could have a fourth engine for the season...

Australia will kick the season off as usual, the Albert Park circuit a great place to get the show on the road. The Bahrain GP will be next up, but the third event is most keenly awaited as it marks the introduction of a new event in a country not previously touched by motor racing: Vietnam. The circuit built for it on the edge of capital city Hanoi is intriguing as it's a combination of

temporary street circuit and permanent race circuit, the former part offering long straights, the latter some sweepers. How well the circuit works for F1 cars will be discovered in spring, but the ingredients look very interesting.

The Chinese GP marks the last of the early-season flyaway races before F1 comes back to its European hub. The first race of the mainly European stretch - Canada apart - will be greeted with considerable fanfare, as Max Verstappen's fans will be out in force at Zandvoort to pack out the first Dutch GP since 1985.

It was thought last year that it was going to be the last Spanish GP, but the Circuit de Catalunya-Barcelona has struck a one-year deal. Monaco retains, as it should, its regular spot, while in 2020 the Azerbaijan GP has moved back to June rather than last year's April slot. The Canadian GP also keeps its regular place in the calendar.

The second run of races in Europe has been complicated by other events, with the French, Austrian and British GPs made tricky by the Tour de France starting in Nice on the Saturday of the French GP, with clear logistical inconveniences if the trucks are to be able to get to Austria in time for the following weekend's race. The British GP was pushed back to avoid clashing with the tennis at Wimbledon. The Hungarian GP marks the last race before the much needed summer break before F1 swings back into action at majestic Spa-Francorchamps, followed by Monza.

The Singapore GP adds a splash of colour with its night race before a quick scurry to Sochi for the Russian GP. The Japanese GP offers its regular challenge at Suzuka.

Then comes a part of the season that really appeals to Liberty Media, a run of three races in the Americas, vital to its push to expand interest in the USA. Despite money problems, the US GP continues at Austin, although Miami remains in the picture for after 2021, possibly as a second US event, with a circuit laid out around the Miami Dolphins' stadium rather than the previously proposed one that was on a street circuit in the city centre.

The Mexican GP was in doubt, but signed a new five-year deal, which is great news as it's such a well-supported event. The Brazilian GP will continue at Interlagos before a proposed move to a new circuit in Rio de Janeiro in 2021. Then, as has become traditional, the season comes to a close in Abu Dhabi, hopefully with a fierce championship battle.

MELBOURNE

Hosting the opening grand prix of the season gives this Australian city-parkland venue kudos and a great backdrop as it circles a lake but, although the cars can run close together, overtaking is hard to achieve.

The Australians' support of sport is legendary, and Melbourne shades Sydney as the nation's sporting capital, its populace happy to take time out from its passion for Australian Rules Football to watch world-class cricket, tennis, golf, horse racing rugby league and rugby union. This is why they have opened their arms to F1 ever since the Australian GP was transferred from Adelaide in 1996.

There were local protests about laying out this temporary circuit in Albert Park, but the sheer number of fans who poured in to fill the grandstands for all three days drowned them out.

The circuit is unusual in having next to no gradient change, which isn't surprising as it's only a handful of blocks in from the beach. The first corner effectively combines the second as well, as the right flick feeds into a more open left, and it's the key overtaking location on lap 1. What becomes a feature of much of the lap is the feeling of being penned in by concrete barriers, as the track then enters a blast between the trees on the run towards Turn 3. The tight right at the end is still remembered for Martin Brundle's aerial attack there, but then the lap broadens through the left at Turn 4 and then another run through the trees.

Out of the tight right at Turn 6, the track finally opens out and, apart from the tight right at Turn 9, it's flat-out all the way through the long arcing left around the back of the lake until the drivers drop down to sixth gear for Turn 12.

The end of the lap, from Turn 13, is more like the first third of the lap, as it goes between the trees again and twists its way back to the tight final two corners.

INSIDE TRACK

AUSTRALIAN GRAND PRIX

Date:	**15 March**
Circuit name:	**Albert Park**
Circuit length:	**3.295 miles/5.300km**
Number of laps:	**58**
Email:	**enquiries@grandprix.com.au**
Website:	**www.grandprix.com.au**

PREVIOUS WINNERS

2010	**Jenson Button** McLAREN
2011	**Sebastian Vettel** RED BULL
2012	**Jenson Button** McLAREN
2013	**Kimi Raikkonen** LOTUS
2014	**Nico Rosberg** MERCEDES
2015	**Lewis Hamilton** MERCEDES
2016	**Nico Rosberg** MERCEDES
2017	**Sebastian Vettel** FERRARI
2018	**Sebastian Vettel** FERRARI
2019	**Valtteri Bottas** MERCEDES

Its best corner: The Turn 11/12 combination, a fast left into a fast right, is the pick of the corners from a driver's perspective, unless their car set-up isn't spot on. It's the sort of corner that challenges them in a manner that Silverstone's Becketts sweepers do.

Its first grand prix: The Australian GP was non-championship when F1 first visited the city in 1956 and Stirling Moss won in a Maserati. However, 1996 marked Melbourne's World Championship debut and Damon Hill won for Williams after team-mate Jacques Villeneuve's engine started losing oil on his F1 debut.

A race in time: McLaren was so dominant in 1998 that it was a question of which driver would win. Mika Hakkinen was leading from David Coulthard when he misheard a radio message and pitted. The team waved him through and Coulthard honoured an agreement that whichever of them had led into the first corner would win, so let him past.

Location: It's hard to imagine an F1 circuit without a traffic jam to get in but this one, situated a mile to the south of the city centre, can make the claim as it is blessed with a public transport system that brings spectators in by tram to all four sides of the Albert Park circuit.

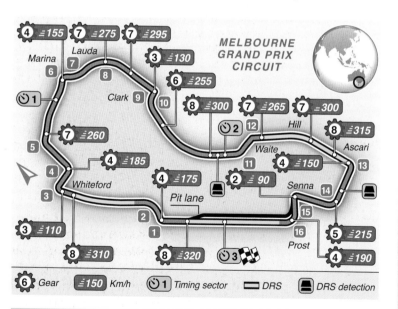

MELBOURNE GRAND PRIX CIRCUIT

Marina · Lauda · Clark · Whiteford · Pit lane · Hill · Waite · Ascari · Senna · Prost

Gear	150 Km/h	Timing sector

DRS · DRS detection

2019 POLE TIME: **HAMILTON (MERCEDES), 1M20.486S, 147.385MPH/237.194KPH**
2019 WINNER'S AVERAGE SPEED: **134.187MPH/215.954KPH**
2019 FASTEST LAP: **BOTTAS (MERCEDES), 1M25.580S, 138.612MPH/223.075KPH**
LAP RECORD: **M SCHUMACHER (FERRARI), 1M24.125S 124.125MPH/226.944KPH, 2004**

SAKHIR

When Bahrain won the scrap to become the first Arab nation to host a grand prix, its race wasn't expected to exist forever. Yet, beating the odds, this two-part circuit is all set for its 16th F1 visit.

BAHRAIN GRAND PRIX

Date:	**22 March**
Circuit name:	**Bahrain International**
Circuit length:	**3.363 miles/5.412km**
Number of laps:	**57**
Email:	**info@bic.com.bh**
Website:	**www.bahraingp.com.bh**

Despite its considerable oil wealth and love of fast cars, Formula 1 and the Middle East had remained mutually exclusive, that was until 2004, when Bahrain made its grand prix debut. It certainly wasn't because there was a rising Bahraini star for which the nation wanted to provide a stage. Instead, it broke onto the F1 scene as the World Championship wanted to spread its reach. Not only did it put the sponsors' brands in front of a wealthy population, but also it provided a race that is usefully between the time zones of far eastern Asia and Europe.

The circuit is distinctive, as it was designed so that one half took the character of the desert and the other – around the pits and paddock – of an oasis. The latter is marked out by watered verges of grass which are in stark comparison to the rocky and dusty area beyond the edges of the track and its run-off out back.

The first corner folds the cars back to the right, feeding almost immediately into a left/right flick that is always very busy on the opening lap, when an overtaking opportunity can open or close in an instant.

Powering out into the desert section, a good length of straight takes the cars out to a hairpin, with the downhill return through a sweeping esse, the circuit's signature section. Like Turn 4, Turn 8 is a possible place for passing, with a further chance into the tight left at Turn 10. Then, after turning uphill at Turn 11, drivers try to get the optimum line out of Turn 13 for a speedy entry onto the return straight, then a tidy run onto the pit straight to line up a rival into Turn 1.

PREVIOUS WINNERS

2009	**Jenson Button** BRAWN
2010	**Fernando Alonso** FERRARI
2012	**Sebastian Vettel** RED BULL
2013	**Sebastian Vettel** RED BULL
2014	**Lewis Hamilton** MERCEDES
2015	**Lewis Hamilton** MERCEDES
2016	**Nico Rosberg** MERCEDES
2017	**Sebastian Vettel** FERRARI
2018	**Sebastian Vettel** FERRARI
2019	**Lewis Hamilton** MERCEDES

Its best corner: The downhill esses through Turns 5, 6 and 7 are where the drivers really have to keep their throttle foot planted. The sixth-gear entry is taken at around 150mph, and they have to hang on and hope for the best.

Its first grand prix: In 2004, Bahrain really did break the mould, and Ferrari left the circuit that had been built with no expense spared smiling because its cars lined up first and second on the grid. They then raced to the end holding down those places, Michael Schumacher finishing ahead of Rubens Barrichello, with Jenson Button best of the rest, but far behind in his BAR.

A race in time: Without a doubt, last year's Bahrain GP was the best in its history. Not just because a rising star laid down a marker – Charles Leclerc on his second outing for Ferrari – but also because the scrapping for the lead was magnificent until the Monegasque suffered the late-race disappointment of his engine dropping a cylinder and the loss of power demoted him to third place.

Location: Head south from Bahrain's capital city, Manama, and you will reach a previously unused rocky, scrubby area, and this is where the government placed the circuit.

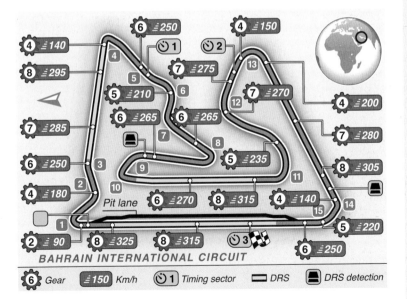

BAHRAIN INTERNATIONAL CIRCUIT

Pit lane

6 Gear | 150 Km/h | ⏱1 Timing sector | DRS | DRS detection

2019 POLE TIME: **LECLERC (FERRARI), 1M27.866S, 137.781MPH/221.737KPH**
2019 WINNER'S AVERAGE SPEED: **121.793MPH/196.007KPH**
2019 FASTEST LAP: **LECLERC (FERRARI), 1M33.411S, 129.602MPH/208.575KPH**
LAP RECORD: **M SCHUMACHER (FERRARI), 1M30.252S 134.262MPH/216.074KPH, 2004**

HANOI

The World Championship's expansion through Asia continues apace with the addition of Vietnam to the Formula 1 trail, hoping, as ever, to attract new fans to a country looking for an image boost.

The best way to take F1 to a new audience is to take it to a country that hasn't held a grand prix before and to run the race on a street circuit in that nation's capital city. This is precisely what Vietnam is doing this year, with a circuit laid out around the heart of Hanoi in the Nam Tur Liem district.

There are two key features, one that the circuit will offer one of the longest straights in use in F1 as it's just under a mile long, and the other that a purpose-built section of the track will be retained to be used as a permanent racing facility after the road sections have been returned to their regular use.

With 23 corners fitted into its 3.458-mile (5.565km) lap, the new street circuit is a busy place to go racing and, like Bahrain's circuit at Sakhir, it will be one of distinct parts as the street section from Turn 4 to Turn 9 will feel precisely like a converted road, while the purpose-built section will contain corners that mimic famous turns at Monaco, Suzuka and the Nurburgring.

The lap starts with a short straight to a tight left and this is followed immediately by a long loop like a giant roundabout, out of which it hits the street section with a long run down to a chicane then a loop and it's back up the other side, like on a motorway.

After a fast kink level with Turn 4, the track arcs right until it reaches a hairpin in front of grandstands. A right turn off the return leg feeds the cars into a sequence of esses that runs all the way to the double apex final corner.

INSIDE TRACK

VIETNAMESE GRAND PRIX

Date:	**5 April**
Circuit name:	**Hanoi Street Circuit**
Circuit length:	**3.484 miles/5.607km**
Number of laps:	**55**
Email:	**info@f1vietnamgp.com**
Website:	**www.f1vietnamgp.com**

PREVIOUS WINNERS

First race

Its best corner: The pick of the corners looks set to be Turn 10 at the far end of the main straight. After hitting 210mph before the end of this 0.95 mile/1.5km blast, with plenty of time to use a tow from a rival, there will definitely be overtaking into this lefthand hairpin.

Flattered by comparison: One of the design features requested when the circuit was commissioned was for various stretches of the track to ape sections of others. The first two corners are intended to mimic the opening complex at the Nurburgring. The run of esses from Turns 12 to 15 have been made to echo the snaking climb from Ste Devote to Massenet at Monaco. Then, as the esses become more sweeping, from Turn 16 to 19, these are meant to be like those running uphill early in the lap at Suzuka. The final three corners of the lap are said to have been inspired by a section of the Sepang circuit that hosted the Malaysian GP from 1999 until 2017.

Location: This all-new street circuit designed by F1's regular circuit architect Hermann Tilke has been laid out next to the My Dinh National Stadium in the outer suburbs of capital city Hanoi.

Local heroes: With Vietnam joining the World Championship, the Vietnamese fans would love to have a local hero to cheer. However, the country has no up-and-coming stars and it will be years until any will be able to make their presence felt. Having the permanent section of the Hanoi circuit will be a start as they develop their craft but, to have a chance of reaching F1, they will have to rise through the ranks in the Asian racing series.

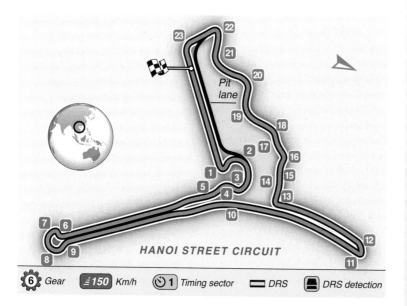

HANOI STREET CIRCUIT

Pit lane

6 Gear   **150** Km/h   **1** Timing sector   DRS   DRS detection

DESIGNED BY CIRCUIT ARCHITECT HERMANN TILKE, WHO PENNED TRACKS LIKE THE CIRCUIT OF THE AMERICAS AND ABU DHABI'S YAS MARINA, THIS CIRCUIT LOOKS PRIMED TO BECOME ONE OF THE MOST CHALLENGING IN F1 WITH ITS MIX OF TURNS, WHILE ALSO FEATURING ONE OF THE LONGEST STRAIGHTS IN THE SPORT AT 1.5KM.

SHANGHAI

The sheer scale of the infrastructure of this purpose-built circuit is only apparent when one sees the size of the aerofoil-shaped bridges mounted eight storeys up above the main straight.

With a lap length of 3.390 miles, the Shanghai International Circuit is in line with most modern grand prix circuits, yet it feels larger. That is because the buildings around the pit straight and paddock are built on the sort of gargantuan scale that can only be achieved when the bill is being picked up by a government that wants to make an impression. And, indeed, this is what it did when it opened in 2004.

The lap starts with a trio of interconnected corners. The first is an uphill right, followed immediately by a tighter right at the crest, after which the cars plunge back down the slope into a lefthander that is tighter still. Just as the track levels out, a left kink feeds the cars onto a dogleg straight. On the opening lap, there can be a lot of passing, and wing-bending contact through Turns 1 to 3.

Drivers can also try to overtake into the righthand hairpin at Turn 6. After that, though, passing is a rarity through the sweepers behind the paddock down to Turn 9. The track then unfolds for a short straight up to Turn 11 where it mimics a reverse copy of the first three corners, albeit on flat terrain, before firing the drivers onto the long and wide back straight. Not surprisingly, the highest speeds recorded come at the end of this straight, with 210mph being reached before heavy braking for the hairpin at Turn 14. This is where most passing moves happen.

The final corner catches a few out, especially in the wet, but many go in right on the edge as they look to gain a tow past the pits to try a passing move into Turn 1.

INSIDE TRACK

CHINESE GRAND PRIX

Date:	**19 April**
Circuit name:	**Shanghai International Circuit**
Circuit length:	**3.390 miles/5.450km**
Number of laps:	**56**
Email:	**f1@china-sss.com**
Website:	**www.f1china.com.cn**

PREVIOUS WINNERS

2010	**Jenson Button** McLAREN
2011	**Lewis Hamilton** McLAREN
2012	**Nico Rosberg** MERCEDES
2013	**Fernando Alonso** FERRARI
2014	**Lewis Hamilton** MERCEDES
2015	**Lewis Hamilton** MERCEDES
2016	**Nico Rosberg** MERCEDES
2017	**Lewis Hamilton** MERCEDES
2018	**Daniel Ricciardo** RED BULL
2019	**Lewis Hamilton** MERCEDES

Its best corner: From a driver's perspective, the sequence of combined corners behind the paddock, Turns 7 and 8, stand out as a challenge. Taken in sixth gear, these esses reward drivers for commitment, and for having found a balance for their car.

Its first grand prix: Rubens Barrichello of Ferrari came to China in 2004 boosted by his victory at Monza in front of the *tifosi*, and this confidence helped him to score his first back-to-back F1 successes. The Brazilian qualified on pole and controlled proceedings.

A race in time: The Chinese GP that sticks in the mind is the one in 2007, when Lewis Hamilton was heading for the F1 title as a rookie. All was going well, but the weather had a role to play and he stayed out too long on rain tyres on a drying track. On finally entering the pitlane, his tyres shot, he slid into the gravel trap and the lost time cost him victory, allowing Ferrari's Kimi Raikkonen to line up a title challenge.

Location: When the circuit was built, it was beyond the northern boundaries of Shanghai, yet rampant growth has meant that although 20 miles from the city centre, it's now within the urban sprawl.

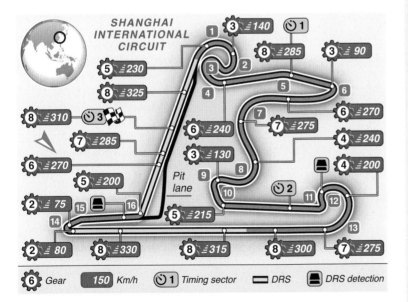

SHANGHAI INTERNATIONAL CIRCUIT

6	Gear	150 Km/h

(⏱)1 Timing sector ▭ DRS 🔲 DRS detection

2019 POLE TIME: **BOTTAS (MERCEDES), 1M31.547S, 133.193MPH/214.355KPH**
2019 WINNER'S AVERAGE SPEED: **123.483MPH/198.727KPH**
2019 FASTEST LAP: **GASLY (RED BULL), 1M34.742S, 128.702MPH/207.126KPH**
LAP RECORD: **M SCHUMACHER (FERRARI), 1M32.238S 132.202KPH/212.759KPH, 2004**

ZANDVOORT

It will provide few options for overtaking, but F1's overdue return to Zandvoort after 35 years is sure to provide the amazing backdrop of a circuit snaking through sand dunes lined with Max Verstappen fans.

INSIDE TRACK

DUTCH GRAND PRIX

Date:	3 May
Circuit name:	Zandvoort
Circuit length:	2.676miles/4.307km
Number of laps:	71
Email:	info@circuitzandvoort.nl
Website:	www.circuitzandvoort.nl

The Dutch GP always used to be one of the most popular when the F1 circus ran its European summer tour for three main reasons. Firstly, the track was interesting. Secondly, the track is a seaside resort. Thirdly, the Dutch are such fun people. In 2020, these three factors will be combined again, but boosted by a massive dose of Max Verstappen fever and the thought of a first home win will be intoxicating.

As it's been three decades since F1 last raced here, a few nips and tucks were required to make the track safer for cars travelling at F1 speeds. The first corner, Tarzan, remains as it ever was, a lightly banked righthand hairpin where drivers always fancy their chances of passing. The first of the modifications comes just after Gerlachbocht, with the track turning sooner after its exit to move the original tight left at Hugenholtzbocht to the left. This means there won't be such a deep dip into the curve and, importantly, more run-off beyond where before there was none.

The track then begins its undulating passage across rolling dunes, with Scheivlak, a seventh-gear dipping right over a crest the pick of the lap. The second modification is at the second part of the Hans Ernst Bocht, with the addition of a tarmac run-off area to give more elbow space.

The biggest change of all is at the final corner of the lap, the Arie Luyendykbocht, with the corner named after Holland's only winner of the Indianapolis 500 being made banked. Tilted by 18 degrees, it means a three-metre drop from upper rim to apex and will ensure a fantastic slingshot onto the start/finish straight.

PREVIOUS WINNERS

1976	**James Hunt** McLAREN
1977	**Niki Lauda** FERRARI
1978	**Mario Andretti** LOTUS
1979	**Alan Jones** WILLIAMS
1980	**Nelson Piquet** BRABHAM
1981	**Alain Prost** RENAULT
1982	**Didier Pironi** FERRARI
1983	**Rene Arnoux** FERRARI
1984	**Alain Prost** McLAREN
1985	**Niki Lauda** McLAREN

Its best corner: Scheivlak stands out for its curving approach that rises, offering drivers the sight of the giant sand dune ahead, then cuts right and down in a high-speed righthand curve that becomes ever more tucked into the dunes as it drops away into a compression.

Its first grand prix: After four years running a race for grand prix cars, Alberto Ascari was dominant for Ferrari when the World Championship first visited the Netherlands in 1952. Team-mates Nino Farina and Luigi Villoresi were the only other drivers on the lead lap at the finish.

A race in time: In 1975, with Niki Lauda and Ferrari setting the pace, the Dutch GP was seen as the next victory to be claimed. This proved not to be the case, though, as the aristocratically-funded Hesketh team not only took the race to the Austrian on a wet but drying track in the opening dozen laps, with James Hunt pushing hard, but also beat him to the finish to trigger wild partying led by Lord Hesketh.

Location: The circuit is tucked into the dunes on the northern edge of the North Sea resort of Zandvoort, lying eight miles to the west of Haarlem and 15 miles west of Amsterdam.

CIRCUIT ZANDVOORT

Pit lane

6	Gear	
≡150	Km/h	
⏱1	Timing sector	
▭	DRS	
◼	DRS detection	

1985 POLE TIME: **PIQUET (BRABHAM)**, 1M11.074S, 133.821MPH/215.365KPH

1985 WINNER'S AVERAGE SPEED: 119.977MPH/193.085KPH

1985 FASTEST LAP: **PROST (McLAREN)**, 1M16.538S, 124.268MPH/199.990KPH

LAP RECORD: **NOT YET APPLICABLE**

BARCELONA

The Spanish GP looked set to be dropped from the World Championship after 2019, but Catalunya's regional government put up $25 million to keep its flagship event on the calendar, for 2020 at least.

With Carlos Sainz Jr going better and better, Spanish fans have a new hero to cheer following Fernando Alonso's recent departure to challenges new. Perhaps with this in mind, or perhaps aware that a World Championship slot is easier to lose than to gain, Catalunya's government voted to stay on board, though this may not be for long.

The Circuit de Catalunya-Barcelona used almost to be the second home for F1 teams, as its combination of corners provided scope to test set-ups for most other circuits. In-season F1 testing has since been curtailed almost to the point of non-existence. However, having been used by F1 since 1991, changing little in that time, it's a known quantity.

The lap starts with a downhill run to the esse that forms the opening corner and, year in, year out, the gravel trap sucks in a few drivers on the opening lap.

Then comes a long parabola curving uphill to the right. A good run through here can offer a slim chance of passing into Turn 4. The nature of the circuit, of short straights into tight corners prevails with the exception of the rise to a fast right over a crest at Campsa, Turn 9.

The downhill infield straight that follows isn't long enough for passing before the track climbs and twists its way to Turn 12. In the interest of safety, the run home from there that was once a wonderful downhill right onto the start/finish straight has been curtailed with a tighter right then a chicane, both of which limit the likelihood of a chasing driver gaining a tow on the run to Turn 1, thus diminishing the likelihood of overtaking.

INSIDE TRACK

SPANISH GRAND PRIX

Date:	**10 May**
Circuit name:	**Circuit de Barcelona-Catalunya**
Circuit length:	**2.892 miles/4.654km**
Number of laps:	**66**
Email:	**info@circuitcat.com**
Website:	**www.circuitcat.com**

PREVIOUS WINNERS

2010	**Mark Webber**	RED BULL
2011	**Sebastian Vettel**	RED BULL
2012	**Pastor Maldonado**	WILLIAMS
2013	**Fernando Alonso**	FERRARI
2014	**Lewis Hamilton**	MERCEDES
2015	**Nico Rosberg**	MERCEDES
2016	**Max Verstappen**	RED BULL
2017	**Lewis Hamilton**	MERCEDES
2018	**Lewis Hamilton**	MERCEDES
2019	**Lewis Hamilton**	MERCEDES

Its best corner: The long final corner used to be the lap's most exciting turn, but the best since it was chopped is the Campsa righthander, with its uphill approach hiding the apex until drivers are almost upon it in fifth gear.

Its first grand prix: Spain's first grand prix was held at Pedralbes in downtown Barcelona in 1951, and was won by Alfa Romeo's Juan Manuel Fangio. The first held at the contemporary circuit, in 1991, was won by Nigel Mansell for Williams after Gerhard Berger had led the early laps from pole for McLaren. With the Austrian being passed then retiring, it was Mansell who triumphed, winning by 11s from Alain Prost's Ferrari.

A race in time: For making a nation wild with delight, few results anywhere can match that here in 2016 when Max Verstappen became Holland's first F1 winner. The fact that he achieved this on his first outing after an in-season promotion from Scuderia Toro Rosso to Red Bull Racing made it all the more remarkable.

Location: Although there have been two grand prix circuits in Barcelona, at Pedralbes and Montjuich Park, the Circuit de Catalunya-Barcelona is 15 miles to the north near the industrial zone at Montmelo.

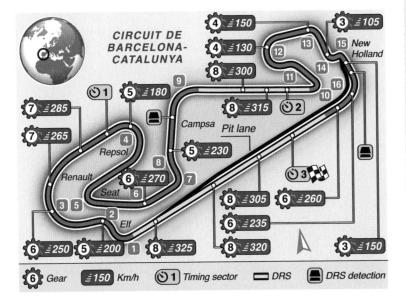

CIRCUIT DE BARCELONA-CATALUNYA

4 ≡ 150	3 ≡ 105	15 New Holland		
4 ≡ 130				
8 ≡ 300				
1	5 ≡ 180			
7 ≡ 285	8 ≡ 315	2		
7 ≡ 265				
Campsa	Pit lane			
Repsol	5 ≡ 230			
Renault	6 ≡ 270	3		
Seat	8 ≡ 305	6 ≡ 260		
Elf	6 ≡ 235			
6 ≡ 250	5 ≡ 200	1	8 ≡ 325	8 ≡ 320	3 ≡ 150

Key: 6 Gear | ≡ 150 Km/h | 🕐 1 Timing sector | ▭ DRS | ▪ DRS detection

2019 POLE TIME: **BOTTAS (MERCEDES), 1M15.406S, 138.091MPH/222.236KPH**
2019 WINNER'S AVERAGE SPEED: **119.463MPH/192.258KPH**
2019 FASTEST LAP: **HAMILTON (MERCEDES), 1M18.492S, 132.662MPH/213.499KPH**
LAP RECORD: **RICCIARDO (RED BULL), 1M18.441S 132.748KPH/213.638KPH, 2018**

This view of the field negotiating the drop from Mirabeau through the Grand Hotel Hairpin to Mirabeau Bas is almost timeless as Monaco has held a grand prix since 1929.

MONACO

As the World Championship expands, Monaco is a reassuring anachronism. If proposed today, its entry wouldn't be accepted, its confines too tight and lap too short, but its entity provides glamour.

It you walk around Monte Carlo when the World Championship isn't in town you'll recognize the famous landmarks but it's still almost impossible to imagine F1 cars hurtling around them. Yet, clear the parked cars, erect the barriers, and there it is, the narrow, twisting challenge that has changed remarkably little since its first race in 1929.

Certainly, there have been nips and tucks, the building of a hotel over the track to create the trademark tunnel and the modernization of the cramped pits, but the feel of the lap remains little changed.

From the moment the drivers accelerate from the grid, there can be no mistaking where they are. Hemmed in by barriers, they turn right at Ste. Devote, then climb steeply. The ascent is long, twists slightly then challenges them with the blind entry to Massenet before the cars are fired out across Casino Square before descending. The right at Mirabeau is tight, the hairpin that follows tighter still. Then, with a high wall on one side and a building on the other, the drivers take a sharp right before another one at Portier.

The tunnel used to plunge the drivers into darkness, but powerful lights make it less of a contrast now as they accelerate through, hoping for a shot at passing into the harbourside chicane. Blasting past the super-yachts, offers little chance of passing as they turn left at Tabac and then go left/right, right/left around Piscine. With the end of the lap as tight as the start, drivers know that their best chance of passing comes at the pitstops, but they live in hope, knowing a win here has more prestige than any other race.

INSIDE TRACK

MONACO GRAND PRIX

Date:	**24 May**
Circuit name:	**Circuit de Monaco**
Circuit length:	**2.075 miles/3.339km**
Number of laps:	**78**
Email:	**info@acm.mc**
Website:	**www.acm.mc**

PREVIOUS WINNERS

2010	**Mark Webber** RED BULL
2011	**Sebastian Vettel** RED BULL
2012	**Mark Webber** RED BULL
2013	**Nico Rosberg** MERCEDES
2014	**Nico Rosberg** MERCEDES
2015	**Nico Rosberg** MERCEDES
2016	**Lewis Hamilton** MERCEDES
2017	**Sebastian Vettel** FERRARI
2018	**Daniel Ricciardo** RED BULL
2019	**Lewis Hamilton** MERCEDES

Its best corner: Monaco is short on corners that test the drivers. However, the left/right, right/left combination around the swimming pool, Piscine, is the trickiest, with the narrowness of the racing line feeling very claustrophobic for the drivers as they try to keep their cars away from the barriers in this sixth-gear balancing act.

Its first grand prix: The first grand prix held on the streets dates back to 1929 when Bugattis were the cars to have and British driver William Grover Williams was first to the finish.

A race in time: For relentless surprise, the 1982 Monaco GP will never be beaten, as its final three laps were the ultimate lottery. Alain Prost crashed his Renault out of the lead and then no fewer than three drivers held the lead before Riccardo Patrese recovered from a spin to win for Brabham. In terms of no holds barred racing, then it has to be Ayrton Senna resisting a charging Nigel Mansell in the final laps in 1992.

Location: First find Monaco, then home in on its heart, Monte Carlo. Look for the harbour and the track is centred on that, venturing away only to make the climb up to Casino Square and then down again to the waterfront before the tunnel.

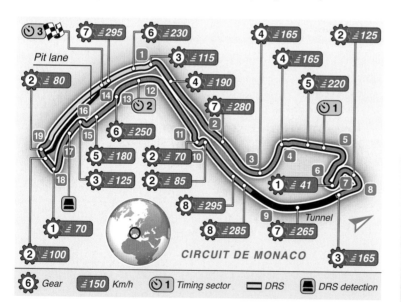

CIRCUIT DE MONACO

6 Gear   **150** Km/h   **1** Timing sector   DRS   DRS detection

2019 POLE TIME: **HAMILTON (MERCEDES), 1M10.166S, 106.385MPH/171.211KPH**
2019 WINNER'S AVERAGE SPEED: **93.391MPH/150.298KPH**
2019 FASTEST LAP: **GASLY (RED BULL), 1M14.279S, 100.494MPH/161.730KPH**
LAP RECORD: **VERSTAPPEN (RED BULL), 1M14.260S 100.520MPH/161.772KPH, 2018**

BAKU

The novelty or racing in Azerbaijan has passed after five years and now the teams see the Baku City Circuit principally for the challenge that it is: a tricky street circuit of two distinct halves.

The spectacular backdrop of Caspian Sea and the mountains beyond stunned the teams when they turned up in Baku in 2016, not necessarily with high hopes for the venue, feeling that it had been forced upon them as the World Championship turned its back on traditional venues.

Yet, the circuit proved to be much better than they had expected, with the challenge of two distinct halves, split between the newer parts of the city down on the seafront and the citadel above, alternating between wide open and narrow, all photographers' dreams.

The first three corners are 90-degree lefthanders, offering nothing special, but wide enough at least for drivers to largely keep out of trouble on the opening lap. Then, after a 90-degree right at Turn 4, the track jinks through a run of medium-speed corners before reaching Turn 8. At this point, it reaches the walls of the citadel and any feeling of space disappears, the walls looming above the drivers. Then it opens out again when it turns right in front of some grandstands at Turn 11 and runs across a square.

Azerbaijan financed the grand prix to give itself a global image and so the upper part of the track runs along the wide streets in front of its finest buildings, largely arcing in an anti-clockwise direction until its nature changes with an abrupt drop out of Turn 16. Then, unlike many street circuits, the cars can really hit some impressive speeds as they power their way through a series of four high-speed kinks on their way back to the lengthy start/finish straight, with the fastest cars reaching more than 200mph before the end of the lap.

AZERBAIJAN GRAND PRIX

Date:	**7 June**
Circuit name:	**Baku City Circuit**
Circuit length:	**3.753 miles/6.006km**
Number of laps:	**51**
Email:	**info@bakugp.az**
Website:	**www.bakugp.az**

PREVIOUS WINNERS

2016	**Nico Rosberg** MERCEDES
2017	**Daniel Ricciardo** RED BULL
2018	**Lewis Hamilton** MERCEDES
2019	**Lewis Hamilton** MERCEDES

Its best corner: For a circuit with a lap made up of a large number of 90-degree bends, it's not easy for drivers to find a flow, but Turn 16 offers gradient change as the drivers turn left and then plunge towards the run of three ever faster kinks leading to the pit straight.

Its first grand prix: The teams and drivers hadn't much of a clue what the street circuit was going to be like until they arrived there in 2016. Nico Rosberg won easily for dominant Mercedes after team-mate Lewis Hamilton qualified only 10th after clipping a wall.

A race in time: Many longstanding circuits have races other than grands prix that stand as their most exciting races, but the Baku City Circuit is used just once a year and so the greatest race held there to date has to be a grand prix. The one held in 2017 stands out for Sebastian Vettel ramming Lewis Hamilton's Mercedes behind the safety car which was odd.

Its closest finish: The most recent visit, last year, wasn't the most exciting race, as it was a Merceces masterclass in which Valtteri Bottas got ahead and stayed there to beat team-mate Lewis Hamilton by 1.524s.

Location: Baku Boulevard is one of the city's prime thoroughfares, a broad street with a prime view out onto the Caspian Sea. It is here that the temporary pit complex is based, with the track winding way back towards the citadel on a tour past the city's grandest buildings.

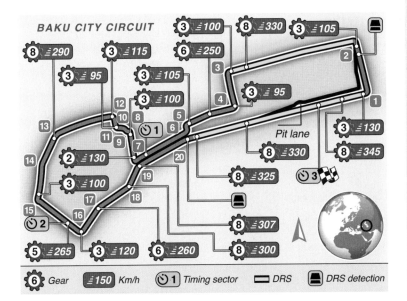

BAKU CITY CIRCUIT

Pit lane

| Gear | | Km/h | Timing sector | DRS | DRS detection |

2019 POLE TIME: **BOTTAS (MERCEDES), 1M40.495S, 133.621MPH/215.043KPH**
2019 WINNER'S AVERAGE SPEED: **124.182MPH/199.852KPH**
2019 FASTEST LAP: **LECLERC (FERRARI), 1M43.009S, 130.360MPH/209.795KPH**
LAP RECORD: **LECLERC (FERRARI), 1M43.009S 130.360MPH/209.795KPH, 2019**

>> **MONTREAL**

This is a car-breaker, with near-constant walls lining its flanks and an unusually large proportion of each lap spent at full throttle combined with an exceptional amount of heavy braking.

INSIDE TRACK

CANADIAN GRAND PRIX

Date:	**14 June**
Circuit name:	**Circuit Gilles Villeneuve**
Circuit length:	**2.710 miles/4.361km**
Number of laps:	**70**
Email:	**info@circuitgillesvilleneuve.ca**
Website:	**www.circuitgillesvilleneuve.ca**

Space is at a premium on the Ile de Notre Dame, and this gives the track its characteristics as it weaves around the parkland setting, usually with the St Lawrence River as a backdrop. Yet, there are parts when the track stops twisting between river and trees to open up and this is the other side of its coin.

The lap starts with a kink to the right and then a bunching of cars into the 80-degree left that follows. Many drivers run wide here and contact is not a rarity, with Alexander Wurz's Benetton being rolled in 1997. Accordingly, many drivers are out of position for the long right that follows, Virage Senna.

At Turn 3, with the river now to drivers' left, the track starts to twist and continues to do so to tight Turn 6. The start of this sequence gained extra

fame last year, when Sebastian Vettel got onto the grass at Turn 3 and rejoined, collecting Lewis Hamilton, into Turn 4.

From Turn 7, drivers have more space to play with as they run through the esse at Turn 8/9 and on down to the hairpin at Turn 10. The entrance to this righthander is a definite passing opportunity.

Get a clean exit from the hairpin, though, and drivers can use a tow all the way up the lap's longest straight to Turn 13 in their quest to line up a passing move into the final sequence of corners.

The maximum speed achieved comes at the end of this lengthy straight that runs alongside the 1976 Olympic Games rowing lake, with the fastest cars hitting 340kph. Then, it's hard on the brakes and into the final chicane.

PREVIOUS WINNERS

2010	**Lewis Hamilton**	McLAREN
2011	**Jenson Button**	McLAREN
2012	**Lewis Hamilton**	McLAREN
2013	**Sebastian Vettel**	RED BULL
2014	**Daniel Ricciardo**	RED BULL
2015	**Lewis Hamilton**	MERCEDES
2016	**Lewis Hamilton**	MERCEDES
2017	**Lewis Hamilton**	MERCEDES
2018	**Sebastian Vettel**	FERRARI
2019	**Lewis Hamilton**	MERCEDES

Its best corner: It's not often that a chicane will be picked as a track's best corner, but the final corner, a right/left flick almost always supplies incident. This is a frequent place for an attempt pass, but it has also been when drivers crash on the way out, often when under pressure, with the wall on the exit once dubbed "Champions' Wall", as it even snared Michael Schumacher.

Its first grand prix: If there was a perfect script for Montreal's first grand prix in 1978, it would have been centred on Gilles Villeneuve winning for Ferrari. Well, that is precisely what happened as the Canadian raced clear after runaway leader Jean-Pierre Jarier's Lotus failed.

A race in time: Sometimes a race stands out for brilliant racing action, other times for the significance of its outcome. For BMW Sauber, the 2008 race will always stand out, for its was here that it not only took its only win, but claimed a one-two as Robert Kubica led home Nick Heidfeld.

Location: Built on an island on the far side of the St Lawrence River from Montreal, the circuit has little space for car parking, but this doesn't matter as it's connected to the city centre by a metro train line.

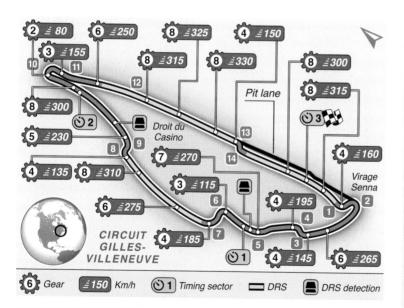

CIRCUIT GILLES-VILLENEUVE

Virage Senna

Droit du Casino

Pit lane

6 Gear	150 Km/h	⏱1 Timing sector	▭ DRS	▪ DRS detection

2019 POLE TIME: **VETTEL (FERRARI), 1M10.240S, 138.884MPH/223.513PH**
2019 WINNER'S AVERAGE SPEED: **127.708MPH/205.527KPH**
2019 FASTEST LAP: **BOTTAS (MERCEDES), 1M13.078S, 133.491MPH/214.833KPH**
LAP RECORD: **BOTTAS (MERCEDES), 1M13.078S 133.491MPH/214.833KPH, 2019**

PAUL RICARD

This revived and modernized former home of the French GP stepped up and improved its traffic flow after a debacle in 2018, and now needs to be judged on whether it provides enough of a challenge.

With the sun expected to shine, a picturesque mountain backdrop plus modern and elegant facilities, this circuit on a high plateau in the south of France should be a sure-fire winner. Yet, on the evidence of the first two grands prix held there since Circuit Paul Ricard's rebirth, the accolades have yet to flow as it is perhaps not enough of a challenge to the drivers to provide the spectacle fans want even to get close to matching the great races held there in the 1970s and 1980s.

The approach to the first corner on the opening lap is always a concern for drivers, as the entry is slightly blind. However this, like all other stretches of the track, is surrounded by considerable expanses of run-off areas to catch any who fall. These are marked with coloured bands of ever coarser tarmac to slow them.

The track then twists its way down a gentle slope all the way to Virage de la Ste. Baume before finally opening out when it reaches the start of the Mistral Straight. Infuriatingly, to keep speeds in check on the approach to Signes corner at its distant far end, there's a chicane midway along the straight. As it is, they still reach Signes at 200mph, and hang on through this top gear thriller, but the chicane breaks the flow and separates the battlers, limiting overtaking.

From this the highest point, the track then folds its way back to the start/finish straight, with drivers able to harry a rival but seldom make a meaningful attack. Then, with the final corner being extra tight, the chances of catching a tow past the pits to try and overtake into Turn 1 are limited.

INSIDE TRACK

FRENCH GRAND PRIX

Date:	28 June
Circuit name:	Circuit Paul Ricard
Circuit length:	3.630 miles/5.842km
Number of laps:	53
Email:	circuit@circuitpaulricard.com
Website:	www.circuitpaulricard.com

PREVIOUS WINNERS

1982	**Rene Arnoux** RENAULT
1983	**Alain Prost** RENAULT
1985	**Nelson Piquet** BRABHAM
1986	**Nigel Mansell** WILLIAMS
1987	**Nigel Mansell** WILLIAMS
1988	**Alain Prost** McLAREN
1989	**Alain Prost** McLAREN
1990	**Alain Prost** FERRARI
2018	**Lewis Hamilton** MERCEDES
2019	**Lewis Hamilton** MERCEDES

Its best corner: Whatever the layout of the circuit, Signes has always been one of those very rare things, a flat-out, top-gear corner. Uphill on approach, but with the terrain flattening by its exit, the famous righthander is taken at close on an impressive 200mph.

Its first grand prix: Paul Ricard really was the brave new world for F1 when it broke onto the scene in 1971 as a tailor-made circuit with safety features and fabulous facilities. Jackie Stewart stuck his Tyrrell on pole position with Clay Regazzoni's Ferrari alongside. However, it was Stewart all the way, followed home by his French team-mate Francois Cevert after Regazzoni spun off on spilt oil.

A race in time: The 1986 French GP was a good one for Nigel Mansell as he mounted a title challenge in his Williams. The English racer took the lead at the start, with poleman Ayrton Senna leading the chase, but the Brazilian hit oil in his Lotus and spun off at the same spot he had in 1985, leaving Mansell clear to win.

Location: Head inland some 20 miles from Toulon on the French Riviera, and the circuit is located near the village of Le Castellet on a broad plateau in a clearing between swathes of pine trees.

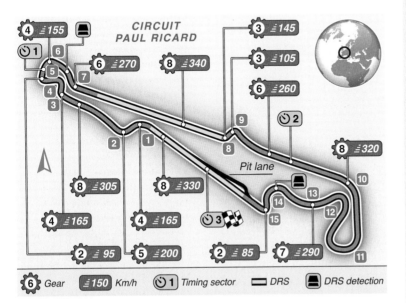

CIRCUIT PAUL RICARD

Pit lane

6 Gear	150 Km/h	1 Timing sector	DRS	DRS detection

2019 POLE TIME: **HAMILTON (MERCEDES), 1M28.319S, 147.965MPH/238.127KPH**
2019 WINNER'S AVERAGE SPEED: **136.606MPH/219.846KPH**
2019 FASTEST LAP: **VETTEL (FERRARI), 1M32.740S, 140.911MPH/226.775KPH**
LAP RECORD: **VETTEL (FERRARI), 1M32.740S 140.911MPH/226.775KPH, 2019**

RED BULL RING

On a summer's day, no circuit visited by F1 has a better setting than this Styrian beauty, with its lap made up of climbs and drops laid out in a stunning mountainside landscape.

Tracks suitable for modern day F1 have changed considerably over the decades and the sweeping parabolas of the original circuit on the site of the Red Bull Ring are still clear to see. The Osterreichring, as it was known, was one of the most wonderful tracks on the F1 tour, its high-speed flow a fabulous challenge for the drivers.

The Red Bull Ring is the majority of that lap, but shorn of the very best bits. As it exists today, it is still a thing of beauty visually, but it will never be as good either as an examination of drivers or as a racing spectacle.

The run to the first turn is exceptionally steep, with drivers having to turn sharp right just over its crest, with contact far from rare here on the opening lap. Then comes the circuit's fastest part, the kinked ascent to Remus. This tight right is again just over a crest and the generous width on approach is suddenly halved in terms of the racing line. Many a driver still dives across the apex kerbs like a torpedo.

The run across the face of the hillside is rapid, then the track starts dropping through Schlossgold and starts to twist for its descent towards the rear of the paddock. After two lefthanders, there's a slight esse and then the run through the trees to the final two turns.

These are critical for a good run onto the start/finish straight and even though it is occasionally possible to make a passing move into Rindtkurve, most drivers prefer to concentrate on getting the optimum run out of the final corner in the hope of getting a tow past the pits to make a passing bid up the slope into Turn 1. Fortunately, there is plenty of run-off area there.

INSIDE TRACK

AUSTRIAN GRAND PRIX

Date:	5 July
Circuit name:	Red Bull Ring
Circuit length:	2.688 miles/4.326km
Number of laps:	71
Email:	information@projekt-spielberg.at
Website:	www.projekt-spielberg.at

PREVIOUS WINNERS

2000	**Mika Hakkinen** McLAREN
2001	**David Coulthard** McLAREN
2002	**Michael Schumacher** FERRARI
2003	**Michael Schumacher** FERRARI
2014	**Nico Rosberg** MERCEDES
2015	**Nico Rosberg** MERCEDES
2016	**Lewis Hamilton** MERCEDES
2017	**Valtteri Bottas** MERCEDES
2018	**Max Verstappen** RED BULL
2019	**Max Verstappen** RED BULL

Its best corner: The greatest corner on the original Osterreichring was the Bosch Curve. The corner was curtailed, and the one installed further away from the foot of the grandstand there, Schlossgold, is still a tricky, downhill left but now offers the chance to pass too.

Its first grand prix: The first grand prix on the Osterreichring was in 1970, but the first on the current circuit, as the A1-Ring, came in 1997 when Prost's Jarno Trulli led the first half, but was passed by Williams' Jacques Villeneuve. Trulli then retired with engine failure, which allowed McLaren's David Coulthard to finish second.

A race in time: The greatest grand prix held on the Osterreichring was also its closest finish, and this came in 1982 when Keke Rosberg and Elio de Angelis were fighting for victory, with the Finn closing in fast, but the Italian driver swept his Lotus 91 out of the final corner just in front of Rosberg's Williams FW08 to win by 0.050s.

Location: Austria is a wide country and the Red Bull Ring is fairly centrally located, so it is far from capital city Vienna close to the country's eastern border. The closest city is Graz, which is 45 miles to the south-east.

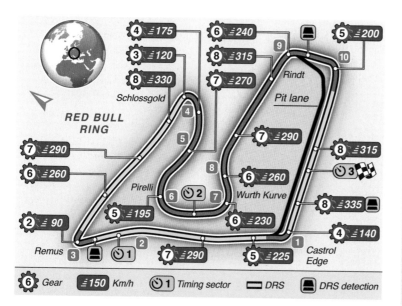

2019 POLE TIME: **LECLERC (FERRARI), 1M03.003S, 153.311MPH/246.731KPH**
2019 WINNER'S AVERAGE SPEED: **139.280MPH/224.150KPH**
2019 FASTEST LAP: **VERSTAPPEN (RED BULL), 1M07.475S, 143.150MPH/230.378KPH**
LAP RECORD: **RAIKKONEN (FERRARI), 1M06.957S, 144.257MPH/232.160KPH, 2018**

SILVERSTONE

It's fast, it's flat, it's open, it was the venue for the opening round of the inaugural World Championship in 1950 and it has been a backbone of F1 since then, always packed with fervent fans.

A long run hosting a round of the World Championship imbues a circuit with the allure of history and this becomes greater still if the event is well attended and the fans become an integral part of the show. At Silverstone, this is certainly the case, with some of the largest and best informed crowds of the season, fans who have been making this pilgrimage for decades.

Furthermore, take the best corners from F1 circuits around the world and Silverstone can lay claim to one of the very best of all, a corner that really challenges the drivers: Becketts.

The construction of the Wing pit building moved the start of the lap from before Copse to before Abbey, so there is bunching through the tight right at Village and then through the Loop, often resulting in a little contact. Then the lap opens out down the Wellington Straight, allowing drivers the space to consider a passing move into the tight left at Brooklands.

After the double right at Luffield and the kink at Woodcote, it's a challenging righthander at Copse and then the circuit's signature corner: Becketts. It's entered directly after a left kink at Maggotts and it's a truly wonderful esse, made all the more fearsome as it's taken at prodigious speed. In qualifying, it's awesome, the fastest cars seeming to defy the laws of physics with the speed at which they change direction.

The Hangar Straight is good for 210mph and then it's all about balance as the drivers set their cars up for a passing bid into Stowe before the track drops into Vale. At the end of this dip, there's a passing opportunity at the sharp lefthander that feeds into a lengthy right onto the start/finish straight.

INSIDE TRACK

BRITISH GRAND PRIX

Date:	**19 July**
Circuit name:	**Silverstone**
Circuit length:	**3.659 miles/5.900km**
Number of laps:	**52**
Email:	**sales@silverstone-circuit.co.uk**
Website:	**www.silverstone-circuit.co.uk**

PREVIOUS WINNERS

2010	**Mark Webber** RED BULL
2011	**Fernando Alonso** FERRARI
2012	**Mark Webber** RED BULL
2013	**Nico Rosberg** MERCEDES
2014	**Lewis Hamilton** MERCEDES
2015	**Lewis Hamilton** MERCEDES
2016	**Lewis Hamilton** MERCEDES
2017	**Lewis Hamilton** MERCEDES
2018	**Sebastian Vettel** FERRARI
2019	**Lewis Hamilton** MERCEDES

Its best corner: Copse remains fearsome, but no corner comes close to offering the thrill, for drivers and fans alike, of Becketts. This is a right/left/right combination taken in top gear before dropping to sixth midway through, the car changing direction in a flash.

Its first grand prix: Although opened only in 1948 after a track layout was devised using the runways and perimeter roads of a World War Two airfield, Silverstone hosted its first grand prix in 1950, to kick off the inaugural World Championship. It was dominated by Alfa Romeo as Giuseppe Farina led home a 1–2–3–4 finish for the Italian marque.

A race in time: This choice depends on your age, but few televised battles can have been as frenetic and as spectacular as that between the Williams team-mates Nigel Mansell and Nelson Piquet in 1987. They were vying for honours and sparks flew as they rocketed down the straights in their FW11Bs. Mansell had pitted for fresh rubber and said afterwards that he'd driven the last 20 laps flat out. His jinking one way, diving the other move to get back past Piquet into Stowe sent the crowd wild.

Location: Silverstone is in the heart of England, just to the west of Towcester in Northamptonshire.

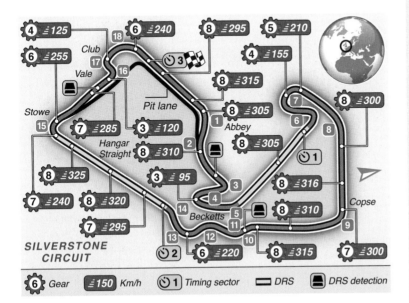

SILVERSTONE CIRCUIT

Club, Vale, Stowe, Hangar Straight, Pit lane, Abbey, Becketts, Copse

Symbol	Meaning
6 Gear	**150** Km/h
1 Timing sector	DRS
	DRS detection

2019 POLE TIME: BOTTAS (MERCEDES), 1M25.093S, 154.863MPH/249.228KPH

2019 WINNER'S AVERAGE SPEED: 140.690MPH/226.419KPH

2019 FASTEST LAP: HAMILTON (MERCEDES), 1M27.369S, 150.828MPH/242.735KPH

LAP RECORD: HAMILTON (MERCEDES), 1M27.369S, 150.828MPH/242.735KPH, 2019

HUNGARORING

Despite a lap that is so tight and almost constantly twisting that it makes overtaking a near impossibility, this Hungarian circuit regularly manages to provide a race of incident.

The raw ingredients of the land selected when the Hungaroring was built in the 1980s were extremely promising, as there was a valley and the track was to be spread across it. This meant that the track would benefit from gradient changes that make it fun for drivers and brilliant for spectators. Sadly, though, the track was narrow and thus overtaking has always been limited.

Starting on one side of the valley, the track dips towards the first corner and continues dropping all the way through the exit. Passing is possible, but the lack of width means that blocking is easier.

On the opening lap, when the traffic is at its busiest, and drivers are having both to defend and attack, cars are side by side so there is often overtaking and sometimes contact at the tight left that follows.

From here, the cars have to negotiate a dipping right before the track drops to the valley floor before rising again to the best corner, Turn 4, a fast flick to the left. After a little more ascent, the track snakes its way across the opposite side of the valley, again sadly without the width required even to consider a passing move through the esses.

Finally, the track opens out as it dips at Turn 11 and the drivers dive back down the slope, cross the valley and then, again sadly, twist through the final three corners, climbing as they go, to return to the start/finish straight. If the approach to the final corner was less restricted, then drivers would have a better chance to catch a tow to enable them to mount a passing move into Turn 1. As it is, it remains their best chance.

INSIDE TRACK

HUNGARIAN GRAND PRIX

Date:	**2 August**
Circuit name:	**Hungaroring**
Circuit length:	**2.722 miles/4.381km**
Number of laps:	**70**
Email:	**office@hungaroring.hu**
Website:	**www.hungaroring.hu**

PREVIOUS WINNERS

2010	**Mark Webber** RED BULL
2011	**Jenson Button** McLAREN
2012	**Lewis Hamilton** McLAREN
2013	**Lewis Hamilton** MERCEDES
2014	**Daniel Ricciardo** RED BULL
2015	**Sebastian Vettel** FERRARI
2016	**Lewis Hamilton** MERCEDES
2017	**Sebastian Vettel** FERRARI
2018	**Lewis Hamilton** MERCEDES
2019	**Lewis Hamilton** MERCEDES

Its best corner: For attempted overtaking, it's Turn 1. From a drivers' perspective, it has to be Turn 4, with its uphill and slightly blind approach making it all the more difficult for the drivers to commit to this lefthand arc in fifth gear at 250kph.

Its first grand prix: It really was a toe in the water on F1's first visit in 1986, as teams had to learn the circuit on arrival in the days before serious telemetry and simulation could give them a head start. It was an all-Brazilian scrap for the lead, with Williams' Nelson Piquet beating Ayrton Senna who had started on pole for Lotus.

A race in time: Due to its format, the Hungaroring is known for trains of cars, as passing is always at a premium. The races that stand out, though, are the ones in which the order is scrambled by changing conditions, and the best of these came in 2006 when Honda pulled off a huge surprise by making all the right calls and Jenson Button delivering thanks to his uncanny ability in wet/dry conditions.

Location: The circuit is in rolling hills a dozen miles north-east of capital Budapest by the village of Mogyorod.

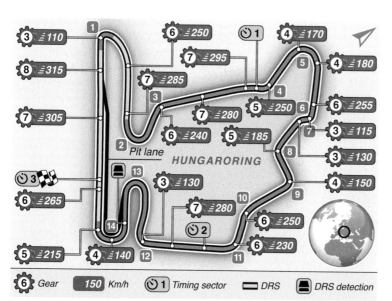

HUNGARORING

Pit lane

Gear | Km/h | Timing sector | DRS | DRS detection

2019 POLE TIME: **VERSTAPPEN (RED BULL), 1M14.572S, 131.416MPH/211.494KPH**
2019 WINNER'S AVERAGE SPEED: **120.255MPH/193.532KPH**
2019 FASTEST LAP: **VERSTAPPEN (RED BULL), 1M17.103S, 127.102MPH/204.552KPH**
LAP RECORD: **VERSTAPPEN (RED BULL), 1M17.103S, 127.102MPH/204.552KPH, 2019**

SPA-FRANCORCHAMPS

One look at this tree-lined circuit that has hosted racing since 1924 and it's clear that it's something special, a place that challenges racing drivers and thrills viewers in equal measure.

When describing most international class circuits, there are sections where the drivers can enjoy the challenge of a stretch of the lap that really flows. At this Belgian classic, the whole lap offers flow, its passage up and down the wooded slopes a continuous change of scenic aspect and gradient. Also, being in the Ardennes, changing weather too. That it has a history dating back almost 100 years makes it all the more magical.

The lap starts with one of F1's shortest runs to a first corner. La Source is a hairpin that makes the likelihood of contact on the opening lap all the greater. From there, it's steeply downhill to Eau Rouge, where the track jinks left then right, then sharply uphill. At Raidillon, it flicks left again, with the cars at the limit of adhesion as the drivers try to carry as much speed as possible onto the straight that follows.

Get a tow up the Kemmel Straight, and overtaking is definitely on into the righthand entry to Les Combes, the point at which the modern Spa-Francorchamps turns off the original route that used to take the track into the next valley between Malmedy and Stavelot. Then the track drops away to the downhill Rivage hairpin. It opens out a little at Speakers' Corner, then offers a challenge with the long, long left called Pouhon.

Having snaked its way down to Curve Paul Frere, where the modern circuit rejoins the return leg of the original layout, the track then opens out for a magnificent run back up the valley, with eighth-gear Blanchimont a challenge. The final chicane is less constricting than the previous Bus Stop combination, and so passing can be attempted on the way in.

BELGIAN GRAND PRIX

Date:	**30 August**
Circuit name:	**Spa-Francorchamps**
Circuit length:	**4.352 miles/7.004km**
Number of laps:	**44**
Email:	secretariat@spa-francorchamps.be
Website:	www.spa-francorchamps.be

PREVIOUS WINNERS

2010	**Lewis Hamilton** McLAREN
2011	**Sebastian Vettel** RED BULL
2012	**Jenson Button** McLAREN
2013	**Sebastian Vettel** RED BULL
2014	**Daniel Ricciardo** RED BULL
2015	**Lewis Hamilton** MERCEDES
2016	**Nico Rosberg** MERCEDES
2017	**Lewis Hamilton** MERCEDES
2018	**Sebastian Vettel** FERRARI
2019	**Charles Leclerc** FERRARI

Its best corner: The Eau Rouge/Raidillon combination isn't as fearsome as it was, but watching any racing car take this uphill twister in top gear with just a slight lift off the throttle can only excite.

Its first grand prix: Having opened for racing in 1924 and then run a grand prix from 1925, Spa-Francorchamps was more than ready to be part of the inaugural World Championship in 1950. On that occasion, Alfa Romeo continued its domination of the first year of F1, with Juan Manuel Fangio jousting for the lead with team-mate Nino Farina before coming home 14s clear of Alfa's Luigi Fagioli.

A race in time: There have been many brilliant Belgian GPs at Spa-Francorchamps, but older racing fans still eulogize about a World Championship sportscar race held here in 1971 when the Porsche 917 shared by Pedro Rodriguez and Jackie Oliver set a winning average speed of 154.579mph when the full 8.761-mile circuit was used, beating the similar 917 of Jo Siffert/Derek Bell by just 0.4s after four hours of racing.

Location: Situated in the Ardennes hills in the east of the country, the circuit is a few miles south of the elegant resort town of Spa, just down the hill from Francorchamps village.

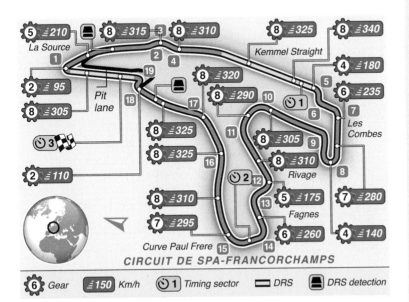

CIRCUIT DE SPA-FRANCORCHAMPS

6 Gear	**≡150** Km/h	**⏱1** Timing sector	**▭** DRS	**◼** DRS detection

2019 POLE TIME: **LECLERC (FERRARI)**, 1M42.519S, 152.835MPH/245.948KPH
2019 WINNER'S AVERAGE SPEED: **137.113MPH/220.662KPH**
2019 FASTEST LAP: **VETTEL (FERRARI)**, 1M46.409S, 147.238MPH/236.957KPH
LAP RECORD: **BOTTAS (MERCEDES)**, 1M46.286S 147.422MPH/237.290KPH, 2018

Making the most of its wooded hillside setting, Spa-Francorhamps has a wonderful flow. This is the descent from Turn 9 towards Pouhon, with the pits at the top of the photo.

MONZA

You can build the greatest sporting venue in the world but, without passionate fans to bring it to life, it will never be special. Monza has those passionate fans, the *tifosi*, and thus a magic of its own.

With close on a century of racing under its belt, Monza is a circuit with history oozing from its every pore as the hunting ground for Italian favourites Alfa Romeo and especially Ferrari across the decades. The fans are loud and passionate, one-eyed even in their love for Ferrari, but this makes a febrile atmosphere and adds edge.

Until the early 1970s, Monza was all about slipstreaming, with drivers needing to master the art of using the car ahead to gain a tow down the straights and then burst out to go past. Then, with speeds getting too high and accidents too frequent, the lap's flow was broken up by the insertion of three chicanes. This changed the nature of this great Italian circuit for ever, but it's still a great place for F1 to go racing.

The first of these chicanes has since been reshaped several times and still provides the best overtaking spot, although it's often a wing-bender on the opening lap. Curva Biassone is not the challenge it was in pre-chicane days when it was called fittingly the Curva Grande, but it sweeps the cars to the second chicane, where passing is also an option.

The trees have been cut back between the Lesmos, making these fast rights less fearsome in feel. Then comes the kinked straight that dips under a bridge carrying part of the old banked circuit. Then comes the third chicane. Get a good exit from here and a driver will benefit on the blast to the Parabolica, from which a good exit will benefit them further, all the way past the pits to the first chicane and a possible passing move.

INSIDE TRACK

ITALIAN GRAND PRIX

Date:	**6 September**
Circuit name:	**Autodromo Nazionale Monza**
Circuit length:	**3.600 miles/5.793km**
Number of laps:	**53**
Email:	**infoautodromo@monzanet.it**
Website:	**www.monzanet.it**

PREVIOUS WINNERS

2010	**Fernando Alonso** FERRARI
2011	**Sebastian Vettel** RED BULL
2012	**Lewis Hamilton** McLAREN
2013	**Sebastian Vettel** RED BULL
2014	**Lewis Hamilton** MERCEDES
2015	**Lewis Hamilton** MERCEDES
2016	**Nico Rosberg** MERCEDES
2017	**Lewis Hamilton** MERCEDES
2018	**Lewis Hamilton** MERCEDES
2019	**Charles Leclerc** FERRARI

Its best corner: The Parabolica is not the challenge it was, as there's now a gravel trap to catch any fallers rather than just a band of grass then trees, but the final corner is still a challenge as a good exit from this double-apex righthander is critical, offering a driver the chance to line up an overtaking move into the first chicane.

Its first grand prix: The first grand prix here, in 1922, wasn't competitive as only the two works Fiats finished on the lead lap after 5h45m of racing – and the only other finisher was four laps in arrears. In the World Championship era, inaugural champion Giuseppe Farina won for Alfa Romeo in 1950.

A race in time: Some of Monza's most exciting races were F3 encounters in the pre-chicane era, when massed groups of cars would hunt in packs. Since the chicanes were inserted in 1972, one of the most surprising races in F1 was in 2008 when Sebastian Vettel put his Toro Rosso on pole. It was also wet in the race and he gave the team its first win, and his too.

Location: There's a royal park in Monza, 10 miles to the north-west of Milan, and the grand prix circuit was built within its walls in 1922.

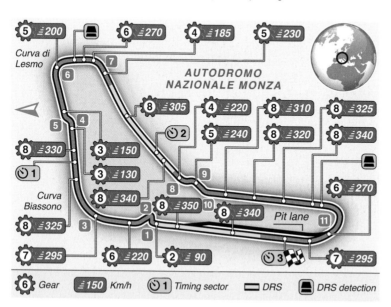

Curva di Lesmo

AUTODROMO NAZIONALE MONZA

Curva Biassono

Pit lane

6	Gear	150	Km/h
1	Timing sector		DRS
	DRS detection		

2019 POLE TIME: **LECLERC (FERRARI)**, 1M19.307S, 163.397MPH/262.902KPH

2019 WINNER'S AVERAGE SPEED: 151.571MPH/243.930KPH

2019 FASTEST LAP: **HAMILTON (MERCEDES)**, 1M21.779S, 158.458MPH/255.014KPH

LAP RECORD: **M SCHUMACHER (FERRARI)**, 1M21.046S 159.909MPH/257.349KPH, 2004

MARINA BAY

Run at night around a circuit laid out on the streets of Singapore's central business district, this race offers a feeling like no other as it challenges drivers with high-speed blasts through the dark.

It no longer seems surprising either to have a round of the World Championship on the streets of Singapore or, even more surprisingly, for the race to be run after nightfall, but this has been a relatively recent development in the 70-year-old World Championship.

A race in Singapore had long been mooted, but it took dynamic leadership to make it happen. This was in 2008 and the first visit earned many plaudits, proving how efficient Singapore can be.

The track, a temporary layout of course, is unusual in that it's a street circuit on which drivers can really get a move on. The start of the lap invariably provides drama as there's an esse feeding directly into a hairpin. From there, it's up through the gears and then the first of many 90-degree bends, but the blast down Raffles Boulevard

that follows is very fast indeed, hitting top gear before a tight corner.

Despite bright floodlights illuminating the circuit, it's still possible to make out the city's landmarks and even the regular road vehicles as they pass by, oblivious to the racing action. One of the best viewing points is from high up in Swissotel the Stanford at Turn 9. From here, the track makes its way around the Singapore Cricket Club and Raffles Hotel, then over the Anderson Bridge before opening out again.

The final section is a little more stop/go as the cars need to be fed through a series of tight esses, one of which takes them under a grandstand at Turn 19. Then the lap finishes with a flourish through a fifth-gear final corner for the blast past the pits towards Turn 1 all over again.

INSIDE TRACK

SINGAPORE GRAND PRIX

Date:	**20 September**
Circuit name:	**Marina Bay Circuit**
Circuit length:	**3.152 miles/5.073km**
Number of laps:	**61**
Email:	**info@singaporegp.sg**
Website:	**www.singaporegp.sg**

PREVIOUS WINNERS

2010	**Fernando Alonso** FERRARI
2011	**Sebastian Vettel** RED BULL
2012	**Sebastian Vettel** RED BULL
2013	**Sebastian Vettel** RED BULL
2014	**Lewis Hamilton** MERCEDES
2015	**Sebastian Vettel** FERRARI
2016	**Daniel Ricciardo** RED BULL
2017	**Lewis Hamilton** MERCEDES
2018	**Lewis Hamilton** MERCEDES
2019	**Sebastian Vettel** FERRARI

Its best corner: As with most street circuits, there are few great corners that really challenge the drivers, but one that requires precision so that not even a second of momentum is lost is fourth-gear Turn 5, the righthander onto the lap's longest straight.

Its first grand prix: The teams didn't really know what to expect other than heat and humidity when they raced here for the first time in 2008. What they wouldn't have expected was that a street race would be won by a driver starting 15th on the grid. This was Fernando Alonso, but he was given a helping hand when Renault team-mate Nelson Piquet Jr. spun off intentionally just as Alonso had completed an unusual strategy to take the lead, earning the team victory but punishment followed.

A race in time: In 2008, Ferrari's pole-sitter Felipe Massa was set fair for victory but a malfunction of his steering wheel meant he needed a pitstop, and he pulled away before his fuel hose had been detached.

Location: Singapore has long been the commercial hub of south-east Asia and the circuit is laid out at the foot of the city-state's main office buildings and most prestigious hotels in the Marina Bay district.

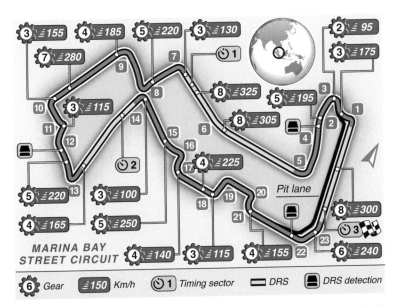

MARINA BAY STREET CIRCUIT

6 Gear	**≡150** Km/h	**⏱1** Timing sector	🔲 DRS	🔳 DRS detection	

2019 POLE TIME: LECLERC (FERRARI), 1M36.217S, 117.709MPH/189.434KPH
2019 WINNER'S AVERAGE SPEED: 97.074MPH/156.226KPH
2019 FASTEST LAP: MAGNUSSEN (HAAS), 1M42.301S, 110.708MPH/178.168KPH
LAP RECORD: MAGNUSSEN (HAAS), 1M41.905S, 109.900MPH/178.860KPH, 2018

SOCHI

Russia transformed an area of this Black Sea resort into a venue for the country's first grand prix in 2014, just after the region hosted the Olympic Winter Games with a track that's nothing special.

It took decades of attempts by F1 ringmaster Bernie Ecclestone before Russia got to host a round of the World Championship in 2014. However, it was neither in Moscow nor St Petersburg, but in a year-round holiday resort, Sochi.

Building a circuit, even a temporary one, in a city is incredibly expensive, so it came as no surprise that it took government finance to make the event happen, with many of the facilities that had just been used for the Sochi Olympic Winter Games being given a new purpose.

The circuit is unusual in that the first corner is simply an open kink that is taken at 190mph on subsequent laps. Turn 2 is thus the first time that the drivers have to hit the brakes as the drivers haul their cars down from more than 200mph and this 90-degree righthander is the

principal place for overtaking, fortunately with a large expanse of tarmac beyond to catch the fallers.

What follows is an unusual open loop that keeps arcing left for nigh on 180 degrees before drivers have to hit the brakes again for a sharp right. The next section, all the way to Turn 10, is nondescript, with short straights and a scattering of low-speed corners, offering few chances for even thinking about passing.

From Turn 10, the drivers get to hit top gear for this first time since before Turn 4, with the fastest cars hitting 210mph just before the left swerve at Turn 12, with heavy braking into Turn 13. The end of the lap is tight and twisty as it snakes through six corners around the back of the paddock before emerging onto the start/finish straight.

INSIDE TRACK

RUSSIAN GRAND PRIX

Date:	**27 September**
Circuit name:	**Sochi Autodrom**
Circuit length:	**3.634 miles/5.848km**
Number of laps:	**53**
Email:	**info@sochiautodrom.ru**
Website:	**www.sochiautodrom.ru**

PREVIOUS WINNERS

2014	**Lewis Hamilton**	MERCEDES
2015	**Lewis Hamilton**	MERCEDES
2016	**Nico Rosberg**	MERCEDES
2017	**Valtteri Bottas**	MERCEDES
2018	**Lewis Hamilton**	MERCEDES
2019	**Lewis Hamilton**	MERCEDES

Its best corner: Turn 13 is the pick of the pack, as this third-gear righthander is a rare spot on the Sochi Autodrom where it's possible to attempt an overtaking manoeuvre if a good exit has been achieved from Turn 10 to help the driver to get a tow. Precision is everything, as the track is surrounded by walls and fences and is thus unforgiving.

Its first grand prix: Lewis Hamilton dominated on F1's first visit in 2014, winning easily, while his Mercedes team-mate Nico Rosberg had a far trickier run to second as he fell to the rear of the field when he had to pit for repairs at the end of the opening lap.

A race in time: Valtteri Bottas took his first F1 win here in 2017, but his next visit to Sochi was less happy as he was asked by Mercedes to let team-mate Lewis Hamilton through to ensure that Ferrari's Sebastian Vettel couldn't catch him in the closing laps of the grand prix.

Location: Best known for being a summer and winter resort popular with the country's top politicians, Sochi is on the northern shore of the Black Sea, offering skiing on the Caucasus Mountains. Favoured by President Putin, Sochi was earmarked for development and the circuit was built on the eastern edge of town.

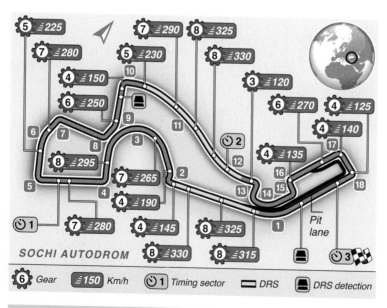

SOCHI AUTODROM

Symbol	Meaning
6 Gear	Gear
150 Km/h	Km/h
1 Timing sector	Timing sector
DRS	DRS
DRS detection	DRS detection

2019 POLE TIME: LECLERC (FERRARI), 1M31.628S, 142.768MPH/229.763KPH
2019 WINNER'S AVERAGE SPEED: 123.310MPH/198.448KPH
2019 FASTEST LAP: HAMILTON (MERCEDES), 1M35.761S, 136.606MPH/219.847KPH
LAP RECORD: HAMILTON (MERCEDES), 1M35.761S 136.606MPH/219.847KPH, 2019

SUZUKA

Brand new circuits have been created over the past two decades to gain a slot on the World Championship calendar, but none as yet offer anything as challenging and admired as Suzuka.

INSIDE TRACK

JAPANESE GRAND PRIX

Date:	11 October
Circuit name:	Suzuka Circuit
Circuit length:	3.608 miles/5.806km
Number of laps:	53
Email:	info@suzukacircuit.co.up
Website:	www.suzukacircuit.co.jp

Ask any driver which circuit they dream about and Suzuka is almost invariably the answer. Visualization of the flow through the lap is key to plotting the perfect line around its swerves, pushing right to the edge but not beyond. Few seldom ever get it spot-on, but they can earn the respect of their peers if they rise to the challenge of doing so.

What makes the challenge so great? Mainly, it's the gradient and a notable lack of space. By contemporary standards, the drivers have limited room to play in, with the barriers hemming them in in a way that is almost claustrophobic.

The track drops towards the first corner, with drivers needing to run a wide line so that they can, traffic allowing, complete the arc as the track turns uphill at Turn 2. On the opening lap, hugging the inside is often the only way to hold position.

Then come the esses, a left/right, left/right combination where the slope steepens, through which the consequence of any error is magnified at each further turn. Flattening out over a crest, the drivers get to breathe briefly before taking the two Degner turns and then diving under a bridge that carries the return leg of the lap.

There's a definite passing spot into the lefthand hairpin, before a fabulous sweep that climbs to the right before drivers have to focus on the most critical exit point of all. This is out of Spoon curve, onto the return straight on which they can achieve their highest speed and, more importantly, line up a passing manoeuvre into the unusually tight chicane. Moves into here are tricky, and not guaranteed to succeed, but they make F1 what it is: gladiatorial.

PREVIOUS WINNERS

2010	**Sebastian Vettel** RED BULL
2011	**Jenson Button** McLAREN
2012	**Sebastian Vettel** RED BULL
2013	**Sebastian Vettel** RED BULL
2014	**Lewis Hamilton** MERCEDES
2015	**Lewis Hamilton** MERCEDES
2016	**Nico Rosberg** MERCEDES
2017	**Lewis Hamilton** MERCEDES
2018	**Lewis Hamilton** MERCEDES
2019	**Valtteri Bottas** MERCEDES

Its best corner: 130R used to be revered for the speed at which it was taken, as the lap's fastest corner but, in these days of high-downforce racing cars, the lap's 15th turn offers little of the challenge of the esses. These run from Turn 3 to Turn 6, the track rising and twisting as it goes, making the drivers work really hard to stay on the racing line.

Its first grand prix: Suzuka first hosted a round of the World Championship in 1987, when Japan made it back onto the calendar for the first time since Fuji Speedway had hosted the race in 1977. The race was won by Gerhard Berger for Ferrari as Williams stumbled and the Italian team came on strong at the end of the season.

A race in time: Some reckon that Kimi Raikkonen pulled off the passing move of the decade in 2005 when he capped his pursuit of Giancarlo Fisichella's Renault by driving his McLaren around the outside of it at the final corner of the penultimate lap.

Location: The circuit is 30 miles south-west of the coastal city of Nagoya, built opposite a permanent funfair on a hillside that runs down to a band of mixed agricultural and industrial land by the sea.

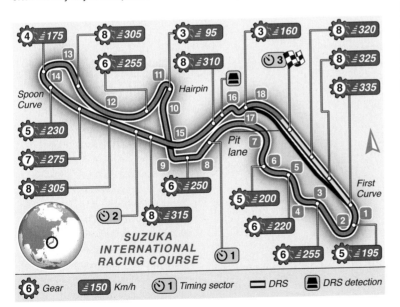

Spoon Curve

Hairpin

Pit lane

First Curve

SUZUKA INTERNATIONAL RACING COURSE

6 Gear	**≡150** Km/h	**⟳1** Timing sector	▭ DRS	▣ DRS detection

2019 POLE TIME: **VETTTEL (FERRARI), 1M27.064S, 149.199MPH/240.113KPH**

2019 WINNER'S AVERAGE SPEED: **137.525MPH/221.325KPH**

2019 FASTEST LAP: **HAMILTON (MERCEDES), 1M30.983S, 142.772MPH/229.770KPH**

LAP RECORD: **HAMILTON (MERCEDES), 1M30.983S 142.772MPH/229.770KPH, 2019**

CIRCUIT OF THE AMERICAS

The United States of America has proved one of F1's hardest nuts to crack, with this purpose-built Texan track its 10th home since the nation's first grand prix at Sebring in 1959.

The USA had tried races on road circuits, races on street circuits and then on a purpose-built circuit laid out on the infield of its greatest circuit of all, the Indianapolis Motor Speedway. Yet none managed to become home for its annual taste of F1 and stick with it for long. The Circuit of the Americas in Texas hosts the United States GP for the ninth time in 2020, hoping that this spell will continue for years to come.

Built to order outside Austin, the circuit made the most of the possibility of gradient change enabled by its rolling location. A track of character, as long as it keeps drawing in the crowds, then it will retain its place on the calendar, although this would be helped hugely by F1 having an American driver.

The lap starts with a stiff climb. Then, at the apex of this tight lefthander, it plateaus before the cars plunge down through the fabulously fast flick through Turn 2 as it flattens out. Then, although chances of passing are limited, comes a wonderful series of esses all the way down to Turn 9.

Turn 11 is a hairpin, with a slight chance for passing, but the main overtaking spot of the entire lap comes at Turn 12, after the drag down the circuit's longest straight culminates in this 105-degree left. A series of tight turns follow before the track opens out over a crest at Turn 17 and drops slightly through a fifth-gear corner that takes the drivers around to the final bend. This is taken in third gear and is tight, so a tidy exit is essential to get to the power down for the sprint to the first corner where a passing move is often on.

INSIDE TRACK

UNITED STATES GRAND PRIX

Date:	**25 October**
Circuit name:	**Circuit of the Americas**
Circuit length:	**3.400 miles/5.472km**
Number of laps:	**56**
Email:	**info@circuitoftheamericas.com**
Website:	**www.circuitoftheamericas.com**

PREVIOUS WINNERS

2012	**Lewis Hamilton** McLAREN
2013	**Sebastian Vettel** RED BULL
2014	**Lewis Hamilton** MERCEDES
2015	**Lewis Hamilton** MERCEDES
2016	**Lewis Hamilton** MERCEDES
2017	**Lewis Hamilton** MERCEDES
2018	**Kimi Raikkonen** FERRARI
2019	**Valtteri Bottas** MERCEDES

Its best corner: Turn 1 is probably the best turn as it not only provides a clear overtaking chance on the way in as the drivers brake hard on the steep approach. Then, it has a sting in the tail as the drivers need to get into position for a good exit as the track dives back down the hill to get a fast run into the sixth-gear Turn 2.

Its first grand prix: Lewis Hamilton started his affinity with this Texan circuit on F1's first visit in 2012, winning for McLaren by half a second from Red Bull's Sebastian Vettel after first overhauling the German's team-mate Mark Webber and then Vettel himself. It was the first of five wins in his first six visits.

A race in time: Any time that Kimi Raikkonen smiles is worth noting and the taciturn Finn was beaming on F1's 2018 visit. The reason was that he had just won a three-way scrap, keeping his Ferrari ahead of Max Verstappen's Red Bull and Lewis Hamilton's Mercedes. It was the first win since the 2013 season-opener in Australia and would be the only win in his final stint with Ferrari.

Location: The Circuit of the Americas is situated beyond the south-eastern edge of Austin, state capital of Texas, just where the land starts to roll in a series of small hills.

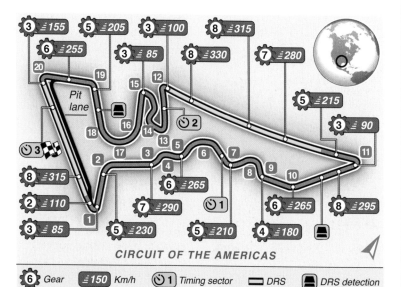

CIRCUIT OF THE AMERICAS

6 Gear	**150** Km/h	**1** Timing sector	DRS	DRS detection

2019 POLE TIME: **BOTTAS (MERCEDES), 1M32.029S, 134.003MPH/215.658KPH**
2019 WINNER'S AVERAGE SPEED: **122.414MPH/197.006KPH**
2019 FASTEST LAP: **LECLERC (FERRARI), 1M36.169S, 128.235MPH/206.374KPH**
LAP RECORD: **LECLERC (FERRARI), 1M36.169S 128.235MPH/206.374KPH, 2019**

MEXICO CITY

There were question marks against this race happening in 2020, but Mexican F1 fans can breathe a sigh of relief as it has signed on for 15 years more of World Championship action.

The passion of the fans has always made racing in Mexico a little bit special. Back in the early 1960s, when the Rodriguez brothers were the rising stars of F1, the atmosphere was electric. Sadly, Ricardo was killed in practice here in 1962 and brother Pedro would die in a sportscar race in 1971. However, the nation's love for racing remains, in noisy abundance.

Crowd control issues led to Mexico City's circuit being dropped from the calendar after 1970. When Mexico was given a second shot, from 1986, with the circuit now named after the Rodriguez brothers, little had changed to the track other than fences having been erected to keep the crowd under control.

The lap starts with a long, wide straight through this municipal park. The first corner complex is a three-corner combination that offers plenty of scope for passing on the opening lap.

A good length straight follows down to the Lake Esses before the hairpin at Turn 6. Returning from there, there's a wonderful sweep of esses between the trees at the edge of the park.

When the track turns into the baseball stadium at Turn 12, steeply-raked grandstands make the arena below feel like a coliseum. The hairpin at Turn 13 is a definite passing place, although ambition can often override accuracy.

Then, coming out behind the grandstands, the lap is completed by a sharp right onto the gentle banking halfway around the famed Peraltada of old. Then, it's all about getting a good tow down the start/finish straight.

INSIDE TRACK

MEXICAN GRAND PRIX

Date:	1 November
Circuit name:	Autodromo Hermanos Rodriguez
Circuit length:	2.674 miles/4.303km
Number of laps:	71
Email:	Rosario@cie.com.mx
Website:	www.autodromohermanosrodriguez.com.mx

PREVIOUS WINNERS

1988	**Alain Prost**	McLAREN
1989	**Ayrton Senna**	McLAREN
1990	**Alain Prost**	FERRARI
1991	**Riccardo Patrese**	WILLIAMS
1992	**Nigel Mansell**	WILLIAMS
2015	**Nico Rosberg**	MERCEDES
2016	**Lewis Hamilton**	MERCEDES
2017	**Max Verstappen**	RED BULL
2018	**Max Verstappen**	RED BULL
2019	**Lewis Hamilton**	MERCEDES

Its best corner: The first corner complex is the best place for overtaking, as it offers drivers scope to try various lines through the right/left/right combination, whether taking the quick in, slow out approach or vice versa in the quest to get ahead of a rival.

Its first grand prix: After trying out with a non-championship event in 1962, Mexico's first World Championship round was held the following year, with Jim Clark triumphant for Lotus, and only Jack Brabham (Brabham) and Richie Ginther (BRM) finishing on the same lap.

A race in time: Ayrton Senna didn't make many mistakes, but one that he couldn't deny was when he famously inverted his McLaren at Peraltada during qualifying in 1991, having hit one of the bumps that made it such a challenge. He was already carrying injuries from a jet ski accident, but he emerged unscathed from this mishap, so must have felt somewhat fortunate.

Location: Mexico City is a considerable sprawl, with the circuit located inside the Magdalena Mixhuca park towards the south-eastern edge of the metropolis, a facility that also includes a baseball stadium, a running track, football pitches and tennis courts.

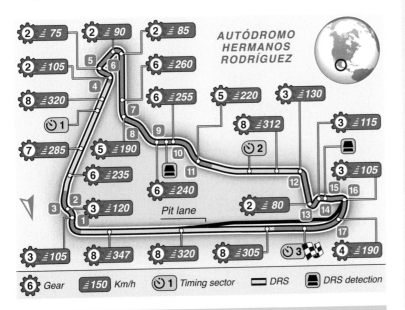

AUTÓDROMO HERMANOS RODRÍGUEZ

Pit lane

6 Gear	150 Km/h
1 Timing sector	DRS
DRS detection	

2019 POLE TIME: LECLERC (FERRARI), 1M15.024S, 128.328MPH/206.525KPH

2019 WINNER'S AVERAGE SPEED: 117.587MPH/189.239KPH

2019 FASTEST LAP: LECLERC (FERRARI), 1M19.232S, 121.532MPH/195.557KPH

LAP RECORD: BOTTAS (MERCEDES), 1M18.741S 122.271MPH/196.776KPH, 2018

INTERLAGOS

The president of Brazil said last year that the Brazilian GP would move to Rio de Janeiro in 2020, but Sao Paulo's Interlagos has hung on to host it for one last time while the new circuit is made ready for 2021.

INSIDE TRACK

BRAZILIAN GRAND PRIX

Date:	**15 November**
Circuit name:	**Autodromo Jose Carlos Pace Interlagos**
Circuit length:	**2.667 miles/4.292km**
Number of laps:	**71**
Email:	**info@gpbrazil.com**
Website:	**www.gpbrazil.com**

PREVIOUS WINNERS

2010	**Sebastian Vettel**	RED BULL
2011	**Mark Webber**	RED BULL
2012	**Jenson Button**	McLAREN
2013	**Sebastian Vettel**	RED BULL
2014	**Nico Rosberg**	MERCEDES
2015	**Nico Rosberg**	MERCEDES
2016	**Lewis Hamilton**	MERCEDES
2017	**Sebastian Vettel**	FERRARI
2018	**Lewis Hamilton**	MERCEDES
2019	**Max Verstappen**	RED BULL

The Brazilian GP's slot at Interlagos had long been in question for two reasons. One was that its facilities were increasingly tired and outmoded. The other reason was that it was losing money and the politicians no longer wanted to dip into the public coffers to keep it afloat.

Then, its fate seemed confirmed last May when Brazil's recently appointed president Jair Bolsonaro said that the grand prix would be moved to Rio de Janeiro, with private finance being used to build an all-new circuit to host it.

Yet, Interlagos has hung on and its famed challenges around its hillside setting lie ahead for one more go. The first corner has a relatively blind entry over a brow and is the start of the steeply dipping Senna esse. Coming out of the compression, the drivers accelerate hard through Curva do Sol then continue down a straight at up to 210mph before balancing their cars for the two lefts that make up Descida do Lago and turn them back up the slope.

The run back up to beneath the paddock offers a tricky right at the crest, Ferradura, before the track drops away again out of Turn 8, Laranja.

Making the most of the slope, the track snakes its way down, then up to the tight right at Cotovelo, down again through Mergulho then along to Juncao.

Juncao is critical as it's the point at which drivers start accelerating and keep their throttle planted all the way to the end of the lap, with the rising, curving straight nestled between walls and barriers to give the drivers a feeling of being enclosed as they top 200mph before having to brake heavily for Turn 1.

Its best corner: The Senna S is a real challenge for numerous reasons. The approach is all but blind, as drivers arrive at 200mph over a crest, with limited ability to see into the corner. Dropping to third gear, drivers have to turn hard left then almost immediately hard right as the track drops away.

Its first grand prix: After a non-championship event in 1972, Interlagos welcomed the World Championship in 1973 and Emerson Fittipaldi sent the crowd wild by winning on home ground, getting the jump on pole-starting Lotus team-mate Ronnie Peterson to lead all the way to beat Jackie Stewart's Tyrrell to the chequered flag.

A race in time: Max Verstappen was set to win for Red Bull in 2018. Then he suffered the fate of being pushed into a spin by a driver unlapping himself. This was Force India's Esteban Ocon who'd just come out on fresh rubber and tried to go past at the Senna S. It didn't work and Lewis Hamilton made the most of this to win.

Location: Interlagos was built between lakes on a hillside on the southern outskirts of Sao Paulo, but the city has continued its expansion and the fields surrounding it have been enveloped by industrial and suburban developments.

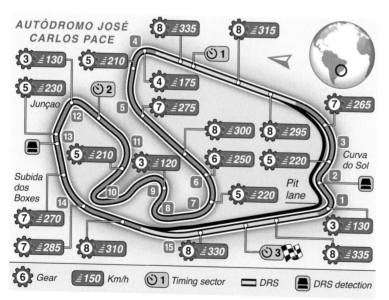

AUTÓDROMO JOSÉ CARLOS PACE

Juncão

Subida dos Boxes

Curva do Sol

Pit lane

Gear | Km/h | Timing sector | DRS | DRS detection

2019 POLE TIME: VERSTAPPEN (RED BULL), 1M07.508S, 142.782MPH/229.786KPH
2019 WINNER'S AVERAGE SPEED: 122.312MPH/196.842KPH
2019 FASTEST LAP: BOTTAS (MERCEDES), 1M10.698S, 136.339MPH/219.417KPH
LAP RECORD: BOTTAS (MERCEDES), 1M10.540S 136.645MPH/219.909KPH, 2018

YAS MARINA

The now traditional home for the end of season grand prix, this circuit was opened with high hopes, designed to provide passing aplenty, but sadly this hasn't proved to be the case.

Money was never going to be in question when Abu Dhabi decided that it wanted to host a grand prix. As the senior member of the United Arab Emirates, it had oil wealth galore and was naturally determined that its purpose-built track was going to be the most upmarket on the World Championship circuit.

Built around a marina and hotel complex, the Yas Marina Circuit came from the design offices of circuit architect Hermann Tilke and its lap is dotted with his regular features, notably long straights into a complex of tight corners. These excited the crews before they made their first visit, but sadly they have not produced the amount of overtaking that was expected of them.

The lap starts with a simple left which is wide enough to allow drivers to take it side-by-side and thus keep a move going all the way to the esse that starts at Turn 2.

Hard braking is required for the entry to the chicane at Turn 5/6 and then it's all about lining up a slick exit from Turn 7, as this leads onto the lap's longest straight. Using the DRS zone along the straight ought to produce a possible pass into Turn 8 as the cars are slowed from more than 200mph as the track twists into Turn 9.

If drivers have no luck there, they can try to get a quick exit from Turn 9 onto the lap's second longest straight down to tight Turn 11.

The remainder of the lap is more medium-speed in nature, made interesting only by ducking under a covered bridge between two parts of the Viceroy Hotel and for passing the marina that gives the track its name.

INSIDE TRACK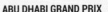

ABU DHABI GRAND PRIX

Date:	**29 November**
Circuit name:	**Yas Marina Circuit**
Circuit length:	**3.451 miles/5.554km**
Number of laps:	**56**
Email:	customerservice@yasmarinacircuit.com
Website:	**www.yasmarinacircuit.com**

PREVIOUS WINNERS

2010	**Sebastian Vettel**	RED BULL
2011	**Lewis Hamilton**	McLAREN
2012	**Kimi Raikkonen**	LOTUS
2013	**Sebastian Vettel**	RED BULL
2014	**Lewis Hamilton**	MERCEDES
2015	**Nico Rosberg**	MERCEDES
2016	**Lewis Hamilton**	MERCEDES
2017	**Valtteri Bottas**	MERCEDES
2018	**Lewis Hamilton**	MERCEDES
2019	**Lewis Hamilton**	MERCEDES

Its best corner: Turn 8 offers drivers their chief chance to overtake. A good tow is essential to make this happen, and the ability to brake later than their rival into this second-gear left. Making it even more appealing for drivers, is the fact that there is a grandstand looming over the corner so their racecraft can be appreciated at close quarters.

Its first grand prix: Sebastian Vettel marked the first race here in 2009 by winning for Red Bull Racing after McLaren's pole-starting Lewis Hamilton was slowed, then forced to retire by a brake problem. After a first lap clash with Rubens Barrichello, Mark Webber brought the other Red Bull home second.

A race in time: Hosting the final round of the year invariably adds the spice of the settling of the drivers' title and 2010 was exceptional in this, as it was a four-way fight and the driver who left smiling wasn't either of the lead duo coming into the event – Fernando Alonso and Mark Webber – but instead Webber's Red Bull team-mate Vettel who won from pole.

Location: Built at the eastern end of Abu Dhabi's main island, the Yas Marina Circuit contains a marina, of course, and is alongside the Ferrari World theme park.

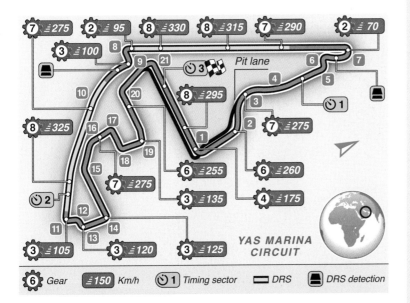

YAS MARINA CIRCUIT

6 Gear	150 Km/h	1 Timing sector	DRS	DRS detection

2019 POLE TIME: **HAMILTON (MERCEDES), 1M34.779S, 131.083MPH/210.958KPH**
2019 WINNER'S AVERAGE SPEED: **120.987MPH/194.710KPH**
2019 FASTEST LAP: **HAMILTON (MERCEDES), 1M39.283S, 125.136MPH/201.387KPH**
LAP RECORD: **HAMILTON (MERCEDES), 1M39.283S, 125.136MPH/201.387KPH, 2019**

This fabulous photo taken from above Scheivlak (bottom right) shows how the Zandvoort circuit nestles in the sand dunes just in from the Netherlands' North Sea coast.

REVIEW OF THE 2019 SEASON

You might reckon that it was all about Mercedes last year, but there was far more to the 2019 season than that, as Ferrari and Red Bull Racing had their moments when their cars were the pick of the field. As a result of this, the racing was the best that it has been for years and provided many memorable moments. Yet, responding to the challenge, Lewis Hamilton put his rivals in their place.

Another year, another title for Mercedes and Lewis Hamilton. This fact will hurt Ferrari as it had a car capable of taking the top prize in 2019 and drivers capable of going for the title and yet a loss of form and a series of clashes laid the way clear for Hamilton to claim his sixth F1 crown.

Mercedes had been concerned by Ferrari's pre-season pace, but still won

the opening round. This wasn't one for Hamilton but one for Valtteri Bottas who showed his desire not to be cast as "wingman" again. He added another win two rounds later, but Hamilton had the momentum and so led Mercedes' attack.

Mercedes took a step up at Barcelona, its revised aero package pulling it further clear. This punctured Ferrari's hopes and

Hamilton made the most of it.

Thwarted ambition at Ferrari is nothing new, and 2019's antics were twofold, as the management and drivers had roles to play in their collective failure. Charles Leclerc was denied by a control system glitch in Bahrain. In Canada, Sebastian Vettel was first to the finish but was hit with a 5s penalty for rejoining the track in

a dangerous manner. That was nothing to the chaos of the German GP when drivers fell like skittles. With competition growing, most notably as Ferrari hit form, Hamilton and Mercedes kept scoring, and the title was Hamilton's with two rounds to go.

Ferrari principal Mattia Binotto is an engineer, and the SF90 was proof of his expertise as it took a run of poles and three wins. However, he had taken control after Sergio Marchionne died and must have wished for more management experience when Vettel and Leclerc clashed. On top of this, Max Verstappen suggested that Ferrari had found a performance advantage through oil burning and that put them under extra attention.

Red Bull Racing advanced as its Honda engine got ever more competitive, and claimed the first of its wins after a scrap between Verstappen and Leclerc in Austria. Two races later, Verstappen won the crazy wet race at Hockenheim, and would win again at Interlagos. Team-mate Pierre Gasly failed to get close and so was dropped. Coming up from Scuderia Toro Rosso, rookie Alex Albon did far better and was denied a first podium in Brazil.

McLaren made strides to rise from sixth in 2018 to rank fourth, with Carlos Sainz Jr peaking with third in Brazil, while rookie Lando Norris did well.

Renault had a mixed year, with Daniel Ricciardo and Nico Hulkenberg regularly shining but often falling short. This left Ricciardo's fourth at Monza the highlight.

Scuderia Toro Rosso had its final shout before being retitled. Daniil Kvyat was brought back and took a surprise third in Germany, but newcomer Albon looked faster and was moved to Red Bull Racing when Gasly was dropped. The French racer then had a huge fillip when he finished second in Brazil.

Racing Point remained seventh in its first year since being renamed and Sergio Perez continued to lead, with cameo drives by Lance Stroll. Alfa Romeo also had a new name. It seemed that it was not like forebear Sauber as points flowed, with Kimi Raikkonen leading the way.

Ninth was disappointing for Haas F1 as the team had kicked off with sixth for Kevin Magnussen, but he and Romain Grosjean failed to improve on that.

Williams was in disarray, with technical director Paddy Lowe fired before the opening race. The car was slow and there was nothing that the returning Robert Kubica or George Russell could do.

Pre-season testing had suggested that Ferrari was the team on form, but 2019 started as 2018 ended, with Mercedes on top. The big change, though, was that it was a revitalized Valtteri Bottas who was first home, not Lewis Hamilton, and he was 20s clear.

Midway through 2018, Bottas was beaten for pace and form by team-mate Hamilton and damned by faint praise when Toto Wolff the described him as "the perfect wing man". The winter break must have done the Finn a power of good, as he was clearly recalibrated and determined not to have to play the supporting role again.

Although Hamilton beat him to pole by 0.1s, Bottas got his start just right and was ahead by the first corner. Four laps in, Hamilton suffered floor damage and then had to make his pitstop earlier than planned to cover Sebastian Vettel who came in on lap 14. This left Bottas to motor on until lap 23 before he came in and then win as he pleased.

If Ferrari was disappointed that it couldn't turn its test form into victory, it was a shock that neither driver even made it to the podium. Instead, Red Bull's Max Verstappen finished third. He made it hard for himself by falling behind Charles Leclerc at the start, but fought back immediately to regain the position in Turn 2. He then emerged from his pitstop, caught Vettel and passed him at Turn 3 six laps later and went off after Hamilton.

There had been raised eyebrows when Daniel Ricciardo left Red Bull for Renault and it looked a poor move when he qualified only 12th for his home grand prix, bounced across the grass on the run to the first corner and tore off his front wing. At least team-mate Nico Hulkenberg took home the points for seventh place, right on the tail of Kevin Magnussen as he and the Haas driver fought to be best of the rest behind the big three teams.

Williams' woes were plain to see when it was late to start testing. Technical chief Paddy Lowe had been fired and drivers George Russell and Robert Kubica were always going to be also-rans, 3s per lap off race pace.

Everyone expected Ferrari to win the first race, but Bottas came first for Mercedes.

ALBERT PARK ROUND 1

DATE: **17 MARCH 2019**

Laps: **58** · Distance: **191.117 miles/307.574km** · Weather: **Warm & sunny**

Pos	Driver	Team	Result	Stops	Qualifying Time	Grid
1	Valtteri Bottas	Mercedes	1h25m27.325s	1	1m20.598s	2
2	Lewis Hamilton	Mercedes	1h25m48.211s	1	1m20.486s	1
3	Max Verstappen	Red Bull	1h25m49.845s	1	1m21.320s	4
4	Sebastian Vettel	Ferrari	1h26m24.434s	1	1m21.190s	3
5	Charles Leclerc	Ferrari	1h26m25.555s	1	1m21.442s	5
6	Kevin Magnussen	Haas	1h26m54.481s	1	1m22.099s	7
7	Nico Hulkenberg	Renault	57 laps	1	1m22.562s	11
8	Kimi Raikkonen	Alfa Romeo	57 laps	1	1m22.314s	9
9	Lance Stroll	Racing Point	57 laps	1	1m23.017s	16
10	Daniil Kvyat	Toro Rosso	57 laps	1	1m22.774s	15
11	Pierre Gasly	Red Bull	57 laps	1	1m23.020s	17
12	Lando Norris	McLaren	57 laps	1	1m22.304s	8
13	Sergio Perez	Racing Point	57 laps	1	1m22.781s	10
14	Alex Albon	Toro Rosso	57 laps	1	1m22.636s	13
15	Antonio Giovinazzi	Alfa Romeo	57 laps	1	1m22.714s	14
16	George Russell	Williams	56 laps	2	1m24.360s	19
17	Robert Kubica	Williams	55 laps	3	1m26.067s	20
R	Romain Grosjean	Haas	29 laps/suspension	1	1m21.826s	6
R	Daniel Ricciardo	Renault	28 laps/crash damage	1	1m22.570s	12
R	Carlos Sainz Jr	McLaren	9 laps/power unit	0	1m23.084s	18

FASTEST LAP: **BOTTAS, 1M25.580S, 138.612MPH/223.075KPH ON LAP 57** · RACE LEADERS: **BOTTAS 1-22 & 25-58, VERSTAPPEN 23-24**

BAHRAIN GP

Lewis Hamilton bounced back from being the second-best Mercedes driver in Australia to assume control in Bahrain, but all the talk after the race was the searing pace of Charles Leclerc. He could easily have won for Ferrari but for an engine blip, having completely outperformed his team-mate Sebastian Vettel.

The signs had been there through 2018 that Leclerc had star quality when he propelled his Sauber higher up the order than expected. His speed at the Australian GP had all but matched Vettel's.

At Sakhir, though, the Monegasque racer really showed his hand. Fastest in two of the three practice sessions, Leclerc grabbed pole, 0.3s ahead of Vettel. However, he was passed by his team-mate on the charge to the first corner after suffering from wheelspin, and then demoted further by Valtteri Bottas through Turn 4, with Hamilton attacking him at Turn 8, where they touched.

Having held on to third, Leclerc then passed Bottas for second at Turn 1 on lap 2, before chasing off after Vettel. Hamilton also profited from the Finn's loss of momentum to grab third at Turn 4 of the same lap. Leclerc then caught Vettel and went past at Turn 2 on lap 6.

From there, Leclerc had everything under control until, on lap 46 of 57, his Ferrari's engine dropped a cylinder and he was hobbled by the subsequent inability to employ the MGU-H. Hamilton didn't seek a second invitation and moved past into the lead. Then, with three laps to go, Bottas also passed Leclerc.

Leclerc might have fallen to fourth behind Max Verstappen, but both Renaults had their engines shut down on lap 54 and the deployment of the safety car annulled Leclerc's mechanical woes and so he was able to hold on for his first F1 podium.

It was a cruel turn, but Leclerc had the satisfaction of easily beating his team-mate, with Vettel's day getting worse when he spun at Turn 4 when tussling with Hamilton on lap 37.

British F1 rookies Lando Norris and Alex Albon took home their first points for sixth and ninth, for McLaren and Toro Rosso, respectively.

SAKHIR ROUND 2

DATE: 31 MARCH 2019

Laps: **57** • Distance: **191.530 miles/308.238km** • Weather: **Hot & sunny**

Pos	Driver	Team	Result	Stops	Qualifying Time	Grid
1	**Lewis Hamilton**	Mercedes	1h34m21.295s	2	1m28.190s	3
2	**Valtteri Bottas**	Mercedes	1h34m24.275s	2	1m28.256s	4
3	**Charles Leclerc**	Ferrari	1h34m27.426s	2	1m27.866s	1
4	**Max Verstappen**	Red Bull	1h34m27.703s	2	1m28.752s	5
5	**Sebastian Vettel**	Ferrari	1h34m57.363s	3	1m28.160s	2
6	**Lando Norris**	McLaren	1h35m07.049s	2	1m29.043s	9
7	**Kimi Raikkonen**	Alfa Romeo	1h35m08.765s	2	1m29.022s	8
8	**Pierre Gasly**	Red Bull	1h35m19.389s	2	1m29.526s	13
9	**Alex Albon**	Toro Rosso	1h35m23.992s	2	1m29.513s	12
10	**Sergio Perez**	Racing Point	1h35m24.991s	2	1m29.756s	14
11	**Antonio Giovinazzi**	Alfa Romeo	1h35m35.894s	2	1m30.026s	16
12	**Daniil Kvyat**	Toro Rosso	56 laps	2	1m29.854s	15
13	**Kevin Magnussen**	Haas	56 laps	2	1m28.757s	6
14	**Lance Stroll**	Racing Point	56 laps	2	1m30.217s	18
15	**George Russell**	Williams	56 laps	2	1m31.759s	19
16	**Robert Kubica**	Williams	55 laps	2	1m31.799s	20
17	**Nico Hulkenberg**	Renault	53 laps/power unit	2	1m30.034s	17
18	**Daniel Ricciardo**	Renault	53 laps/power unit	1	1m29.488s	10
19	**Carlos Sainz Jr**	McLaren	53 laps/crash damage	3	1m28.813s	7
R	**Romain Grosjean ***	Haas	16 laps/crash damage	1	1m29.015s	11

FASTEST LAP: **LECLERC, 1M33.411S, 129.602MPH/208.575KPH ON LAP 38** • RACE LEADERS: **VETTEL 1-5 & 14, LECLERC 6-13 & 15-47, HAMILTON 48-57**
* 3-PLACE GRID PENALTY FOR DRIVING TOO SLOWLY AND IMPEDING A RIVAL

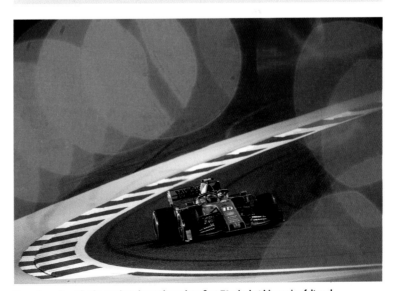
Ferrari new boy Charles Leclerc desrved to take a first F1 win, but his engine faltered.

CHINESE GP

Ferrari continued to wonder where its preseason form had gone as Mercedes came, saw and conquered in China. Valtteri Bottas started from pole, showing that his new-found form put him equal with Lewis Hamilton, but his British team-mate got ahead and stayed there.

The margins between success and failure in F1 can be tiny. Take the gap between the Mercedes drivers after the final qualifying session. It was just 0.023s, but it was advantage Bottas, as he matched his 2018 pole tally in the third round of 2019.

At the start, though, it was advantage Hamilton as he was quicker off the mark and opened out a 2s lead by the end of the opening lap. What followed was Hamilton at his best as he stretched his lead through the first stint to 5s before he called in for the first of two planned pitstops. Bottas had no answer to this.

Nor did Ferrari, and the Italian team had every reason to feel confused, as the potentially race-winning pace Charles Leclerc had displayed in Bahrain was gone. Indeed, as the Mercedes duo edged clear, Ferrari decided that it was time for Leclerc to cede third to Vettel, something he wasn't at all pleased about.

Red Bull had reason to feel frustrated too, but this related to qualifying when Max Verstappen and three others were unable to start their planned final flier because of traffic. As it was, he started fifth and was only able to rise to fourth really thanks to Ferrari not getting its tactics right for Leclerc by leaving him out too long on his first set of tyres. Pierre Gasly finished almost a minute further back in sixth.

No other car finished on the leading lap, with Daniel Ricciardo scoring points with Renault on his third attempt.

One of the more notable performances came from Toro Rosso's Alex Albon who had to start from the pitlane after a massive shunt in third practice and yet came through to 10th after a one-stop run.

One of the less impressive drives came from team-mate Daniil Kvyat. He clattered into both McLarens on the opening lap, forcing the pair to pit for repairs and earning a drive-through penalty.

SHANGHAI ROUND 3

DATE: **14 APRIL 2019**

Laps: **56** • Distance: **189.559 miles/305.066km** • Weather: **Warm & overcast**

Pos	Driver	Team	Result	Stops	Qualifying Time	Grid
1	**Lewis Hamilton**	Mercedes	1h32m06.350s	2	1m31.570s	2
2	**Valtteri Bottas**	Mercedes	1h32m12.902s	2	1m31.547s	1
3	**Sebastian Vettel**	Ferrari	1h32m20.094s	2	1m31.848s	3
4	**Max Verstappen**	Red Bull	1h32m33.977s	2	1m32.089s	5
5	**Charles Leclerc**	Ferrari	1h32m37.626s	2	1m31.865s	4
6	**Pierre Gasly**	Red Bull	1h33m35.657s	3	1m32.930s	6
7	**Daniel Ricciardo**	Renault	55 laps	1	1m32.958s	7
8	**Sergio Perez**	Racing Point	55 laps	1	1m33.299s	12
9	**Kimi Raikkonen**	Alfa Romeo	55 laps	1	1m33.419s	13
10	**Alex Albon ***	Toro Rosso	55 laps	1	no time	20
11	**Romain Grosjean**	Haas	55 laps	2	no time	10
12	**Lance Stroll**	Racing Point	55 laps	2	1m34.292s	16
13	**Kevin Magnussen**	Haas	55 laps	2	no time	9
14	**Carlos Sainz Jr**	McLaren	55 laps	2	1m33.523s	14
15	**Antonio Giovanizzi**	Alfa Romeo	55 laps	2	no time	19
16	**George Russell**	Williams	54 laps	2	1m35.253s	17
17	**Robert Kubica**	Williams	54 laps	1	1m35.281s	18
18	**Lando Norris**	McLaren	50 laps/crash damage	3	1m33.967s	15
R	**Daniil Kvyat**	Toro Rosso	41 laps/ saving engine life	3	1m33.236s	11
R	**Nico Hulkenberg**	Renault	16 laps/MGUK	1	1m32.962s	8

FASTEST LAP: **GASLY, 1M34.742S, 128.702MPH/207.126KPH ON LAP 55** • RACE LEADER: **HAMILTON 1-56**
* STARTED FROM THE PITLANE

Lewis Hamilton got the jump on team-mate Bottas and was in control from then on.

AZERBAIJAN GP

Four races in, and it became four wins for Mercedes, with two each for both Lewis Hamilton and now Valtteri Bottas. However, the team deserved as much praise as the drivers, as its strategy gave them a helping hand to beat the potentially faster Ferraris.

Mercedes knew coming into the 2019 season that Ferrari's SF90 was a quick car. The Italian team had mismanaged the opening races and then, just as it was setting the pace on the streets of Baku, did so again. This time, Charles Leclerc hampered his chances with a shunt in the second qualifying session. Then Sebastian Vettel was unable to find a tow in final qualifying and so lost a chance to prevent Mercedes from filling the front row of the grid, Bottas ahead of Hamilton.

While this was a talking point, another was the shocking incident early in the first practice session when a loose manhole cover was sucked up to clatter against the underside of George Russell's Williams. Understandably, this left all drivers less than comfortable about the state of the temporary venue.

Bottas took the lead at the start, but only just, after being a little cautious in order to avoid wheelspin, and had to ride it out on the outside line through Turns 1 and 2, relying on Hamilton giving him space. Despite Ferrari's pace in practice, the first stint of the race was all about Mercedes, as the silver cars stretched clear.

While Vettel was losing ground and was the first of the top three to pit, Leclerc, starting from eighth, was making progress up the order. He had lost two places to Carlos Sainz Jr and Daniel Ricciardo on lap 1, but was up to fourth by lap 9. Having a fresh set of tyres to start on, he kept going as his rivals pitted, and stayed in the lead, but with an ever-smaller margin, hoping for a safety car intervention. On lap 31, Bottas motored past, followed by Hamilton and Vettel.

Sergio Perez has an affinity for the Baku circuit, as he backed up his third place for Force India with a "best of the rest" sixth in 2019, the team now competing as Racing Point.

Taking pole helped Valtteri Bottas into a winning position in the dash to the first corner.

BAKU ROUND 4

DATE: 28 APRIL 2019

Laps: **51** · Distance: **190.170 miles/306.049km** · Weather: **Warm & sunny**

Pos	Driver	Team	Result	Stops	Qualifying Time	Grid
1	Valtteri Bottas	Mercedes	1h31m52.942s	1	1m40.495s	1
2	Lewis Hamilton	Mercedes	1h31m54.466s	1	1m40.554s	2
3	Sebastian Vettel	Ferrari	1h32m04.681s	1	1m40.797s	3
4	Max Verstappen	Red Bull	1h32m10.435s	1	1m41.069s	4
5	Charles Leclerc	Ferrari	1h33m02.049s	2	no time	8
6	Sergio Perez	Racing Point	1h33m09.358s	1	1m41.593s	5
7	Carlos Sainz Jr	McLaren	1h33m16.768s	1	1m42.398s	9
8	Lando Norris	McLaren	1h33m33.210s	2	1m41.886s	7
9	Lance Stroll	Racing Point	1h33m36.758s	1	1m42.630s	13
10	Kimi Raikkonen *	Alfa Romeo	50 laps	1	no time	19
11	Alex Albon	Toro Rosso	50 laps	1	1m42.494s	11
12	Antonio Giovinazzi !!	Alfa Romeo	50 laps	1	1m42.424s	17
13	Kevin Magnussen	Haas	50 laps	2	1m42.699s	12
14	Nico Hulkenberg	Renault	50 laps	2	1m43.427s	15
15	George Russell	Williams	49 laps	2	1m45.062s	16
16	Robert Kubica *	Williams	49 laps	3	1m45.455s	18
R	Pierre Gasly !*	Red Bull	38 laps/driveshaft	0	no time	20
R	Romain Grosjean	Haas	38 laps/brakes	1	1m43.407s	14
R	Daniil Kvyat	Toro Rosso	33 laps/crash damage	1	1m41.681s	6
R	Daniel Ricciardo	Renault	33 laps/crash damage	1	1m42.477s	10

FASTEST LAP: LECLERC, 1M43.009S, 130.360MPH/209.795KPH ON LAP 50 · RACE LEADERS: BOTTAS 1-11 & 32-51, HAMILTON 12, LECLERC 13-31
* REQUIRED TO START FROM PITLANE, ! 5-PLACE GRID PENALTY FOR REPLACING GEARBOX, !! 10-PLACE GRID PENALTY FOR USING NEW POWER UNIT

» SPANISH GP

Lewis Hamilton made it three Spanish GP wins in a row and, in so doing, took the championship lead from Mercedes team-mate Valtteri Bottas, who had qualified in pole position, but whose chances were scuppered by a brilliant start from Hamilton.

The Circuit de Barcelona-Catalunya is a hard track on which to pass and so the prospects were good for Bottas. Fastest in two of the three practice sessions, then in all three qualifying sessions, he looked well set to extend his one-point championship lead.

Then came the start and Hamilton was better away, and able to pull alongside on the inside line into Turn 1. Matters got more complicated for Bottas as Sebastian Vettel also challenged him on the outside, and this was enough of a distraction for Hamilton to get his nose in front. Max Verstappen was able to slip into third as Vettel sorted himself out.

Vettel then struggled with a flatspotted right front tyre and he fell to fifth when finally asked by the team to allow team-mate Charles Leclerc to overtake him. Ferrari's slow reaction to letting the quicker Leclerc pass Vettel hurt their hopes of a podium finish. The German was the first of the top drivers to pit and, to compound his unhappiness, it was a very slow first stop after a wheelnut was cross-threaded.

Hamilton proved to be the better Mercedes driver in race trim, controlling proceedings thereafter to win by 4s.

Verstappen's drive was a strong one, taking third, but Ferrari helped him in the middle stint when it again took an age to let its faster driver through, this time with Vettel, running on soft tyres, being held back by Leclerc on hards.

For the rival teams, and most notably Ferrari and Red Bull, Mercedes' continued dominance was hugely dispiriting, as it made it clear that the upgrades all teams introduce for the first race of the year in Europe had found them no advantage.

In a race short on incident after the first corner tussle, Lance Stroll and Lando Norris were the only retirements when they clashed in Turn 2 on lap 45.

Lewis Hamilton is delighted as his third win of 2019 helped him into the points lead.

BARCELONA ROUND 5

DATE: **12 MAY 2019**

Laps: **66** · Distance: **190.825 miles/307.104km** · Weather: **Warm & sunny**

Pos	Driver	Team	Result	Stops	Qualifying Time	Grid
1	Lewis Hamilton	Mercedes	1h35m50.553s	2	1m16.040s	2
2	Valtteri Bottas	Mercedes	1h35m54.517s	2	1m15.406s	1
3	Max Verstappen	Red Bull	1h35m58.122s	2	1m16.357s	4
4	Sebastian Vettel	Ferrari	1h36m03.804s	2	1m16.272s	3
5	Charles Leclerc	Ferrari	1h36m10.019s	2	1m16.588s	5
6	Pierre Gasly	Red Bull	1h36m18.602s	2	1m16.708s	6
7	Kevin Magnussen	Haas	1h36m22.785s	2	1m16.922s	8
8	Carlos Sainz Jr	McLaren	1h36m23.499s	2	1m17.599s	12
9	Daniil Kvyat	Toro Rosso	1h36m25.084s	2	1m17.573s	9
10	Romain Grosjean	Haas	1h36m25.888s	2	1m16.911s	7
11	Alex Albon	Toro Rosso	1h36m27.201s	2	1m17.445s	11
12	Daniel Ricciardo *	Renault	1h36m29.684s	2	1m18.106s	13
13	Nico Hulkenberg !!	Renault	1h36m32.246s	1	1m18.404s	20
14	Kimi Raikkonen	Alfa Romeo	1h36m37.320s	2	1m17.788s	14
15	Sergio Perez	Racing Point	1h36m38.134s	2	1m17.886s	15
16	Antonio Giovinazzi !	Alfa Romeo	1h36m50.228s	2	1m18.664s	18
17	George Russell !	Williams	65 laps	2	1m19.072s	19
18	Robert Kubica	Williams	65 laps	2	1m20.254s	17
R	Lance Stroll	Racing Point	44 laps/accident	1	1m18.471s	16
R	Lando Norris	McLaren	44 laps/accident	1	1m17.338s	10

FASTEST LAP: HAMILTON, 1M18.492S, 132.662MPH/213.499KPH ON LAP 54 · RACE LEADER: HAMILTON 1-66
* 3-PLACE GRID PENALTY FOR COLLISION IN PREVIOUS RACE,
! 5-PLACE GRID PENALTY FOR REPLACING GEARBOX, !! MADE TO START FROM PITLANE FOR CHANGING WING IN PARC FERME

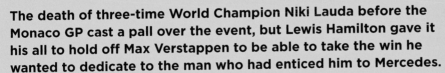

MONACO GP

The death of three-time World Champion Niki Lauda before the Monaco GP cast a pall over the event, but Lewis Hamilton gave it his all to hold off Max Verstappen to be able to take the win he wanted to dedicate to the man who had enticed him to Mercedes.

Considering that Hamilton started this his 13th F1 campaign with 73 grand prix wins to his name, it seemed an anomaly that he had but two Monaco wins – in 2008 and 2016 – in his tally. So, there was extra incentive to add to that number, and even more so as Lewis was clearly emotionally overwrought by the Austrian great's death.

As the race would prove, Hamilton would need every fraction of resilience to stay in front as Verstappen was determined to get past him.

First step to glory was to qualify on pole, which Hamilton did, by 0.086s from Valtteri Bottas. Next step was to lead into Ste. Devote on the opening lap, which he did. Verstappen led the chase

Charles Leclerc had the speed but not the precision that Ferrari needed and he failed even to reach the second qualifying session after flatspotting his tyres. This left him to fight his way forward from 15th on the grid and he didn't find the space he needed, scoring no points after colliding with Nico Hulkenberg's Renault.

For many, this changed their races, as it triggered a safety car period and the first four – Hamilton, Bottas, Verstappen and Sebastian Vettel – all dived for the pits. This meant that the Mercedes drivers arrived at the same time and caused a delay for Bottas and, with Red Bull eager to get Verstappen out ahead of him, there was a clash as the Dutchman squeezed the Finn against the pit wall. A 5s penalty for an unsafe release would have a major effect on Verstappen's race result.

That was in the future, though, and Verstappen set about catching then trying to pass Hamilton. He tried every move and lunge imaginable, but Hamilton wasn't for shifting and would just keep the Mercedes in front. With the penalty applied, Verstappen was classified fourth as Vettel took second and Bottas third.

MONTE CARLO ROUND 6

DATE: **26 MAY 2019**

Laps: **78** · Distance: **161.734 miles/260.286km** · Weather: **Overcast but warm**

Pos	Driver	Team	Result	Stops	Qualifying Time	Grid
1	**Lewis Hamilton**	Mercedes	1h43m28.437s	1	1m10.166s	1
2	**Sebastian Vettel**	Ferrari	1h43m31.039s	1	1m10.947s	4
3	**Valtteri Bottas**	Mercedes	1h43m31.599s	2	1m10.252s	2
4	**Max Verstappen ***	Red Bull	1h43m33.974s	1	1m10.641s	3
5	**Pierre Gasly !**	Red Bull	1h43m38.383s	2	1m11.041s	8
6	**Carlos Sainz Jr**	McLaren	1h44m21.891s	1	1m11.417s	9
7	**Daniil Kvyat**	Toro Rosso	1h44m23.011s	1	1m11.271s	7
8	**Alex Albon**	Toro Rosso	1h44m23.637s	1	1m11.653s	10
9	**Daniel Ricciardo**	Renault	1h44m29.331s	1	1m11.218s	6
10	**Romain Grosjean ****	Haas	1h44m29.471s	1	1m12.027s	13
11	**Lando Norris**	McLaren	1h44m35.238s	1	1m11.724s	12
12	**Kevin Magnussen !!**	Haas	77 laps	1	1m11.109s	5
13	**Sergio Perez**	Racing Point	77 laps	1	1m12.233s	16
14	**Nico Hulkenberg**	Renault	77 laps	1	1m11.670s	11
15	**George Russell**	Williams	77 laps	1	1m13.477s	19
16	**Lance Stroll !!**	Racing Point	77 laps	1	1m12.846s	17
17	**Kimi Raikkonen**	Alfa Romeo	77 lap	1	1m12.115s	14
18	**Robert Kubica**	Williams	77 laps	1	1m13.751s	20
19	**Antonio Giovanizzi !**	Alfa Romeo	76 laps	1	1m12.185s	18
R	**Charles Leclerc**	Ferrari	16 laps/crash damage	1	1m12.149s	15

FASTEST LAP: GASLY, 1M14.279S, 100.494MPH/161.730KPH ON LAP 72 · RACE LEADER: HAMILTON 1-78
* 5S PENALTY FOR UNSAFE PIT RELEASE, ** 5S PENALTY FOR CROSSING THE PIT EXIT LINE !! 5S PENALTY FOR LEAVING TRACK & GAINING ADVANTAGE ! 3-PLACE GRID PENALTY FOR IMPEDING ANOTHER DRIVER

Hamilton took the lead and was never headed as he raced to his second Monaco win.

CANADIAN GP

Sebastian Vettel's Ferrari was first to the finish, but a five-second penalty for rejoining the track in what was adjudged to be a dangerous manner after he'd gone onto the grass handed the victory to arch-rival Lewis Hamilton, to Vettel's evident displeasure.

Whether the stewards were right or wrong to censure Vettel was the only conversation after the race, with the internet awash with contrasting opinions.

Vettel had put the smile back on the faces at Ferrari by qualifying on pole for the first time since the 2018 German GP and he converted that into the lead ahead of Hamilton. So far so good, and there he stayed until the pitstops.

Better still, Hamilton dropped to almost 5s behind by the time he re-emerged. In the second part of the race, though, Hamilton closed in on the Ferrari. Just as he got to within DRS-opening range, Vettel picked up the pace. Then Hamilton came back and, on lap 48 of 70, Vettel got loose in Turn 3, leaving the Ferrari to scoot across the grass before rejoining the track out of Turn 4. Hamilton had to brake to avoid being squeezed into the outside wall. It was close, but there was no contact, and Vettel was able to race on to the finish. Sadly for him, he was told on lap 57 that he'd been given a 5s penalty for "unsafe re-entry to the track and forcing another driver off track." He was livid. His only hope of victory came when team-mate Charles Leclerc caught Hamilton, but he couldn't exert enough pressure to delay him and Hamilton's 3.658s deficit was enough for him to take victory.

The memory that will endure wasn't so much the manoeuvre, but Vettel's action when he reached parc ferme and swapped around the first and second place finishing markers in a visual display of his fury. To many, F1 looked foolish at a time that they thought it should be doing everything in its power to encourage the gladiatorial racing that has always been a feature of its greatest years. To his credit, uncomfortable about the punishment meted out, Hamilton pulled Vettel up to join him on the top step of the podium.

MONTREAL ROUND 7

DATE: 9 JUNE 2019

Laps: 70 · Distance: **189.686 miles/305.270km** · Weather: **Hot & sunny**

Pos	Driver	Team	Result	Stops	Qualifying Time	Grid
1	**Lewis Hamilton**	Mercedes	1h29m07.084s	1	1m10.446s	2
2	**Sebastian Vettel** *	Ferrari	1h29m10.742s	1	1m10.240s	1
3	**Charles Leclerc**	Ferrari	1h29m11.780s	1	1m10.920s	3
4	**Valtteri Bottas**	Mercedes	1h29m58.127s	2	1m11.101s	6
5	**Max Verstappen**	Red Bull	1h30m04.739s	1	1m11.800s	9
6	**Daniel Ricciardo**	Renault	69 laps	1	1m11.071s	4
7	**Nico Hulkenberg**	Renault	69 laps	1	1m11.324s	7
8	**Pierre Gasly**	Red Bull	69 laps	1	1m11.079s	5
9	**Lance Stroll**	Racing Point	69 laps	1	1m12.266s	17
10	**Daniil Kvyat**	Toro Rosso	69 laps	1	1m11.921s	10
11	**Carlos Sainz Jr** !	McLaren	69 laps	1	1m13.981s	11
12	**Sergio Perez**	Racing Point	69 laps	1	1m12.197s	15
13	**Antonio Giovinazzi**	Alfa Romeo	69 laps	1	1m12.136s	12
14	**Romain Grosjean**	Haas	69 laps	1	no time	14
15	**Kimi Raikkonen**	Alfa Romeo	69 laps	2	1m12.230s	16
16	**George Russell**	Williams	68 laps	1	1m13.617s	18
17	**Kevin Magnussen** !!	Haas	68 laps	1	no time	20
18	**Robert Kubica**	Williams	67 laps	2	1m14.393s	19
R	**Alex Albon**	Toro Rosso	59 laps/ saving engine life	1	1m12.193s	13
R	**Lando Norris**	McLaren	8 laps/brakes	0	1m11.863s	8

FASTEST LAP: BOTTAS, 1M13.078S, 133.491MPH/214.833KPH ON LAP 69 · RACE LEADERS: VETTEL 1-25 & 33-70, HAMILTON 26-27, LECLERC 28-32 * 5S PENALTY FOR REJOINING TRACK UNSAFELY & FORCING ANOTHER CAR OFF TRACK, ! 3-PLACE GRID PENALTY FOR IMPEDING ANOTHER DRIVER, !! MADE TO START FROM PITS FOR CHANGING SURVIVAL CELL

It would have been a first Ferrari win of 2019, but Sebastian Vettel was hit with a penalty.

FRENCH GP

Lewis Hamilton made it four wins in a row to stamp his authority on the 2019 Drivers World Championship. Mercedes, meanwhile, continued its dominance of the Constructors Cup standings as Valtteri Bottas followed him home at a distance, with Ferrari's Charles Leclerc the best of the rest.

It was always likely that Hamilton was going to be at the front of the field again when the F1 circus moved to the Paul Ricard circuit in France. And so it proved as he put his Mercedes on pole position by almost 0.3s over Bottas.

The race proved to be another example of Hamilton's competitive edge as he got away well and he and Bottas edged clear of the rest. Max Verstappen tried to pass Leclerc for third, but was resisted.

Thereafter, Hamilton was wholly in control, his main problem being that one of the stays for his seat broke. Bottas wasn't able to profit and, indeed, only just held off Leclerc over the closing laps.

Having challenged Leclerc in the early laps of the race, Max Verstappen fell back and admitted that he had pushed too hard early on, thus taking the edge of his tyres. That said, the Dutchman was still able to finish ahead of Sebastian Vettel, with Ferrari's nominal number one driver able to progress only from seventh on the grid to fifth.

Behind him, Carlos Sainz Jr was next to the finish as McLaren continued its mid-season advance up through the field. Rookie team-mate Lando Norris looked set to finish seventh behind him, but a hydraulic problem began to deny him use of his DRS and then made his steering extra heavy, and so he fell back to ninth, allowing the Renaults of Daniel Ricciardo and Nico Hulkenberg plus Alfa Romeo's Kimi Raikkonen to get past him on the final lap. However, the Australian was later hit with two 5s penalties, and those dropped him to a final classification of 11th.

Thus, the final point went to the second Red Bull Racing driver, Pierre Gasly, but the Frenchman was far from happy after being comprehensively outdriven by his team-mate Verstappen yet again.

Hamilton and Leclerc clcebrate on the podium after Mercedes' ace made it four in a row.

101

PAUL RICARD ROUND 8

DATE: **23 JUNE 2019**

Laps: **53** • Distance: **192.432 miles/309.690km** • Weather: **Hot & sunny**

Pos	Driver	Team	Result	Stops	Qualifying Time	Grid
1	**Lewis Hamilton**	Mercedes	1h24m31.198s	1	1m28.319s	1
2	**Valtteri Bottas**	Mercedes	1h24m49.254s	1	1m28.605s	2
3	**Charles Leclerc**	Ferrari	1h24m50.183s	1	1m28.965s	3
4	**Max Verstappen**	Red Bull	1h25m06.103s	1	1m29.409s	4
5	**Sebastian Vettel**	Ferrari	1h25m33.994s	2	1m29.799s	7
6	**Carlos Sainz Jr**	McLaren	1h26m06.660s	1	1m29.522s	6
7	**Kimi Raikkonen**	Alfa Romeo	52 laps	1	1m30.533s	12
8	**Nico Hulkenberg**	Renault	52 laps	1	1m30.544s	13
9	**Lando Norris**	McLaren	52 laps	1	1m29.418s	5
10	**Pierre Gasly**	Red Bull	52 laps	1	1m30.184s	9
11	**Daniel Ricciardo ***	Renault	52 laps	1	1m29.918s	8
12	**Sergio Perez**	Racing Point	52 laps	1	1m30.738s	14
13	**Lance Stroll**	Racing Point	52 laps	1	1m31.726s	17
14	**Daniil Kvyat !**	Toro Rosso	52 laps	1	1m31.564s	19
15	**Alex Albon**	Toro Rosso	52 laps	1	1m30.461s	11
16	**Antonio Giovinazzi**	Toro Rosso	52 laps	2	1m33.420s	10
17	**Kevin Magnussen**	Haas	52 laps	1	1m31.440s	15
18	**Robert Kubica**	Williams	51 laps	1	1m33.205s	18
19	**George Russell !**	Williams	51 laps	1	1m32.789s	20
R	**Romain Grosjean**	Haas	44 laps/withdrew	1	1m31.626s	16

FASTEST LAP: VETTEL, 1M32.740S, 140.911MPH/226.775KPH ON LAP 53 · RACE LEADER: HAMILTON 1-53
* TWO 5S PENALTIES FOR REJOINING TRACK UNSAFELY & LEAVING TRACK TO GAIN AN ADVANTAGE, ! MADE TO START FROM BACK OF GRID FOR USING EXTRA POWER UNIT ELEMENTS

AUSTRIAN GP

The deliberation lasted longer than the race itself but, eventually, Red Bull Racing's Max Verstappen was told that he could keep his hard-won win after a stirring tussle with Charles Leclerc. Engine supplier Honda felt vindicated by its first win since the 2006 Hungarian GP.

Lewis Hamilton turned up in Austria looking to extend his winning streak to five races, yet this wasn't ever really on the cards. Ferrari's Leclerc took pole for the second time, while Hamilton lapped 0.259s slower and was hit with a three-place grid penalty for impeding Kimi Raikkonen. He did gain one of those places back when Kevin Magnussen was put back five positions, to 10th, because his Haas had been fitted with a replacement gearbox.

At the start, Leclerc kept his Ferrari at the head of the field while Verstappen slipped back to seventh. The Monegasque, who had deserved to win in Bahrain, looked to be in control, with even the Mercedes duo unable to topple him, Hamilton's pace affected when he damaged his front wing. Later, both Mercedes would be afflicted by insufficient engine cooling, forcing the drivers to turn them down a notch.

Although Verstappen did some overtaking, he didn't look a threat until he stayed out 10 laps longer than his leading rivals before making a stop for fresh rubber. As Hamilton lost time with a nose replacement, Verstappen was able to come back out in fourth. Then he reeled in Sebastian Vettel and passed him on lap 50 of 71. The German was then brought in for a third set of tyres in a move that removed him from the equation.

Six laps later, Verstappen passed Bottas for second at Remus and then set off after Leclerc. The deficit was 5s with 15 laps to go and Honda in particular urged the Dutchman on. Derided when supplying McLaren with engines, their motor was now in with a shot at winning. Verstappen made his move on lap 68, but Leclerc fought back. Next lap, Verstappen went through, but he had clattered into the Ferrari and this move was investigated for hours after the race before he was allowed to keep his win.

Red Bull broke its 2019 duck when Verstappen won for the Austrian sponsor in Austria.

RED BULL RING ROUND 9   DATE: **30 JUNE 2019**

Laps: **71** • Distance: **190.420 miles/306.452km** • Weather: **Very hot & sunny**

Pos	Driver	Team	Result	Stops	Qualifying Time	Grid
1	**Max Verstappen**	Red Bull	1h22m01.822s	1	1m03.439s	2
2	**Charles Leclerc**	Ferrari	1h22m04.546s	1	1m03.003s	1
3	**Valtteri Bottas**	Mercedes	1h22m20.782s	1	1m03.537s	3
4	**Sebastian Vettel**	Ferrari	1h22m21.432s	2	no time	9
5	**Lewis Hamilton ***	Mercedes	1h22m24.627s	1	1m03.262s	4
6	**Lando Norris**	McLaren	70 laps	1	1m04.099s	5
7	**Pierre Gasly**	Red Bull	70 laps	1	1m04.199s	8
8	**Carlos Sainz Jr !!**	McLaren	70 laps	1	1m13.601s	19
9	**Kimi Raikkonen**	Alfa Romeo	70 laps	1	1m04.166s	6
10	**Antonio Giovanizzi**	Alfa Romeo	70 laps	1	1m04.179s	7
11	**Sergio Perez**	Racing Point	70 laps	1	1m04.789s	13
12	**Daniel Ricciardo**	Renault	70 laps	1	1m04.790s	12
13	**Nico Hulkenberg !**	Renault	70 laps	1	1m04.516s	15
14	**Lance Stroll**	Racing Point	70 laps	1	1m04.832s	14
15	**Alex Albon !!**	Toro Rosso	70 laps	1	1m04.665s	18
16	**Romain Grosjean**	Haas	70 laps	1	1m04.490s	11
17	**Daniil Kvyat**	Toro Rosso	70 laps	1	1m05.324s	16
18	**George Russell *!!**	Williams	69 laps	1	1m05.904s	20
19	**Kevin Magnussen !**	Haas	69 laps	3	1m04.072s	10
20	**Robert Kubica**	Williams	68 laps	1	1m06.206s	17

FASTEST LAP: VERSTAPPEN, 1M07.475S, 143.150MPH/230.378KPH ON LAP 60 • RACE LEADERS: LECLERC 1-22 & 32-68, HAMILTON 23-30, VERSTAPPEN 31 & 69-71
* 3-PLACE GRID PENALTY FOR IMPEDING ANOTHER DRIVER, ! 5-PLACE GRID PENALTY FOR CHANGING ENGINE, !! REQUIRED TO START FROM BACK OF GRID FOR USING ADDITIONAL POWER UNIT

BRITISH GP

This was a fabulous race, and the home fans got the Lewis Hamilton victory that they had hoped for. They saw some brilliant overtaking moves throughout the top half of the field as the drivers put on a great display, even if not all the moves came off.

British F1 fans were already thrilled by the news of the British GP's five-year contract extension, but then had even more reason to be delighted as Silverstone delivered one of the most dramatic grands prix for years.

After failing to be fastest in any of the three practice sessions, qualifying didn't quite go to plan for Hamilton either, as he was edged out of pole by team-mate Valtteri Bottas by 0.006s. Only Ferrari's Charles Leclerc had a realistic shot at pole in qualifying but, come the race, Hamilton would reach the top.

Bottas resisted his challenge through the first corner and all eyes were drawn to the internecine battling between the Haas drivers as they got together, damaging both.

Hamilton was in no mood to run second and got his nose in front at Luffield on lap 3, but Bottas fought back wonderfully and was ahead again before Copse. There he would stay until diving into the pits for a new set of medium compound tyres on lap 16. Hamilton stayed out and immediately upped his pace as he elected to try to make a one-stop strategy work.

Things changed when the safety car was deployed after Antonio Giovinazzi spun his Alfa Romeo at Club and Hamilton chose that moment to pit. The Mercedes were one-two after the safety car withdrew and Hamilton immediately pulled away, which was dispiriting for Bottas as he still had to make a second stop. The Brit finished almost 25 seconds clear, and the day was made even better as Hamilton's fifth British GP win in six years was his sixth overall, moving him one victory clear of Jim Clark and Alain Prost with most British GP wins.

Behind them, though, there was a great scrap between Leclerc and Max

SILVERSTONE ROUND 10

DATE: 14 JULY 2019

Laps: 52 · Distance: 190/262 miles/306.198km · Weather: **Warm & cloudy**

Pos	Driver	Team	Result	Stops	Qualifying Time	Grid
1	**Lewis Hamilton**	Mercedes	1h21m08.452s	1	1m25.099s	2
2	**Valtteri Bottas**	Mercedes	1h21m33.380s	2	1m25.093s	1
3	**Charles Leclerc**	Ferrari	1h21m38.569s	2	1m25.172s	3
4	**Pierre Gasly**	Red Bull	1h21m43.144s	1	1m25.590s	5
5	**Max Verstappen**	Red Bull	1h21m47.910s	2	1m25.276s	4
6	**Carlos Sainz Jr**	McLaren	1h22m02.091s	1	1m26.578s	13
7	**Daniel Ricciardo**	Renault	1h22m02.853s	2	1m26.182s	7
8	**Kimi Raikkonen**	Alfa Romeo	1h22m13.992s	1	1m26.546s	12
9	**Daniil Kvyat**	Toro Rosso	1h22m15.172s	2	1m26.721s	17
10	**Nico Hulkenberg**	Renault	1h22m21.185s	1	1m26.386s	10
11	**Lando Norris**	McLaren	1h22m22.733s	2	1m26.224s	8
12	**Alex Albon**	Toro Rosso	1h22m24.069s	1	1m26.345s	9
13	**Lance Stroll**	Racing Point	1h22m29.538s	2	1m26.762s	18
14	**George Russell**	Williams	51 laps	1	1m27.789s	19
15	**Robert Kubica**	Williams	51 laps	1	1m28.257s	20
16	**Sebastian Vettel ***	Ferrari	51 laps	2	1m25.787s	6
17	**Sergio Perez**	Racing Point	51 laps	3	1m26.928s	15
R	**Antonio Giovinazzi**	Alfa Romeo	18 laps/spun off	0	1m26.519s	11
R	**Romain Grosjean**	Haas	9 laps/crash damage	1	1m26.757s	14
R	**Kevin Magnussen**	Haas	6 laps/crash damage	1	1m26.662s	16

FASTEST LAP: HAMILTON, 1M27.369S, 150.828MPH/242.735KPH ON LAP 52 · RACE LEADERS: BOTTAS 1-16, HAMILTON 17-52
* 10S PENALTY FOR CAUSING A COLLISION

Hamilton is held aloft by the fans after he returned to winning ways in Silverstone.

Verstappen over fourth place, two young guns taking no prisoners. Sebastian Vettel ran third, but Verstappen was flying and passed him around the outside at Stowe to get the crowd onto its feet. Vettel, however, tried to regain the place going into Vale, but instead clattered into the

Red Bull, earning himself a 10s penalty and taking him out of the points places.

Pierre Gasly had his best race for Red Bull, with fourth place taking the pressure off him. His team-mate Verstappen, having had to stop for repairs after being hit by Vettel, did well to recover to finish fifth.

GERMAN GP

Max Verstappen rose to the top for Red Bull Racing in a rare event in the modern World Championship: a race of bedlam. Mercedes' drivers both slid off at the same place and there were four safety car periods as Sebastian Vettel rose from last on the grid to second at the chequered flag.

Five pitstops for any driver would normally spell disaster, yet such was the turmoil, that this was the number of pit visits that led to success for Max Verstappen. It was wet, it was wild, and it was wonderful. Following on from an exciting British GP, it really put F1 back on a good keel as a sporting spectacle after too many races whose outcomes had been dictated by mistakes rather than racing.

Ferrari started the race on the back foot, as Charles Leclerc failed to set a time in Q3 when his engine wouldn't fire, so he qualified 10th. This, however, was 10 places ahead of team-mate Sebastian Vettel, who had to start last after a turbo failure meant he didn't set a time in Q1.

In a race that started on a wet track, Sergio Perez triggered the first safety car spell by spinning off on lap 2. Lewis Hamilton, Valtteri Bottas and Charles Leclerc would later all spin at Turn 17 and the safety car deployments allowed teams to juggle their tactics and Red Bull got it mostly right, as Verstappen would go on to win by 7s from a driver who expected to come away with nothing: Vettel. After his Silverstone disaster, second place was vindication and all the sweeter as it came on home ground.

The biggest smile on the podium belonged to Daniil Kvyat who didn't put a wheel wrong for Toro Rosso and got past Racing Point's Lance Stroll for third. He was helped by Nico Hulkenberg throwing away a potential third place for Renault by joining the ranks of drivers sliding off at Turn 17.

After his off and a slow pitstop, Hamilton chased the Haas drivers across the line in 11th. Later, the Alfa Romeos were hit with 30s penalties for clutch irregularities, and so Hamilton scored after all. The bigger news, though, was that Williams took the first point of its campaign, as Robert Kubica was elevated to 10th.

HOCKENHEIM ROUND 11

Laps: 54 · Distance: 181.897 miles/292.736km · Weather: Hot & wet

DATE: 28 JULY 2019

Pos	Driver	Team	Result	Stops	Qualifying Time	Grid
1	Max Verstappen	Red Bull	1h44m31.275s	5	1m12.113s	2
2	Sebastian Vettel !	Ferrari	1h44m38.608s	5	no time	20
3	Daniil Kvyat	Toro Rosso	1h44m39.580s	4	1m13.135s	14
4	Lance Stroll	Racing Point	1h44m40.241s	5	1m13.450s	15
5	Carlos Sainz Jr	McLaren	1h44m40.858s	3	1m12.897s	7
6	Alex Albon	Toro Rosso	1h44m41.327s	4	1m13.461s	16
7	Romain Grosjean	Haas	1h44m48.113s	5	1m12.851s	6
8	Kevin Magnussen	Haas	1h44m50.040s	6	1m12.789s	12
9	Lewis Hamilton	Mercedes	1h44m50.942s	7	1m11.767s	1
10	Robert Kubica	Williams	1h44m56.262s	5	1m14.839s	18
11	George Russell	Williams	1h44m57.679s	5	1m14.721s	18
12	Kimi Raikkonen *	Alfa Romeo	1h45m13.489s	4	1m12.538s	5
13	Antonio Giovinazzi *	Alfa Romeo	1h45m15.124s	4	1m12.786s	11
14	Pierre Gasly	Red Bull	61 laps/collision	4	1m12.522s	4
R	Valtteri Bottas	Mercedes	56 laps/spun off	3	1m12.129s	3
R	Nico Hulkenberg	Renault	39 laps/spun off	3	1m13.126s	9
R	Charles Leclerc	Ferrari	27 laps/spun off	3	no time	10
R	Lando Norris !!	McLaren	25 laps/power unit	2	1m13.333s	19
R	Daniel Ricciardo	Renault	13 laps/exhaust	1	1m12.799s	13
R	Sergio Perez	Racing Point	1 lap/spun off	0	1m13.065s	8

FASTEST LAP: VERSTAPPEN, 1M16.645S, 133.495MPH/214.839KPH ON LAP 61 · LAP LEADERS: HAMILTON 1-29 & 47, VERSTAPPEN 30-46 & 48-64.
* 30S PENALTY FOR CLUTCH IRREGULARITIES, ! 5-PLACE GRID PENALTY FOR USING ADDITIONAL POWER UNIT, !! MADE TO START FROM BACK OF GRID FOR USING ADDITIONAL POWER UNIT.

Max Verstappen had every reason to smile, as he won and his rivals fell off in a wild race.

HUNGARIAN GP

The European summer was a purple patch for F1 last year and the fabulous scrap between Max Verstappen and Lewis Hamilton in Hungary ran all the way to the chequered flag. Hamilton pulled off a great pass to win, with the rest of the field trailing in their wake.

Max Verstappen's orange-shirted fans, descended on the Hungaroring, boosted with extra enthusiasm after his victory in Germany. When he pipped Valtteri Bottas to pole, their joy was boosted further, and why not? After all, the Hungaroring is a circuit that offers few chances for overtaking.

So, when the Red Bull emerged from Turn 1 in the lead on the opening lap, they roared their approval, especially as Verstappen had resisted a challenge from both Mercedes into that downhill first righthander. Bottas locked up at Turn 3, with Hamilton on the outside, but Hamilton hung on around the outside to claim second as Bottas slipped to fourth, losing a place to Charles Leclerc. With his drive in the balance for 2020, Bottas cursed his luck as his nose wing was damaged and he had to pit to replace it a few laps later.

Verstappen eased clear as he and Hamilton dropped all their rivals, including the Ferraris, which were not able to keep up. Hamilton shadowed Verstappen's moves, having more tyre life when he emerged on his second set of rubber and so closed in. This was when the game of chess they were playing turned into a scrap, as Hamilton went to the outside at Turn 4 after they lapped Daniel Ricciardo on lap 39. He got in front, but ran wide and was back to a more distant second when he rejoined.

A few laps later, Hamilton was closing in again, but then he pitted to change onto mediums. He knew that this would make him faster than Verstappen, but it was a gamble as he had 20 laps to claw back 20s. Progress was slow for the first 10 laps, but then it tumbled as Verstappen had nothing left and, entering lap 67, he could resist no more. Even with a late stop for fresh tyres, Verstappen was still able to finish clear of the Ferraris.

Carlos Sainz Jr scored a second consecutive fifth-place finish as he shone for McLaren.

HUNGARORING ROUND 12 DATE: **4 AUGUST 2019**

Laps: **70** • Distance: **190.531 miles/306.630** • Weather: **Hot & bright**

Pos	Driver	Team	Result	Stops	Qualifying Time	Grid
1	**Lewis Hamilton**	Mercedes	1h35m03.796s	2	1m14.769s	3
2	**Max Verstappen**	Red Bull	1h35m21.592s	2	1m14.572s	1
3	**Sebastian Vettel**	Ferrari	1h36m05.229s	1	1m15.071s	5
4	**Charles Leclerc**	Ferrari	1h36m09.046s	1	1m15.043s	4
5	**Carlos Sainz Jr**	McLaren	69 laps	1	1m15.852s	8
6	**Pierre Gasly**	Red Bull	69 laps	1	1m15.450s	6
7	**Kimi Raikkonen**	Alfa Romeo	69 laps	1	1m16.041s	10
8	**Valtteri Bottas**	Mercedes	69 laps	2	1m14.590s	2
9	**Lando Norris**	McLaren	69 laps	1	1m15.800s	7
10	**Alex Albon**	Toro Rosso	69 laps	1	1m16.687s	12
11	**Sergio Perez**	Racing Point	69 laps	1	1m17.109s	16
12	**Nico Hulkenberg**	Renault	69 laps	1	1m16.565s	11
13	**Kevin Magnussen**	Haas	69 laps	1	1m17.081s	14
14	**Daniel Ricciardo !**	Renault	69 laps	1	1m17.257s	20
15	**Daniil Kvyat**	Toro Rosso	68 laps	1	1m16.692s	13
16	**George Russell**	Williams	68 laps	1	1m17.031s	15
17	**Lance Stroll**	Racing Point	68 laps	2	1m17.542s	18
18	**Antonio Giovinazzi ***	Alfa Romeo	68 laps	1	1m16.804s	17
19	**Robert Kubica**	Williams	67 laps	1	1m18.324s	19
R	**Romain Grosjean**	Haas	49 laps/water leak	1	1m16.013s	9

FASTEST LAP: VERSTAPPEN, 1M17.103S, 127.102MPH/204.552KPH ON LAP 69 • RACE LEADERS: VERSTAPPEN 1-24 & 32-66, HAMILTON 25-31 & 67-70
* 3-PLACE GRID PENALTY FOR IMPEDING ANOTHER DRIVER, ! MADE TO START FROM BACK OF GRID FOR USING ADDITIONAL POWER UNIT ELEMENTS

BELGIAN GP

Emotions were stretched following Formula 2 driver Anthoine Hubert's fatal accident on the Saturday, so it was an emotional moment when his childhood friend and rival Charles Leclerc beat Lewis Hamilton to take his breakthrough F1 win for Ferrari and dedicated it to Anthoine.

Fortunately, modern day racing drivers are not accustomed to any of their number dying. So, when Hubert was killed in the supporting F2 race on Saturday, it put them out of kilter, made it harder for them to focus. For the French contingent who had grown up racing against Anthoine – Leclerc and especially former housemate Pierre Gasly – it was harder still. Yet, Leclerc proved his mettle by stepping up the following day to score his first F1 win.

The race was all about Leclerc resisting everything that Hamilton could throw at him. The Ferrari driver started from pole and was protected by team-mate Sebastian Vettel running second. His main defence came after the leading drivers had made their pitstops and the early pitting Vettel first took the lead and then slotted into second behind Leclerc. As Vettel had pitted on lap 15 and Leclerc and the Mercedes drivers between five and seven laps later, it was likely that Vettel would have to make a second stop, while they wouldn't.

Vettel duly kept Hamilton at bay and so earned Leclerc a cushion. Hamilton heaped on the pressure and finally got past into second on lap 32, leaving him 12 laps to try to reduce the 7s gap to Leclerc. The Mercedes driver got to within 1.1s with just three laps to go, but a cluster of traffic dented Hamilton's charge and Leclerc was able to keep just enough in hand to take a famous win.

Alex Albon had been promoted to Red Bull Racing after a driver swap with Gasly, and starred by finishing fifth – after Lando Norris's McLaren had failed with a lap to go – despite having to start at the back of the grid as additional power unit elements had been used. It gave Red Bull Racing something to smile about in a race in which Max Verstappen was out on lap 1 after a clash at La Source with Kimi Raikkonen.

Charles Leclerc controlled the race with a little help from team-mate Sebastian Vettel.

SPA-FRANCORCHAMPS ROUND 13 DATE: **1 SEPT 2019**

Laps: **44** • Distance: **191.414 miles/308.052km** • Weather: **Warm & cloudy**

Pos	Driver	Team	Result	Stops	Qualifying Time	Grid
1	**Charles Leclerc**	Ferrari	1h23m45.710s	1	1m42.519s	1
2	**Lewis Hamilton**	Mercedes	1h23m46.691s	1	1m43.282s	3
3	**Valtteri Bottas**	Mercedes	1h23m58.295s	1	1m43.415s	4
4	**Sebastian Vettel**	Ferrari	1h24m12.132s	2	1m43.267s	2
5	**Alex Albon !**	Red Bull	1h25m07.035s	1	1m45.799s	17
6	**Sergio Perez**	Racing Point	1h25m10.158s	1	1m44.706s	7
7	**Daniil Kvyat *!**	Toro Rosso	1h25m15.367s	1	1m46.518s	19
8	**Nico Hulkenberg ***	Renault	1h25m32.349s	2	1m44.542s	12
9	**Pierre Gasly**	Toro Rosso	1h25m34.878s	1	1m46.435s	13
10	**Lance Stroll !**	Racing Point	1h25m35.548s	2	1m45.047s	16
11	**Lando Norris**	McLaren	43 laps/power unit	1	1m44.847s	11
12	**Kevin Magnussen**	Haas	43 laps	1	1m45.086s	8
13	**Romain Grosjean**	Haas	43 laps	1	1m44.797s	9
14	**Daniel Ricciardo ***	Renault	43 laps	1	1m44.257s	10
15	**George Russell**	Williams	43 laps	1	1m47.548s	14
16	**Kimi Raikkonen**	Alfa Romeo	43 laps	3	1m44.557s	6
17	**Robert Kubica *!!**	Williams	43 laps	1	no time	20
18	**Antonio Giovinazzi *^**	Alfa Romeo	42 laps/spun off	1	no time	18
R	**Carlos Sainz Jr *+**	McLaren	1 lap/power unit	1	1m46.507s	15
R	**Max Verstappen**	Red Bull	0 laps/collision	0	1m43.690s	5

FASTEST LAP: VETTEL, 1M46.409S, 147.238MPH/236.957KPH ON LAP 36 RACE LEADERS: LECLERC 1-20 & 27-44, HAMILTON 21-22, VETTEL 23-26 * 5-PLACE GRID PENALTY FOR USING ADDITIONAL POWER UNIT, + 10-PLACE GRID PENALTY FOR USING ADDITIONAL POWER UNIT ELEMENTS, ! MADE TO START FROM BACK OF GRID FOR USING ADDITIONAL POWER UNIT ELEMENTS, ^ MADE TO START FROM PIT LANE FOR REPLACING GEARBOX, !! MADE TO START FROM PIT LANE FOR CAR BEING MODIFIED UNDER PARC FERME CONDITIONS

ITALIAN GP

The final qualifying session was a shambles, but Charles Leclerc delighted Ferrari's home fans by claiming pole position and then sent them into paroxysms of delight the following day by winning as he pleased. It was Ferrari's first home win since 2010.

Thank goodness the 2019 Italian GP will be remembered for Ferrari's celebrations, as otherwise it might have been recalled for a peculiar end to qualifying. The sight of nine of the 10 cars in the final session hanging back and jockeying for track position in order to get a tow was ridiculous, but it became farcical when they hung back so much that only one, Carlos Sainz Jr, was able to start his final run before the chequered flag fell. Ferrari's new hero, Leclerc, ended up with pole thanks to a time he'd set earlier in the session.

Leclerc led away, tailed by Hamilton and Bottas. Vettel spun out of fifth place on lap 6, and he then drove straight into the path of Lance Stroll's Racing Point as he rejoined, tipping it into a spin. With a 10s stop-and-go penalty, he was never going to treat the *Tifosi* to points for Ferrari. Additionally, he was rightly given three superlicence penalty points.

Leclerc became increasingly robust in the defence of his lead on the approach to the second chicane on lap 23 and then again at the same point on lap 36, this after making a mistake at the first chicane. Both times he was able to repel the Mercedes driver, but his aggression raised eyebrows.

Mercedes decided that its best hope of getting ahead of Leclerc was to leave Bottas out for a longer first stint. This meant he could attack on fresher tyres near the end when he had already advanced to second after Hamilton slipped off at the first chicane with 12 laps to go, but the Finn's late charge wasn't quite enough.

Renault came away smiling, as Ricciardo and Hulkenberg finished fourth and fifth to move them ahead of Toro Rosso into fifth in the constructors' championship. Sainz Jr might have been able to follow them across the line, but when he pitted from sixth, his crew failed to attach his right front wheel properly.

MONZA ROUND 14

DATE: 8 SEPTEMBER 2019

Laps: 53 • Distance: 190.587miles/306.720km • Weather: Warm & sunny

Pos	Driver	Team	Result	Stops	Qualifying Time	Grid
1	**Charles Leclerc**	Ferrari	1h15m26.665s	1	1m19.307s	1
2	**Valtteri Bottas**	Mercedes	1h15m27.400s	1	1m19.354s	3
3	**Lewis Hamilton**	Mercedes	1h16m01.864s	2	1m19.346s	2
4	**Daniel Ricciardo**	Renault	1h16m12.180s	1	1m19.839s	5
5	**Nico Hulkenberg**	Renault	1h16m24.830s	1	1m20.049s	6
6	**Alex Albon**	Red Bull	1h16m25.980s	1	no time	8
7	**Sergio Perez !**	Racing Point	1h16m40.467s	1	1m21.291s	14
8	**Max Verstappen !**	Red Bull	1h16m41.157s	2	no time	20
9	**Antonio Giovinazzi**	Alfa Romeo	52 laps	1	1m21.068s	18
10	**Lando Norris *!**	McLaren	52 laps	1	1m21.125s	19
11	**Pierre Gasly !**	Toro Rosso	52 laps	1	no time	9
12	**Lance Stroll**	Racing Point	52 laps	2	1m19.457s	4
13	**Sebastian Vettel**	Ferrari	52 laps	3	1m21.800s	16
14	**George Russell**	Williams	52 laps	1	no time	15
15	**Kimi Raikkonen !!**	Alfa Romeo	52 laps	2	1m20.784s	13
16	**Romain Grosjean**	Haas	52 laps	2	1m22.356s	17
17	**Robert Kubica**	Williams	51 laps	2	1m20.615s	11
R	**Kevin Magnussen**	Haas	43 laps/hydraulics	2	1m20.630s	12
R	**Daniel Kvyat**	Toro Rosso	29 laps/oil leak	1	1m20.455s	7
R	**Carlos Sainz Jr**	McLaren	27 laps/wheel	1		

FASTEST LAP: HAMILTON, 1M21.779S, 158.458MPH/255.014KPH ON LAP 51 RACE LEADERS: LECLERC 1-19 & 28-53, BOTTAS 20-27 * 5-PLACE GRID PENALTY FOR USING EXTRA POWER UNIT ELEMENTS, ! MADE TO START FROM BACK OF GRID FOR USING EXTRA POWER UNIT ELEMENTS !! MADE TO START FROM PITLANE FOR CAR BEING MODIFIED UNDER PARC FERME CONDITIONS

A podium shot to gladden the hearts of Ferrari fans all around the world as Leclerc celebrates.

SINGAPORE GP

Ferrari's Sebastian Vettel had been coming under pressure after being outperformed by young team-mate Charles Leclerc, but he delivered in Singapore, heading home a one-two on a circuit that hadn't been expected to suit the characteristics of the Ferrari SF90.

Ferrari travelled to Singapore buoyed by its two wins on the trot, but the team didn't hold out high hopes that it would be able to outpace the Mercedes, feeling that the strengths of their SF90s were less suited to the Yas Marina Circuit.

Yet, they surprised themselves as well as others when not only did Leclerc produce a stunning lap to grab pole – his third in a row – but Vettel was able to lap third fastest, a fraction down on Lewis Hamilton's Mercedes.

Leclerc controlled proceedings after making a tidy start to the race to the extent he was able to back the field up as he ran as slowly as he dared to preserve the soft compound tyres on which he had started. Hamilton was close behind, but couldn't find a way past.

Then Ferrari elected to bring Vettel in early for his tyre change from third. That was on lap 19, and Mercedes responded by bringing Bottas in too. A lap later, Leclerc pitted and was hardly delighted to find that Vettel had been more efficient and was now ahead of him.

Hamilton decided to try a different tactic and didn't pit until a further six laps later, when his tyres' performance "went off a cliff". It didn't work as he re-emerged eighth. Although able to pass Antonio Giovinazzi and Daniel Ricciardo – who'd started from the back of the grid – and having Lance Stroll and Pierre Gasly pit from in front of him, he could climb no higher than fourth.

Vettel got to enjoy being in the lead and he was then given an easier run thanks to no fewer than three safety car interventions. He duly dispatched the 10-lap sprint to the finish to score his first win since the 2018 Belgian GP and so scotch paddock gossip that he had lost his edge after a series of mistakes through 2019.

MARINA BAY ROUND 15

DATE: 22 SEPTEMBER 2019

Laps: **61** • Distance: **191.821 miles/308.706km** • Weather: **Hot & humid**

Pos	Driver	Team	Result	Stops	Qualifying Time	Grid
1	Sebastian Vettel	Ferrari	1h58m33.667s	1	1m36.437s	3
2	Charles Leclerc	Ferrari	1h58m36.308s	1	1m36.217s	1
3	Max Verstappen	Red Bull	1h58m37.488s	1	1m36.813s	4
4	Lewis Hamilton	Mercedes	1h58m38.275s	1	1m36.408s	2
5	Valtteri Bottas	Mercedes	1h58m39.786s	1	1m37.146s	5
6	Alex Albon	Red Bull	1h58m45.330s	1	1m37.411s	6
7	Lando Norris	McLaren	1h58m48.436s	1	1m38.329s	9
8	Pierre Gasly	Toro Rosso	1h58m49.214s	1	1m38.699s	11
9	Nico Hulkenberg	Renault	1h58m50.385s	2	1m38.264s	8
10	Antonio Giovinazzi *	Alfa Romeo	1h59m01.122s	2	1m38.697s	10
11	Romain Grosjean	Haas	1h59m09.103s	2	1m40.277s	17
12	Carlos Sainz Jr	McLaren	1h59m09.641s	2	1m37.818s	7
13	Lance Stroll	Racing Point	1h59m10.086s	3	1m39.979s	16
14	Daniel Ricciardo !!	Renault	1h59m11.327s	1	no time	20
15	Daniil Kvyat	Toro Rosso	1h59m11.845s	2	1m39.957s	14
16	Robert Kubica	Williams	1h59m20.691s	2	1m41.186s	19
17	Kevin Magnussen	Haas	2h00m00.189s	2	1m39.650s	13
R	Kimi Raikkonen	Alfa Romeo	49 laps/collision	1	1m38.858s	12
R	Sergio Perez !	Racing Point	42 laps/oil leak	1	1m38.620s	15
R	George Russell	Williams	34 laps/collision	1	1m40.867s	18

FASTEST LAP: MAGNUSSEN, 1M42.301S, 110.708MPH/178.168KPH ON LAP 58 RACE LEADERS: LECLERC 1-19, HAMILTON 20-26, GIOVINAZZI 27-30, VETTEL 31-61
* 10S PENALTY FOR NOT HEEDING RACE DIRECTORS' ORDERS,
! DISQUALIFIED FROM QUALIFYING FOR MGU-K EXCEEDING POWER LIMIT & 5-PLACE GRID PENALTY FOR REPLACING GEARBOX,
!! 10-PLACE GRID PENALTY FOR USING ADDITIONAL POWER UNIT ELEMENTS

Sebastian Vettel ran a different tactic to his rivals, pitted early and then reaped the benefits.

RUSSIAN GP

A week after becoming Ferrari's hero by returning to winning ways, Sebastian Vettel veered to zero with several bouts of refusing team orders and then the way he retired triggered a virtual safety car period that denied his team-mate Charles Leclerc a shot at victory.

The trouble started on the dash to the first corner when Ferrari's tactic of using a tow from pole-starter Leclerc to help Vettel move past Lewis Hamilton went beyond what they had planned. This was because Vettel used it to take the lead. Radio messages then revealed that he was refusing to drop back to where Ferrari intended him to be, second. The messages between the team, Vettel and Leclerc became more terse, with Vettel refusing to cede. Clearly, Leclerc's ascendancy in the team was riling him and it had become win at all costs for the German.

Vettel has a history of refusing to heed team orders, such as in the 2013 Malaysian GP when team boss Christian Horner told him and Mark Webber to "multi 21", an instruction to back off, and Vettel flouted that, overtook and went on to win.

In Sochi, Ferrari took action by letting Leclerc pit first, on lap 22. This was four laps before Vettel came in and it moved Leclerc ahead. That same lap, Vettel was told to switch off his engine as engine management failure struck. He halted at Turn 15 and, as the car was in the way, it triggered a virtual safety car period. If Vettel had been allowed to continue a few hundred metres further, he would have reached the pitlane and the VSC wouldn't have been needed. This hurt Ferrari more, as Hamilton was able to dive into the pits and come back out in front. It was a gift that set him ever closer to his sixth F1 title and it also means that Mercedes has now won six races from six in Sochi.

A safety car period followed when George Russell hit the wall and Ferrari gambled by bringing Leclerc in again from second for fresh tyres, but this didn't work and he was never able to pass Valtteri Bottas, let alone Hamilton.

Lewis Hamilton celebrates not just victory but something of an explosion in the Ferrari camp.

SOCHI ROUND 16

DATE: **29 SEPTEMBER 2019**

Laps: **53** · Distance: **192.466 miles/309.745km** · Weather: **Bright & warm**

Pos	Driver	Team	Result	Stops	Qualifying Time	Grid
1	Lewis Hamilton	Mercedes	1h33m38.992s	1	1m32.030s	2
2	Valtteri Bottas	Mercedes	1h33m42.821s	1	1m32.632s	4
3	Charles Leclerc	Ferrari	1h33m44.204s	2	1m31.628s	1
4	Max Verstappen !	Red Bull	1h33m53.202s	1	1m32.310s	9
5	Alex Albon !^	Red Bull	1h34m17.340s	1	1m39.197s	18
6	Carlos Sainz Jr	McLaren	1h34m24.881s	1	1m33.222s	5
7	Sergio Perez	Racing Point	1h34m27.720s	1	1m33.958s	11
8	Lando Norris	McLaren	1h34m36.741s	1	1m33.301s	7
9	Kevin Magnussen *	Haas	1h34m37.771s	1	1m34.038s	13
10	Nico Hulkenberg	Renault	1h34m38.833s	2	1m33.289s	6
11	Lance Stroll	Racing Point	1h34m39.813s	1	1m34.233s	14
12	Daniil Kvyat !!	Toro Rosso	1h34m41.488s	2	no time	20
13	Kimi Raikkonen	Alfa Romeo	1h34m47.902s	2	1m34.840s	15
14	Pierre Gasly !	Toro Rosso	1h34m49.068s	1	1m33.950s	16
15	Antonio Giovinazzi	Alfa Romeo	1h34m52.338s	2	1m34.037s	12
R	Robert Kubica !!	Williams	28 laps/withdrawn	1	1m36.474s	19
R	George Russell	Williams	27 laps/accident	2	1m35.356s	17
R	Sebastian Vettel	Ferrari	26 laps/power unit	1	1m32.053s	3
R	Daniel Ricciardo	Renault	24 laps/accident damage	1	1m33.661s	10
R	Romain Grosjean	Haas	0 laps/collision	0	1m33.517s	8

FASTEST LAP: HAMILTON, 1M35.761S, 136.606MPH/219.847KPH ON LAP 51 RACE LEADERS: VETTEL 1-25, HAMILTON 26-53
* 5-SECOND PENALTY FOR LEAVING TRACK & GAINING AN ADVANTAGE, ! 5-PLACE GRID PENALTY FOR USING ADDITIONAL POWER UNIT ELEMENT, !! REQUIRED TO START FROM REAR OF GRID FOR ADDITIONAL POWER UNITS HAVING BEEN USED, ^ REQUIRED TO START FROM PITLANE FOR CAR BEING MODIFIED UNDER PARC FERME RULES

JAPANESE GP

Valtteri Bottas took his third win of the season but this was a race that very nearly didn't take place because Typhoon Hagibis ploughed an awful path of destruction across the country. It cleared in time for both qualifying and race to be held on the Sunday.

Typhoon Hagibis was the most powerful storm to hit Japan in 50 years. All track activity for Saturday was cancelled and qualifying rescheduled to Sunday morning.

This was a wise choice as no one was put in the way of danger and it meant that a representative grid could be achieved rather than having to allocate starting positions according to championship ranking. This pleased Sebastian Vettel, as Ferrari's burgeoning pace helped him to pole position ahead of team-mate Charles Leclerc. The Mercedes filled row two, Bottas ahead of Lewis Hamilton.

Vettel seemed to anticipate the start, then backed off and Bottas didn't need a second invitation, going around the outside to take the lead. Having blocked Hamilton's attempt to go past him for third, Leclerc then went too deep into Turn 1 and hit the side of fast-starting Max Verstappen's Red Bull, pushing it into a half-spin and the Dutch racer into a fury. The Monegasque stayed out for three laps before pitting for repairs and he earned no praise from Hamilton as his reduced pace dropped the Englishman away from the lead pair.

Although Ferrari had had a clear pace advantage in qualifying, it was Bottas who was most comfortable in the race, gradually edging clear of Vettel and responding when the German pitted. Hamilton was kept out a few laps longer and realised that this had removed any chance he had of winning. So, it was Bottas who acted as Mercedes's standard bearer and he didn't put a wheel wrong to win by 13s. By flagfall, Hamilton had closed onto Vettel's tail but simply couldn't find a way past.

This gave Mercedes a record sixth consecutive title, going one better than Ferrari's run from 2000 to 2004.

Ten days after the race, both Renault drivers were disqualified for having an illegal brake bias adjustment system.

Valtteri Bottas leads the Ferraris after making a magnificent getaway at the start of the race.

SUZUKA ROUND 17

DATE: 13 OCTOBER 2019

Laps: **52** · Distance: **187.445 miles/301.664km** · Weather: **Warm & sunny**

Pos	Driver	Team	Result	Stops	Qualifying Time	Grid
1	**Valtteri Bottas**	Mercedes	1h21m46.755s	2	1m27.293s	3
2	**Sebastian Vettel**	Ferrari	1h22m00.098s	2	1m27.064s	1
3	**Lewis Hamilton**	Mercedes	1h22m00.613s	2	1m27.302s	4
4	**Alex Albon**	Red Bull	1h22m46.292s	2	1m27.851s	6
5	**Carlos Sainz Jr**	McLaren	51 laps	1	1m28.304s	7
6	**Charles Leclerc**	Ferrari	51 laps!	3	1m27.253s	2
7	**Pierre Gasly**	Toro Rosso	51 laps	1	1m28.836s	9
8	**Sergio Perez**	Racing Point	51 laps	2	1m30.344s	17
9	**Lance Stroll**	Racing Point	51 laps	1	1m29.345s	12
10	**Daniil Kvyat**	Toro Rosso	51 laps	1	1m29.563	14
11	**Lando Norris**	McLaren	51 laps	2	1m28.464s	8
12	**Kimi Raikkonen**	Alfa Romeo	51 laps	2	1m29.358s	13
13	**Romain Grosjean**	Haas	51 laps	1	1m29.341s	10
14	**Antonio Giovinazzi**	Alfa Romeo	51 laps	2	1m29.254s	11
15	**Kevin Magnussen ***	Haas	51 laps	2	no time	19
16	**George Russell**	Williams	50 laps	1	1m30.364s	18
17	**Robert Kubica *!**	Williams	50 laps	2	no time	20
R	**Max Verstappen**	Red Bull	14 laps/crash damage	0	1m27.851s	5
DQ	**Daniel Ricciardo**	Renault	51 laps	1	1m29.822s	16
DQ	**Nico Hulkenberg**	Renault	51 laps	1	1m30.112s	15

FASTEST LAP: HAMILTON, 1M30.983S, 142.772MPH/229.770KPH ON LAP 45 RACE LEADERS: BOTTAS 1-17, 21-36 & 43-52, HAMILTON 18-20 & 37-42 * 5-PLACE GRID PENALTY FOR REPLACING GEARBOX, ! STARTED FROM PITS FOR CHANGING SURVIVAL CELL, + DISQUALIFIED FOR ILLEGAL BRAKE BIAS ADJUSTMENT SYSTEM

MEXICAN GP

Lewis Hamilton put himself on the brink of landing of landing the 2019 drivers' title by winning in Mexico City, but it was a far from easy victory as he had to accept the challenge of running a very long stint on hard-compound tyres.

Qualifying on pole put a broad grin on Max Verstappen's face, but it was wiped off when he had his time deleted for failing to slow for a yellow flag that was being waved at the final corner as Valtteri Bottas had gone off there and his Mercedes hit the barriers. The misdemeanour demoted the Dutchman to fourth on the grid and promoted Charles Leclerc to pole, ahead of his Ferrari team-mate Sebastian Vettel.

When the race got underway, Leclerc led to the first corner, with Vettel being robust in the way he moved across on Hamilton and forced him to back off. This left Hamilton in a position to be challenged by Verstappen and they clashed in Turn 1. Then in Turn 2 too. This cost the pair momentum, and positions too, as Alex Albon and Carlos Sainz Jr went past. Back in the pack, Romain Grosjean and Kimi Raikkonen came together, leaving debris on the track.

Hamilton was the first to advance, passing the McLaren on lap 4, with Verstappen passing Bottas on that same lap, moments before he had his right rear tyre blow, forcing a slow return to the pits.

The lead trio closed up, with Albon catching Vettel who was closing in on Leclerc. However, the outcome of the race hinged on a strategic decision made by Hamilton's stand-in race engineer. He decided, after Hamilton had pitted on lap 23, that his charge would run a longer than planned second stint on Pirelli's hard-compound tyre and so avoid the need for a second pitstop. Hamilton was far from convinced that this was the right decision, but he got his head down and produced a masterful drive to achieve this aim, making them last through the final 48 laps as he managed to hang on to keep the later-stopping Vettel behind him, while Leclerc's need to pit twice ended his hopes of coming out on top.

MEXICO CITY ROUND 18

DATE: 27 OCTOBER 2019

Laps: **71** • Distance: **189.738 miles/305.354km** • Weather: **Warm & bright**

Pos	Driver	Team	Result	Stops	Qualifying Time	Grid
1	Lewis Hamilton	Mercedes	1h36m48.904s	1	1m15.262s	3
2	Sebastian Vettel	Ferrari	1h36m50.670s	1	1m15.170s	2
3	Valtteri Bottas	Mercedes	1h36m52.457s	1	1m15.338s	6
4	Charles Leclerc	Ferrari	1h36m55.272s	2	1m15.024s	1
5	Alex Albon	Red Bull	1h37m10.303s	2	1m15.336s	5
6	Max Verstappen !	Red Bull	1h37m57.711s	1	1m14.758s	4
7	Sergio Perez	Racing Point	1h38m02.723s	1	1m16.687s	11
8	Daniel Ricciardo	Renault	1h38m03.828s	1	1m16.933s	13
9	Pierre Gasly	Toro Rosso	70 laps	2	1m16.586s	10
10	Nico Hulkenberg	Renault	70 laps	1	1m16.885s	12
11	Daniil Kvyat *	Toro Rosso	70 laps	2	1m16.469s	9
12	Lance Stroll	Racing Point	70 laps	1	1m18.065s	16
13	Carlos Sainz Jr	McLaren	70 laps	2	1m16.014s	7
14	Antonio Giovinazzi	Alfa Romeo	70 laps	1	1m17.269s	15
15	Kevin Magnussen	Haas	69 laps	1	1m18.436s	17
16	George Russell	Williams	69 laps	1	1m18.823s	19
17	Romain Grosjean	Haas	69 laps	1	1m18.599s	18
18	Robert Kubica	Williams	69 laps	2	1m20.179s	20
R	Kimi Raikkonen	Alfa Romeo	58 laps/overheating	2	1m16.967s	14
R	Lando Norris	McLaren	48 laps/withdrew	1	1m16.322s	8

FASTEST LAP: LECLERC, 1M19.232S, 121.513MPH/195.557KPH ON LAP 53 RACE LEADERS: LECLERC 1-14 & 38-43, VETTEL 15-37, HAMILTON 44-71, * 10S PENALTY FOR CAUSING A COLLISION, ! 3-PLACE GRID PENALTY FOR FAILING TO SLOW FOR A WAVED YELLOW FLAG IN QUALIFYING

Lewis Hamilton holds his arms aloft on the podium having all but claimed his sixth F1 title.

UNITED STATES GP

Valtteri Bottas had this race under control all the way from pole position to chequered flag, but it was Mercedes team-mate Lewis Hamilton who attracted all the attention when it was over, as his second place was enough to land him his sixth F1 drivers' title.

Ferrari had become the form team in qualifying, but it couldn't add another pole to make it six in the last seven races as Valtteri Bottas pipped Sebastian Vettel to grab the top spot. The Italian team was at a loss to explain its loss of form. Maybe it was the ever-worsening bumps on the circuit that caused consternation for drivers and race engineers alike. Lewis Hamilton qualified only fifth.

The uphill run to the first corner is always exciting at the Circuit of the Americas and this time was no different as Bottas was able to run through the lefthander at the crest of the slope without trouble, followed by Max Verstappen, but Charles Leclerc was demoted there by Hamilton, while Carlos Sainz Jr and Alex Albon clashed, with the Red Bull suffering damage on landing. Then, within half a lap, Hamilton got by Vettel too, with the German reporting that he might have had contact and his car's handling was deteriorating. He was soon to lose more places before his rear suspension collapsed after seven laps.

His wasn't the only car to suffer as, right at the end of the race, Kevin Magnussen departed because of an exploding brake disc.

With Mercedes covering both of Verstappen's pitstops, the Finn had the race under control. But, like in Mexico, Hamilton was running a one-stop strategy. This time, though, it didn't work as his second stint proved too long for his tyres and he was unable to resist a move from Bottas with four laps to go. Second, on this occasion, would have to do for the new champion.

After the podium ceremony, Bottas was overshadowed as the press all wanted to hear from Hamilton and he was refreshingly fired up by his sixth F1 title, appreciative of the entire Mercedes team and eager to pay tribute to his mentor within the camp: the late Niki Lauda.

CIRCUIT OF THE AMERICAS ROUND 19   DATE: 3 NOVEMBER 2019

Laps: 56 • Distance: 191.634 miles/308.405km • Weather: Warm & sunny

Pos	Driver	Team	Result	Stops	Qualifying Time	Grid
1	**Valtteri Bottas**	Mercedes	1h33m55.653s	2	1m32.029s	1
2	**Lewis Hamilton**	Mercedes	1h33m59.801s	1	1m32.321s	5
3	**Max Verstappen**	Red Bull	1h34m00.655s	2	1m32.096s	3
4	**Charles Leclerc**	Ferrari	1h34m47.892	2	1m32.137s	4
5	**Alex Albon**	Red Bull	1h35m13.691s	3	1m32.548s	6
6	**Daniel Ricciardo**	Renault	1h35m26.019s	1	1m33.488s	9
7	**Lando Norris**	McLaren	1h35m26.417s	2	1m33.175s	8
8	**Carlos Sainz Jr**	McLaren	55 laps	1	1m32.847s	7
9	**Nico Hulkenberg**	Renault	55 laps	2	1m33.815s	11
10	**Sergio Perez !**	Talking Point	55 laps	1	1m35.808s	20
11	**Kimi Raikkonen**	Alfa Romeo	55 laps	2	1m34.369s	17
12	**Daniil Kvyat ***	Toro Rosso	55 laps	2	1m33.989s	13
13	**Lance Stroll**	Talking Point	55 laps	2	1m34.100s	14
14	**Antonio Giovinazzi**	Alfa Romeo	55 laps	2	1m34.226s	16
15	**Romain Grosjean**	Haas	55 laps	1	1m34.158s	15
16	**Pierre Gasly**	Toro Rosso	54 laps/crash damage	2	1m33.601s	10
17	**George Russell**	Williams	54 laps	2	1m35.372s	18
18	**Kevin Magnussen**	Haas	52 laps/brakes	2	1m33.979s	12
R	**Robert Kubica**	Williams	31 laps/hydraulics	1	1m35.889s	19
R	**Sebastian Vettel**	Ferrari	7 laps/suspension	0	1m32.041s	2

FASTEST LAP: LECLERC, 1M36.169S, 128.235MPH/206.374KPH ON LAP 44 RACE LEADERS: BOTTAS 1-14, 24-35 & 52-56, HAMILTON 15-23 & 36-51
! STARTED FROM PIT LANE FOR FAILING TO STOP FOR WEIGHT CHECK, * 5S PENALTY FOR CAUSING A COLLISION

Valtteri Bottas leads the pack up the hill into the first corner and would go on to win the race.

BRAZILIAN GP

Every now and again a race crops up that throws away the script. This was one of those, with a furious finish that involved the Ferraris colliding, Lewis Hamilton knocking Alex Albon out of second and Max Verstappen cruising to his third win of the year.

Verstappen was clear after the tricky first two corners. Behind him, Hamilton went around the outside of Sebastian Vettel's Ferrari into second, while Valtteri Bottas soon fell back, bottling up Albon.

Charles Leclerc had been hit with a 10-place penalty for using a new power unit and had to progress from 14th.

Red Bull had all the answers, while Hamilton wasn't sure that the tyres he'd taken at his first pitstop were the best compound. Verstappen remained ahead after the leaders had made their second stops, too. Then, when Bottas stopped with engine failure and a safety car period was triggered for the removal of his car, Verstappen pitted for a third time. This put Hamilton into the lead, but he knew that the Dutchman's fresher tyres would help him and Verstappen swept around the outside at Turn 1 when the field was released. And that was that, but one thing remained at the forefront of Verstappen's mind; he should have won here in 2018, but Force India's Esteban Ocon – who was unlapping himself – hit his car. On this occasion, the incidents were split between his rivals.

The first to stumble were the Ferrari drivers. When Vettel tried to take third from Albon, Leclerc pounced into Turn 1. They were side by side, then clashed. Leclerc's suspension broke and Vettel had a tyre fail. No points for Ferrari.

Hamilton made a third stop for tyres and came back out third behind Albon. Anxious to pass him, he hit his fellow Briton at Turn 9 on lap 70 and pitched him into a spin. All this let Pierre Gasly climb from sixth to second in just five laps. And, when Hamilton was hit with a 5s penalty, it promoted Carlos Sainz Jr to the final podium position, an amazing result as the McLaren driver had started from the tail of the grid.

Max Verstappen gives his former team-mate Pierre Gasly a hug for his surprise second place.

INTERLAGOS ROUND 20

DATE: **17 NOVEMBER 2019**

Laps: **71** · Distance: **190.064 miles/305.879km** · Weather: **Warm & sunny**

Pos	Driver	Team	Result	Stops	Qualifying Time	Grid
1	**Max Verstappen**	Red Bull	1h33m14.678s	3	1m07.508s	1
2	**Pierre Gasly**	Toro Rosso	1h33m20.755s	2	1m08.837s	6
3	**Carlos Sainz Jr !**	McLaren	1h33m23.574s	1	no time	20
4	**Kimi Raikkonen**	Alfa Romeo	1h33m24.130s	2	1m08.984s	8
5	**Antonio Giovinazzi**	Alfa Romeo	1h33m24.879s	2	1m08.919s	12
6	**Daniel Ricciardo**	Renault	1h33m25.219s	2	1m08.903s	11
7	**Lewis Hamilton ***	Mercedes	1h33m25.817s	3	1m07.699s	3
8	**Lando Norris**	McLaren	1h33m25.882s	2	1m08.868s	10
9	**Sergio Perez**	Racing Point	1h33m26.207s	2	1m09.035s	15
10	**Daniil Kvyat**	Toro Rosso	1h33m26.609s	2	1m09.320s	16
11	**Kevin Magnussen**	Haas	1h33m27.410s	2	1m09.037s	9
12	**George Russell**	Williams	1h33m28.277s	3	1m10.126s	18
13	**Romain Grosjean**	Haas	1h33m28.925s	2	1m08.854s	7
14	**Alex Albon**	Red Bull	1h33m29.605s	2	1m07.935s	5
15	**Nico Hulkenberg ****	Renault	1h33m32.737s	3	1m08.921s	13
16	**Robert Kubica**	Williams	70 laps	4	1m10.614s	19
R	**Sebastian Vettel**	Ferrari	65 laps/collision	2	1m07.631s	2
R	**Charles Leclerc !!**	Ferrari	65 laps/collision	2	1m07.728s	14
R	**Lance Stroll**	Racing Point	65 laps/crash damage	2	1m09.536s	17
R	**Valtteri Bottas**	Mercedes	51 laps/power unit	2	1m07.874s	4

FASTEST LAP: BOTTAS, 1M10.698S, 136.339MPH/219.417KPH ON LAP 43
RACE LEADERS: VERSTAPPEN 1-21, 26-44, 49-53 & 60-71, VETTEL 22-25 & 45-48, HAMILTON 54-59
* 5S PENALTY FOR CAUSING COLLISION WITH ALBON, ** 5S PENALTY FOR OVERTAKING UNDER SAFETY CAR CONDITIONS, ! MADE TO START FROM BACK OF GRID FOR USING ADDITIONAL POWER UNIT ELEMENTS, !! 10-PLACE GRID PENALTY FOR USING ADDITIONAL POWER UNIT ELEMENTS

ABU DHABI GP

Lewis Hamilton couldn't have asked for a more emphatic way to end the 2019 season as he led every one of the 55 laps en route to victory by 17s to complete his sixth title-winning campaign. Max Verstappen drove well to be the best of the rest.

Hamilton started the final race of the year on pole, helped by Ferrari making a hash of things in qualifying as Charles Leclerc felt that he was delayed by team-mate Sebastian Vettel and was thus unable to get around in time to start his final flying lap. Data showed that, on this occasion, it was the team rather than Vettel at fault.

Valtteri Bottas was second fastest, but his car needed an engine change after his retirement from the Brazilian GP and this forced him to start from the tail of the grid. This meant Verstappen lined up alongside Hamilton, with Leclerc ahead of Vettel on the row behind.

Hamilton led into Turn 1. Back in the pack, though, there was trouble as Lance Stroll spun into Pierre Gasly's Toro Rosso which, in turn, bumped into Stroll's Racing Point team-mate Sergio Perez. The Mexican was fortunate not so suffer any damage, but a pitstop for a new nose wrecked Gasly's hopes of another points-scoring result.

Halfway around lap 1, at Turn 8, Leclerc managed to pass Verstappen, with Vettel failing in his attempt to follow suit. After that, Hamilton and Verstappen were able to make appreciably longer runs before their planned pitstop. Such was the Mercedes driver's pace, that he was able to rejoin the track still in the lead. Verstappen was back behind Leclerc when he came back out, but he then hunted him down and was able to dive back into second at Turn 8 seven laps later. That was as far as Verstappen would advance, though, as it was never going to be anyone but Hamilton's day. Abu Dhabi has become a happy hunting ground for Mercedes, as this was the team's sixth win in a row at Yas Marina.

Bottas made it up to fourth place, getting right onto Leclerc's tail on the final lap, while it took Vettel until lap 53 to pass Alex Albon for fifth, with Perez and Carlos Sainz Jr making final lap gains.

Lewis Hamilton leads the way in the fading light as evening turned into night at the final round.

YAS MARINA ROUND 22

DATE: 1 DECEMBER 2019

Laps: 55 • Distance: **189.738 miles/305.355km** • Weather: **Warm & dry**

Pos	Driver	Team	Result	Stops	Qualifying Time	Grid
1	**Lewis Hamilton**	Mercedes	1h34m05.715s	1	1m34.797s	1
2	**Max Verstappen**	Red Bull	1h34m22.487s	1	1m35.139s	2
3	**Charles Leclerc**	Ferrari	1h34m49.150s	2	1m35.219s	3
4	**Valtteri Bottas !**	Mercedes	1h34m50.094s	1	1m34.973s	20
5	**Sebastian Vettel**	Ferrari	1h35m10.072s	2	1m35.339s	4
6	**Alex Albon**	Red Bull	1h35m14.920s	1	1m35.682s	5
7	**Sergio Perez**	Racing Point	54 laps	1	1m37.055s	10
8	**Lando Norris**	McLaren	54 laps	1	1m36.436s	6
9	**Daniil Kvyat**	Toro Rosso	54 laps	1	1m37.141s	13
10	**Carlos Sainz Jr**	McLaren	54 laps	2	1m36.459s	8
11	**Daniel Ricciardo**	Renault	54 laps	2	1m36.456s	7
12	**Nico Hulkenberg**	Renault	54 laps	1	1m36.710s	9
13	**Kimi Raikkonen**	Alfa Romeo	54 laps	1	1m38.383s	17
14	**Kevin Magnussen**	Haas	54 laps	1	1m37.254s	14
15	**Romain Grosjean**	Haas	54 laps	1	1m38.051s	15
16	**Antonio Giovinazzi**	Alfa Romeo	54 laps	2	1m38.114s	16
17	**George Russell**	Williams	54 laps	1	1m38.717s	18
18	**Pierre Gasly**	Toro Rosso	53 laps	1	1m37.089s	11
19	**Robert Kubica**	Williams	53 laps	1	1m39.236s	19
R	**Lance Stroll**	Racing Point	45 laps/brakes	2	1m37.103s	12

FASTEST LAP: HAMILTON, 1M39.283S, 125.136MPH/201.387KPH ON LAP 53 RACE LEADER: HAMILTON 1-55
! MADE TO START FROM BACK OF GRID FOR USING ADDITIONAL POWER UNIT ELEMENTS

Lewis Hamilton didn't need this 11th win of 2019 to land the title, as that was already his, but it gave him a wonderful send-off after a year in which he had serious challenges to repel.

POS	DRIVER	NAT		CAR-ENGINE	R1	R2	R3	R4	R5
1	LEWIS HAMILTON	GBR	🇬🇧	MERCEDES F1 W10	2P	1	1	2	1F
2	VALTTERI BOTTAS	FIN	🇫🇮	MERCEDES F1 W10	1F	2	2P	1P	2P
3	MAX VERSTAPPEN	NED	🇳🇱	RED BULL-HONDA RB15	3	4	4	4	3
4	CHARLES LECLERC	MON	🇲🇨	FERRARI SF90	5	3PF	5	5F	5
5	SEBASTIAN VETTEL	GER	🇩🇪	FERRARI SF90	4	5	3	3	4
6	CARLOS SAINZ JR	SPA	🇪🇸	McLAREN-RENAULT MCL34	R	19	14	7	8
7	PIERRE GASLY	FRA	🇫🇷	RED BULL-HONDA RB15	11	8	6F	R	6
				TORO ROSSO-HONDA STR14	–	–	–	–	–
8	ALEX ALBON	GBR	🇬🇧	TORO ROSSO-HONDA STR14	14	9	10	11	11
				RED BULL-HONDA RB15	–	–	–	–	–
9	DANIEL RICCIARDO	AUS	🇦🇺	RENAULT RS19	R	18	7	R	12
10	SERGIO PEREZ	MEX	🇲🇽	RACING POINT-MERCEDES RP19	13	10	8	6	15
11	LANDO NORRIS	GBR	🇬🇧	McLAREN-RENAULT MCL34	12	6	18	8	R
12	KIMI RAIKKONEN	FIN	🇫🇮	ALFA ROMEO-FERRARI C38	8	7	9	10	14
13	DANIIL KVYAT	RUS	🇷🇺	TORO ROSSO-HONDA STR14	10	12	R	R	9
14	NICO HULKENBERG	GER	🇩🇪	RENAULT RS19	7	17	R	14	13
15	LANCE STROLL	CDN	🇨🇦	RACING POINT-MERCEDES RP19	9	14	12	9	R
16	KEVIN MAGNUSSEN	DEN	🇩🇰	HAAS-FERRARI VF-19	6	13	13	13	7
17	ANTONIO GIOVINAZZI	ITA	🇮🇹	ALFA ROMEO-FERRARI C38	15	11	15	12	16
18	ROMAIN GROSJEAN	FRA	🇫🇷	HAAS-FERRARI VF-19	R	R	11	R	10
19	ROBERT KUBICA	POL	🇵🇱	WILLIAMS-MERCEDES FW42	17	16	17	16	18
20	GEORGE RUSSELL	GBR	🇬🇧	WILLIAMS-MERCEDES FW42	16	15	16	15	17

116

SCORING

1st	25 points
2nd	18 points
3rd	15 points
4th	12 points
5th	10 points
6th	8 points
7th	6 points
8th	4 points
9th	2 points
10th	1 point
Fastest lap	1 point

POS	TEAM-ENGINE	R1	R2	R3	R4	R5
1	MERCEDES (+9 fastest laps)	1/2	1/2	1/2	1/2	1/2
2	FERRARI (+6)	4/5	3/5	3/5	3/5	4/5
3	RED BULL-HONDA (+5)	3/11	4/8	4/6	4/R	3/6
4	McLAREN-RENAULT	12/R	6/19	14/18	7/8	8/R
5	RENAULT	7/R	17/18	7/R	14/R	12/13
6	TORO ROSSO-HONDA	10/14	9/12	10/R	11/R	9/11
7	RACING POINT-MERCEDES	9/13	10/14	8/12	6/9	15/R
8	ALFA ROMEO-FERRARI	8/15	7/11	9/15	10/12	14/16
9	HAAS-FERRARI	6/R	13/R	11/13	13/R	7/10
10	WILLIAMS-MERCEDES	16/17	15/16	16/17	15/16	17/18

SYMBOLS AND GRAND PRIX KEY

ROUND 1 **AUSTRALIAN GP**	ROUND 7 **CANADIAN GP**	ROUND 13 **BELGIAN GP**	ROUND 19 **UNITED STATES GP**
ROUND 2 **BAHRAIN GP**	ROUND 8 **FRENCH GP**	ROUND 14 **ITALIAN GP**	ROUND 20 **BRAZILIAN GP**
ROUND 3 **CHINESE GP**	ROUND 9 **AUSTRIAN GP**	ROUND 15 **SINGAPORE GP**	ROUND 21 **ABU DHABI GP**
ROUND 4 **AZERBAIJAN GP**	ROUND 10 **BRITISH GP**	ROUND 16 **RUSSIAN GP**	
ROUND 5 **SPANISH GP**	ROUND 11 **GERMAN GP**	ROUND 17 **JAPANESE GP**	
ROUND 6 **MONACO GP**	ROUND 12 **HUNGARIAN GP**	ROUND 18 **MEXICAN GP**	

DQ DISQUALIFIED **F** FASTEST LAP **NC** NOT CLASSIFIED **NS** NON-STARTER **P** POLE POSITION **R** RETIRED **W** WITHDRAWN

R6	R7	R8	R9	R10	R11	R12	R13	R14	R15	R16	R17	R18	R19	R20	R21	TOTAL
1P	1	1P	5	1F	9P	1	2	3F	4	1F	3F	1	2	7	1PF	413
3	4F	2	3	2P	R	8	3	2	5	2	1	3	1P	RF	4	326
4	5	4	1F	5	1F	2PF	R	8	3	4	R	6	3	1P	2	278
R	3	3	2P	3	R	4	1P	1P	2P	3P	6	4PF	4F	R	3	264
2	2P	5F	4	16	2	3	4F	13	1	R	2P	2	R	17	5	240
6	11	6	8	6	5	5	R	R	12	6	5	13	8	3	10	96
5F	8	10	7	4	14	6	–	–	–	–	–	–	–	–	–	95
–	–	–	–	–	–	–	9	11	8	14	7	9	16	2	18	
8	R	15	15	12	6	10	–	–	–	–	–	–	–	–	–	92
–	–	–	–	–	–	–	5	6	6	5	4	5	5	14	6	
9	6	11	12	7	R	14	14	4	14	R	DQ	8	6	6	11	54
12	12	12	11	17	R	11	6	7	R	7	8	7	10	9	7	52
11	R	9	6	11	R	9	11	10	7	8	11	R	7	8	8	49
17	15	7	9	8	12	7	16	15	R	13	12	R	11	4	13	43
7	10	14	17	9	3	15	7	R	15	12	10	11	12	10	9	37
13	7	8	13	10	R	12	8	5	9	10	DQ	10	9	15	12	37
16	9	13	14	13	4	17	10	12	13	11	9	12	13	R	R	21
14	17	17	19	R	8	13	12	R	17F	9	15	15	R	11	14	20
19	13	16	10	R	13	18	R	9	10	15	14	14	14	5	16	14
10	14	R	16	R	7	R	13	16	11	R	13	17	15	13	15	8
18	18	18	20	15	10	19	17	17	16	R	17	18	R	16	19	1
15	16	19	18	14	11	16	15	14	R	R	16	16	17	12	17	0

R6	R7	R8	R9	R10	R11	R12	R13	R14	R15	R16	R17	R18	R19	R20	R21	TOTAL
1/3	1/4	1/2	3/5	1/2	9/R	1/8	2/3	2/3	4/5	1/2	1/3	1/3	1/2	7/R	1/4	739
2/R	2/3	3/5	2/4	3/16	2/R	3/4	1/4	1/13	1/2	3/R	2/6	2/4	4/R	R/R	3/5	504
4/5	5/8	4/10	1/7	4/5	1/14	2/6	5/R	6/8	3/6	4/5	4/R	5/6	3/5	1/14	2/6	417
6/11	11/R	6/9	6/8	6/11	5/R	5/9	11/R	10/R	7/12	6/8	5/11	13/R	7/8	3/8	8/10	145
9/13	6/7	8/11	12/13	7/10	R/R	12/14	8/14	4/5	9/14	10/R	DQ/DQ	8/10	6/9	6/15	11/12	91
7/8	10/R	14/15	15/17	9/12	3/6	10/15	7/9	11/R	8/15	12/14	7/10	9/11	12/16	2/10	9/18	85
12/16	9/12	12/13	11/14	13/17	4/R	11/17	6/10	7/12	13/R	7/11	8/9	7/12	10/13	9/R	7/R	73
17/19	13/15	7/16	9/10	8/R	12/13	7/18	16/R	9/15	10/R	13/15	12/14	14/R	11/14	4/5	13/16	57
10/14	14/17	17/R	16/19	R/R	7/8	13/R	12/13	16/R	11/17	9/R	13/15	15/17	15/R	11/13	14/15	28
15/18	16/18	18/19	18/20	14/15	10/11	16/19	15/17	14/17	16/R	R/R	16/17	16/18	17/R	12/16	17/19	1

STARTS

DRIVERS

325	Rubens Barrichello	(BRA)	175	Jacques Laffite	(FRA)	123	Ronnie Peterson	(SWE)
314	Fernando Alonso	(SPA)	171	Niki Lauda	(AUT)	119	Pierluigi Martini	(ITA)
308	Michael Schumacher	(GER)		Daniel Ricciardo	(AUS)	116	Damon Hill	(GBR)
307	Jenson Button	(GBR)	166	Romain Grosjean	(FRA)		Jacky Ickx	(BEL)
305	Kimi Raikkonen	(FIN)	165	Jacques Villeneuve	(CDN)		Alan Jones	(AUS)
270	Felipe Massa	(BRA)	163	Thierry Boutsen	(BEL)	114	Keke Rosberg	(FIN)
256	Riccardo Patrese	(ITA)	162	Mika Hakkinen	(FIN)		Patrick Tambay	(FRA)
	Jarno Trulli	(ITA)		Johnny Herbert	(GBR)	112	Denny Hulme	(NZL)
250	Lewis Hamilton	(GBR)	161	Ayrton Senna	(BRA)		Jody Scheckter	(RSA)
247	David Coulthard	(GBR)	159	Heinz-Harald Frentzen	(GER)	111	Heikki Kovalainen	(FIN)
241	Sebastian Vettel	(GER)	158	Martin Brundle	(GBR)		John Surtees	(GBR)
230	Giancarlo Fisichella	(ITA)		Olivier Panis	(FRA)	109	Philippe Alliot	(FRA)
216	Mark Webber	(AUS)	152	John Watson	(GBR)		Mika Salo	(FIN)
210	Gerhard Berger	(AUT)	149	Rene Arnoux	(FRA)	108	Elio de Angelis	(ITA)
208	Andrea de Cesaris	(ITA)	147	Eddie Irvine	(GBR)	106	Jos Verstappen	(NED)
206	Nico Rosberg	(GER)		Derek Warwick	(GBR)	104	Jo Bonnier	(SWE)
204	Nelson Piquet	(BRA)	146	Carlos Reutemann	(ARG)		Pedro de la Rosa	(SPA)
201	Jean Alesi	(FRA)	144	Emerson Fittipaldi	(BRA)		Jochen Mass	(GER)
199	Alain Prost	(FRA)	139	Valtteri Bottas	(FIN)	103	Kevin Magnussen	(DEN)
194	Michele Alboreto	(ITA)	135	Jean-Pierre Jarier	(FRA)	102	Max Verstappen	(NED)
187	Nigel Mansell	(GBR)	132	Eddie Cheever	(USA)		Carlos Sainz Jr	(SPA)
180	Ralf Schumacher	(GER)		Clay Regazzoni	(SWI)	100	Bruce McLaren	(NZL)
179	Nico Hulkenberg	(GER)	128	Mario Andretti	(USA)			
176	Graham Hill	(GBR)		Adrian Sutil	(GER)			
	Sergio Perez	(MEX)	126	Jack Brabham	(AUS)			

CONSTRUCTORS

991	Ferrari	492	Lotus	383	Arrows
864	McLaren	485	Alfa Romeo (*nee* Sauber,	230	March
783	Williams		including BMW Sauber)	197	BRM
655	Renault* (*nee* Toleman, then	421	Red Bull Racing (*nee* Stewart,	132	Osella
	Benetton, then Renault II, Lotus		then Jaguar Racing)	129	Renault
	II & Renault III)	418	Tyrrell		
609	Scuderia Toro Rosso (*nee*	409	Prost (*nee* Ligier)		
	Minardi)	394	Brabham		
518	Racing Point (*nee* Jordan, then	386	Mercedes GP (*nee* BAR, then		
	Midland, then Spyker & Force India)		Honda Racing & Brawn GP)		

MOST WINS

DRIVERS

91	Michael Schumacher	(GER)	16	Stirling Moss	(GBR)		Jody Scheckter	(RSA)
84	Lewis Hamilton	(GBR)	15	Jenson Button	(GBR)	9	Mark Webber	(AUS)
53	Sebastian Vettel	(GER)	14	Jack Brabham	(AUS)	8	Denny Hulme	(NZL)
51	Alain Prost	(FRA)		Emerson Fittipaldi	(BRA)		Jacky Ickx	(BEL)
41	Ayrton Senna	(BRA)		Graham Hill	(GBR)		Max Verstappen	(NED)
32	Fernando Alonso	(SPA)	13	Alberto Ascari	(ITA)	7	Rene Arnoux	(FRA)
31	Nigel Mansell	(GBR)		David Coulthard	(GBR)		Valtteri Bottas	(FIN)
27	Jackie Stewart	(GBR)	12	Mario Andretti	(USA)		Juan Pablo Montoya	(COL)
25	Jim Clark	(GBR)		Alan Jones	(AUS)		Daniel Ricciardo	(AUS)
	Niki Lauda	(AUT)		Carlos Reutemann	(ARG)	6	Tony Brooks	(GBR)
24	Juan Manuel Fangio	(ARG)	11	Rubens Barrichello	(BRA)		Jacques Laffite	(FRA)
23	Nelson Piquet	(BRA)		Felipe Massa	(BRA)		Riccardo Patrese	(ITA)
	Nico Rosberg	(GER)		Jacques Villeneuve	(CDN)		Jochen Rindt	(AUT)
22	Damon Hill	(GBR)	10	Gerhard Berger	(AUT)		Ralf Schumacher	(GER)
21	Kimi Raikkonen	(FIN)		James Hunt	(GBR)		John Surtees	(GBR)
20	Mika Hakkinen	(FIN)		Ronnie Peterson	(SWE)		Gilles Villeneuve	(CDN)

CONSTRUCTORS

237	Ferrari	23	Tyrrell	3	March
181	McLaren	17	BRM		Wolf
114	Williams	16	Cooper	2	Honda
102	Mercedes GP (including Honda Racing, Brawn GP)	15	Renault	1	BMW Sauber
		10	Alfa Romeo		Eagle
79	Lotus	9	Ligier		Hesketh
62	Red Bull Racing (including Stewart)		Maserati		Penske
			Matra		Porsche
49	Renault* (including Benetton, Renault II, Lotus II & Renault III)		Mercedes		Shadow
			Vanwall		Scuderia Toro Rosso
35	Brabham	4	Jordan		

Clay Regazzoni holds off James Hunt's McLaren and Patrick Depailler's Tyrrell as he heads for victory for Ferrari at Long Beach in 1976.

DRIVERS

	Driver	Year		Driver	Year		Driver	Year
13	Michael Schumacher	2004	8	Mika Hakkinen	1998	6	Mario Andretti	1978
11	Lewis Hamilton	2014		Damon Hill	1996		Alberto Ascari	1952
	Lewis Hamilton	2018		Michael Schumacher	1994		Jim Clark	1965
	Lewis Hamilton	2019		Ayrton Senna	1988		Juan Manuel Fangio	1954
	Michael Schumacher	2002	7	Fernando Alonso	2005		Damon Hill	1994
	Sebastian Vettel	2011		Fernando Alonso	2006		James Hunt	1976
10	Lewis Hamilton	2015		Jim Clark	1963		Nigel Mansell	1987
	Lewis Hamilton	2016		Alain Prost	1984		Kimi Raikkonen	2007
9	Lewis Hamilton	2017		Alain Prost	1988		Nico Rosberg	2015
	Nigel Mansell	1992		Alain Prost	1993		Michael Schumacher	1998
	Nico Rosberg	2016		Kimi Raikkonen	2005		Michael Schumacher	2003
	Michael Schumacher	1995		Ayrton Senna	1991		Michael Schumacher	2006
	Michael Schumacher	2000		Jacques Villeneuve	1997		Ayrton Senna	1989
	Michael Schumacher	2001					Ayrton Senna	1990

CONSTRUCTORS

	Constructor	Year		Constructor	Year		Constructor	Year
19	Mercedes GP	2016		Williams	1992		Renault	2006
16	Mercedes GP	2014		Williams	1993		Williams	1997
	Mercedes GP	2015	9	Ferrari	2001	7	Ferrari	1952
15	Ferrari	2002		Ferrari	2006		Ferrari	1953
	Ferrari	2004		Ferrari	2007		Ferrari	2008
	McLaren	1988		McLaren	1998		Lotus	1963
	Mercedes GP	2019		Red Bull Racing	2010		Lotus	1973
12	McLaren	1984		Williams	1986		McLaren	1999
	Mercedes GP	2017		Williams	1987		McLaren	2000
	Red Bull Racing	2011	8	Benetton	1994		McLaren	2012
	Williams	1996		Brawn GP	2009		Red Bull Racing	2012
11	Benetton	1995		Ferrari	2003		Tyrrell	1971
	Mercedes GP	2018		Lotus	1978		Williams	1991
10	Ferrari	2000		McLaren	1991		Williams	1994
	McLaren	2005		McLaren	2007			
	McLaren	1989		Renault	2005			

MOST POLE POSITIONS

DRIVERS

88	Lewis Hamilton	(GBR)	22	Fernando Alonso	(SPA)	13	Jack Brabham	(AUS)
68	Michael Schumacher	(GER)	20	Damon Hill	(GBR)		Graham Hill	(GBR)
65	Ayrton Senna	(BRA)	18	Mario Andretti	(USA)		Jacky Ickx	(BEL)
57	Sebastian Vettel	(GER)		Rene Arnoux	(FRA)		Juan Pablo Montoya	(COL)
33	Jim Clark	(GBR)		Kimi Raikkonen	(FIN)		Jacques Villeneuve	(CDN)
	Alain Prost	(FRA)	17	Jackie Stewart	(GBR)	12	Gerhard Berger	(AUT)
32	Nigel Mansell	(GBR)	16	Felipe Massa	(BRA)		David Coulthard	(GBR)
30	Nico Rosberg	(GER)		Stirling Moss	(GBR)	11	Mark Webber	(AUS)
29	Juan Manuel Fangio	(ARG)	14	Alberto Ascari	(ITA)	10	Valtteri Bottas	(FIN)
26	Mika Hakkinen	(FIN)		Rubens Barrichello	(BRA)		Jochen Rindt	(AUT)
24	Niki Lauda	(AUT)		James Hunt	(GBR)			
	Nelson Piquet	(BRA)		Ronnie Peterson	(SWE)			

CONSTRUCTORS

228	Ferrari	31	Renault	3	Racing Point (including Jordan, Force India)
154	McLaren	14	Tyrrell		Shadow
128	Williams	12	Alfa Romeo		Toyota
111	Mercedes GP (including BAR, Honda Racing, Brawn GP)	11	BRM	2	Lancia
			Cooper	1	BMW Sauber
107	Lotus	10	Maserati		Scuderia Toro Rosso
62	Red Bull Racing	9	Ligier		
39	Brabham	8	Mercedes		
34	Renault* (including Toleman, Benetton, Renault II, Lotus II & Renault III)	7	Vanwall		
		5	March		
		4	Matra		

Opposite: Hamilton wins in Abu Dhabi in 2016.
Above: Vettel after winning in India in 2011.

Juan Manuel Fangio powers his Ferrari along the harbourfront in Monaco in 1957 for one of the four wins that helped him to land his fifth F1 title.

MOST FASTEST LAPS

DRIVERS

76	Michael Schumacher	(GER)	21	Gerhard Berger	(AUT)	13	Alberto Ascari	(ITA)
47	Lewis Hamilton	(GBR)	20	Nico Rosberg	(GER)		Valtteri Bottas	(FIN)
46	Kimi Raikkonen	(FIN)	19	Damon Hill	(GBR)		Alan Jones	(AUS)
41	Alain Prost	(FRA)		Stirling Moss	(GBR)		Riccardo Patrese	(ITA)
38	Sebastian Vettel	(GER)		Ayrton Senna	(BRA)		Daniel Ricciardo	(AUS)
30	Nigel Mansell	(GBR)		Mark Webber	(AUS)	12	Rene Arnoux	(FRA)
28	Jim Clark	(GBR)	18	David Coulthard	(GBR)		Jack Brabham	(AUS)
25	Mika Hakkinen	(FIN)	17	Rubens Barrichello	(BRA)		Juan Pablo Montoya	(COL)
24	Niki Lauda	(AUT)	16	Felipe Massa	(BRA)	11	John Surtees	(GBR)
23	Juan Manuel Fangio	(ARG)	15	Clay Regazzoni	(SWI)	10	Mario Andretti	(USA)
	Nelson Piquet	(BRA)		Jackie Stewart	(GBR)		Graham Hill	(GBR)
22	Fernando Alonso	(SPA)	14	Jacky Ickx	(BEL)			

CONSTRUCTORS

253	Ferrari	54	Renault* (including Toleman, Benetton, Renault II & Lotus II)	14	Alfa Romeo
161	McLaren			13	Cooper
133	Williams	40	Brabham	12	Matra
75	Mercedes GP (including BAR, Honda Racing & Brawn GP)	22	Tyrrell	11	Prost (including Ligier)
		18	Renault	9	Mercedes
71	Lotus	15	BRM	7	March
65	Red Bull Racing		Maserati	6	Vanwall

MOST POINTS (this figure is gross tally, i.e. including scores that were later dropped)

DRIVERS

3,431	Lewis Hamilton	(GBR)	581	Sergio Perez	(MEX)	289	Graham Hill	(GBR)
2,985	Sebastian Vettel	(GER)	535	David Coulthard	(GBR)	281	Emerson Fittipaldi	(BRA)
1,899	Fernando Alonso	(SPA)	511	Nico Hulkenberg	(GER)		Riccardo Patrese	(ITA)
1,859	Kimi Raikkonen	(FIN)	485.5	Nelson Piquet	(BRA)	277.5	Juan Manuel Fangio	(ARG)
1,594.5	Nico Rosberg	(GER)	482	Nigel Mansell	(GBR)	275	Giancarlo Fisichella	(ITA)
1,566	Michael Schumacher	(GER)	420.5	Niki Lauda	(AUT)	274	Jim Clark	(GBR)
1,289	Valtteri Bottas	(FIN)	420	Mika Hakkinen	(FIN)		Robert Kubica	(POL)
1,235	Jenson Button	(GBR)	389	Romain Grosjean	(FRA)	267	Carlos Sainz Jr	(SPA)
1,167	Felipe Massa	(BRA)	385	Gerhard Berger	(AUT)	261	Jack Brabham	(AUS)
1,047.5	Mark Webber	(AUS)	360	Damon Hill	(GBR)	259	Nick Heidfeld	(GER)
1,040	Daniel Ricciardo	(AUS)		Jackie Stewart	(GBR)	255	Jody Scheckter	(RSA)
948	Max Vertsappen	(NED)	329	Ralf Schumacher	(GER)	248	Denny Hulme	(NZL)
798.5	Alain Prost	(FRA)	310	Carlos Reutemann	(ARG)	246.5	Jarno Trulli	(ITA)
658	Rubens Barrichello	(BRA)	307	Juan Pablo Montoya	(COL)	241	Jean Alesi	(FRA)
614	Ayrton Senna	(BRA)	303	Charles Leclerc	(FRA)	235	Jacques Villeneuve	(CDN)

CONSTRUCTORS

8,239.5	Ferrari	1,514	Lotus	439	BRM
5,614	Mercedes GP (including BAR, Honda Racing, Brawn GP)	1,404	Racing Point (including Jordan, Midland, Spyker, Force India)	424	Prost (including Ligier)
5,330.5	McLaren			333	Cooper
4,812.5	Red Bull Racing (including Stewart, Jaguar Racing)	915	Alfa Romeo* (including Sauber & BMW Sauber)	312	Renault
				278.5	Toyota
3,567	Williams	854	Brabham	197	Haas
2,823.5	Renault* (including Toleman, Benetton, Renault II & Lotus II)	617	Tyrrell	171.5	March
		536	Scuderia Toro Rosso	167	Arrows
				155	Matra

123

CHAMPIONSHIP TITLES

DRIVERS

7	Michael Schumacher	(GER)	1	Mario Andretti	(USA)
6	Lewis Hamilton	(GBR)		Jenson Button	(GBR)
5	Juan Manuel Fangio	(ARG)		Giuseppe Farina	(ITA)
4	Alain Prost	(FRA)		Mike Hawthorn	(GBR)
	Sebastian Vettel	(GER)		Damon Hill	(GBR)
3	Jack Brabham	(AUS)		Phil Hill	(USA)
	Niki Lauda	(AUT)		Denis Hulme	(NZL)
	Nelson Piquet	(BRA)		James Hunt	(GBR)
	Ayrton Senna	(BRA)		Alan Jones	(AUS)
	Jackie Stewart	(GBR)		Nigel Mansell	(GBR)
2	Fernando Alonso	(SPA)		Kimi Raikkonen	(FIN)
	Alberto Ascari	(ITA)		Jochen Rindt	(AUT)
	Jim Clark	(GBR)		Keke Rosberg	(FIN)
	Emerson Fittipaldi	(BRA)		Nico Rosberg	(GER)
	Mika Hakkinen	(FIN)		Jody Scheckter	(RSA)
	Graham Hill	(GBR)		John Surtees	(GBR)
				Jacques Villeneuve	(CDN)

CONSTRUCTORS

16	Ferrari		Renault
9	Williams	1	Benetton
8	McLaren		Brawn
7	Lotus		BRM
6	Mercedes GP		Matra
4	Red Bull Racing		Tyrrell
2	Brabham		Vanwall
	Cooper		

NB. To avoid confusion, the Lotus stats listed are based on the team that ran from 1958 to 1994, whereas those listed as Renault* are for the team based at Enstone that started as Toleman in 1981, became Benetton in 1986, then Renault II in 2002, Lotus II in 2012 and Renault III in 2016. The Renault listings are for the team that ran from 1977 to 1985, the stats for Red Bull Racing include those of the Stewart Grand Prix and Jaguar Racing teams from which it evolved, and those for Mercedes GP for the team that started as BAR in 1999, then ran as Honda GP from 2006 and as Brawn GP in 2009. Racing Point's stats include those of Jordan, Midland, Spyker and Force India, while Scuderia Toro Rosso's include those of its forerunner Minardi and they will be Scuderia Alpha Tauri from 2020. The numbers for Alfa Romeo* are those of the team created in 2019 from Sauber (1993–2018, including BMW Sauber), with no connection to the two iterations of the Alfa Romeo works team that ran 1950–51 and 1979–85.

Lewis Hamilton loves his home grand prix at Silverstone and interacts with the fans from a stage more normally used for concerts during the grand prix weekend.

2020 SEASON FILL-IN CHART

DRIVER	TEAM	Round 1 – 15 March AUSTRALIAN GP	Round 2 – 22 March BAHRAIN GP	Round 3 – 5 April VIETNAMESE GP	Round 4 – 19 April CHINESE GP	Round 5 – 3 May DUTCH GP	Round 6 – 10 May SPANISH GP	Round 7 – 24 May MONACO GP	Round 8 – 7 June AZERBAIJAN GP	Round 9 – 14 June CANADIAN GP	Round 10 – 28 June FRENCH GP
LEWIS HAMILTON	Mercedes										
VALTTERI BOTTAS	Mercedes										
CHARLES LECLERC	Ferrari										
SEBASTIAN VETTEL	Ferrari										
MAX VERSTAPPEN	Red Bull										
ALEX ALBON	Red Bull										
CARLOS SAINZ JR	McLaren										
LANDO NORRIS	McLaren										
DANIEL RICCIARDO	Renault										
ESTEBAN OCON	Renault										
PIERRE GASLY	Alpha Tauri										
DANIIL KVYAT	Alpha Tauri										
SERGIO PEREZ	Racing Point										
LANCE STROLL	Racing Point										
KIMI RAIKKONEN	Alfa Romeo										
ANTONIO GIOVINAZZI	Alfa Romeo										
KEVIN MAGNUSSEN	Haas F1										
ROMAIN GROSJEAN	Haas F1										
GEORGE RUSSELL	Williams										
NICOLAS LATIFI	Williams										

SCORING SYSTEM: 25, 18, 15, 12, 10, 8, 6, 4, 2, 1 POINTS FOR THE FIRST 10 FINISHERS IN EACH GRAND PRIX;
1 POINT FOR DRIVER SETTING THE RACE'S FASTEST LAP (IF FINISHING IN FIRST 10)

Round 11 – 5 July AUSTRIAN GP	Round 12 - 19 July BRITISH GP	Round 13 – 2 August HUNGARIAN GP	Round 14 - 30 August BELGIAN GP	Round 15 - 6 Sept ITALIAN GP	Round 16 – 20 Sept SINGAPORE GP	Round 17 – 27 Sept RUSSIAN GP	Round 18 –11 Oct JAPANESE GP	Round 19 – 25 Oct UNITED STATES GP	Round 20 – 1 Nov MEXICAN GP	Round 21 – 15 Nov BRAZILIAN GP	Round 22 – 29 Nov ABU DHABI GP	POINTS TOTAL

The publishers would like to thank the following sources for their kind permission to reproduce the pictures in this book.

FIA: 59T

McLAREN: 59B

MOTORSPORT IMAGES: 61TR; /A1GP: 57B, 90-91; /Jerry Andre: 10, 16, 22, 31, 37, 45, 59C, 62-63, 70-71; /Carl Bingham: 109; /Sam Bloxham: 34, 46-47, 104, 105, 106, 128; /Charles Coates: 21; /Ercole Colombo/Studio Colombo: 43, 53; /Glenn Dunbar: 17, 20, 39, 40, 42, 94, 100, 111, 121; /Steve Etherington: 11, 61B, 96, 97, 103, 112, 120, 124-125; /Andrew Ferraro: 35; /Simon Galloway: 13, 55, 61TL, 110; /Gareth Harford: 26, 52; /Andy Hone: 6-7, 18-19, 24, 28, 38, 49, 51, 95, 114; /LAT Images: 57T, 57L, 119, 122; /Zak Mauger: 14, 23, 27, 32-33, 41, 80-81, 113; /Lionel Ng: 108; /Joe Portlock: 44, 99, 101; / Rainer Schlegelmilch: 15, 29; /Sutton Images: 25, 57R, 61R; /Mark Sutton: 2, 5, 8-9, 12, 30, 36, 50, 54, 92-93; /Steven Tee: 48, 98, 102, 107, 115

Every effort has been made to acknowledge correctly and contact the source and/ or copyright holder of each picture. Any unintentional errors or omissions will be corrected in future editions of this book.

Another season done, and that's a sixth F1 title in the bag for Lewis Hamilton. In 2020, he will be aiming for a record-equalling seventh F1 crown.